IMPLEMENTING EVIDENCE-INFORMED PRACTICE

IMPLEMENTING
EVIDENCE-INFORMED PRACTICE

International Perspectives

KATHARINE DILL
and
WES SHERA

Canadian Scholars' Press Inc.
Toronto

Implementing Evidence-Informed Practice: International Perspectives
Edited by Katharine Dill and Wes Shera

First published in 2012 by
Canadian Scholars' Press Inc.
180 Bloor Street West, Suite 801
Toronto, Ontario
M5S 2V6

www.cspi.org

Every reasonable effort has been made to identify copyright holders.
CSPI would be pleased to have any errors or omissions brought to its attention.

Canadian Scholars' Press Inc. gratefully acknowledges financial support for our publishing activities from the Government of Canada through the Canada Book Fund (CBF).

Library and Archives Canada Cataloguing in Publication

Implementing evidence-informed practice : international perspectives /
[edited by] Katharine Dill, Wes Shera. — 1st ed.

ISBN 978-1-55130-401-4

1. Evidence-based social work. 2. Social service—Practice. 3. Social service.
I. Dill, Katharine II. Shera, Wes, 1946–

HV10.5.I47 2012   361.3'2   C2011-907291-2

Cover design by EmDash Designs
Text design by Susan MacGregor/Digital Zone

12 13 14 15 16   5 4 3 2 1

Printed and bound in Canada by Webcom

MIX
Paper from
responsible sources
FSC® C004071

TABLE OF CONTENTS

CHAPTER 1

INTRODUCTION

Katharine Dill and Wes Shera

BACKGROUND AND CONTEXT

Around the world, human service organizations have been moving toward a model of evidence-based practice (Chaffin & Friedrich, 2004; Kindler, 2008; Petch, 2009; Stevens, Liabo, Frost, & Roberts, 2005). Barth (2008) has argued that the evidence-based practice movement is no longer a "fad," but has grown in response to both government and funder demands for cost-effective services and increased public requirements for accountability and transparency in clinical decision making (Briggs & McBeath, 2009; Dill & Shera, 2009; Johnson & Austin, 2006). Evidence-based practice refers to a decision-making model in which practitioners competently use interventions that have been proven to be effective by rigorous research studies. Over the past decade, the concept of "evidence-informed" practice (EIP) has expanded this notion of evidence-based practice (EBP) to include practitioner and client knowledge, and recognizes the importance of organizational and cultural contexts (Chaffin & Friedrich, 2004; Dill & Shera, 2009; Petch, 2009).

Petr (2009) has developed a multi-dimensional evidence-based model that utilizes appropriate criteria to assess the efficacy of research evidence, practitioner knowledge, and client perspectives. The model also includes a process of assessing the efficacy of these reviews and uses value criteria to assess the appropriateness of the recommended intervention. Petr's book includes detailed case examples in the areas of preventing maltreatment of children from ages birth to five, engaging parents of children receiving mental health services, and therapeutic foster care. Another significant example of the multi-dimensional approach can be found in the field of adult mental health, where the recent development and implementation of recovery approaches to care were created from a synthesis of research (quantitative, qualitative, and longitudinal), practitioner knowledge, and client narratives (Torrey et al., 2005). Contributing authors to this edited book were asked to reflect upon Petr's (2009) model as they prepared their chapters. They were asked to assess the degree to which their case examples were congruent with this theoretical model.

This shift toward evidence-based and evidence-informed practice has marked an important turning point in the field of human services, in which practitioners have traditionally been separated from academic research and have implemented interventions based on customary practices and clinical wisdom as opposed to what has been demonstrated to be effective within the literature (Chaffin & Friedrich, 2004). The position the authors take in this volume is that both models have impacted practice; however, we believe that evidence-informed practice has the potential to have a greater impact because of its emphasis on the contextualization and the inclusion of multiple sources of knowledge.

The promotion of evidence-informed practice creates an organizational learning culture that supports critical thinking and practice that is firmly rooted in sound evidence, improves links to policy, and promotes future research initiatives (Dill & Shera, 2010). An emphasis on research utilization by human service organizations allows for the creation of informed consumers and practitioners who are able to critically appraise research outcomes and identify the actions required to promote better outcomes for children and families (Aarons & Palinkas, 2007).

Evidence-informed practice has the potential to create both organizational and systemic change. Creating this type of fundamental change can promote efforts to determine if interventions have had the desired effect, ensure that public money is spent efficiently, and make certain that practitioners intervene in the lives of others on the basis of the best available related evidence (Aarons & Palinkas, 2007; Dill & Shera, 2009). Figure 1.1 displays the fundamental dimensions of a multi-dimensional, multi-level model of evidence-informed practice. This model was used as the organizing framework for the international conference held in April, 2010.

MOVING EVIDENCE-INFORMED PRACTICE INTO THE REAL WORLD

In March 2008, Research in Practice (RiP: www.rip.org.uk/) and Research in Practice for Adults (RiPfA: www.ripfa.org.uk) believed that there was a need to create an international network of emerging experts in the area of evidence-informed practice as it relates to work with vulnerable children and families. In 2008, international teams met at Dartington Hall, Totnes, the UK, where RiP and RiPfA are located. This first ever conference became the "incubator" for a network of international experts from Australia, Norway, Finland, Sweden, Ireland, the UK, the US, and Canada. At this event, *Beyond the Rhetoric: International*

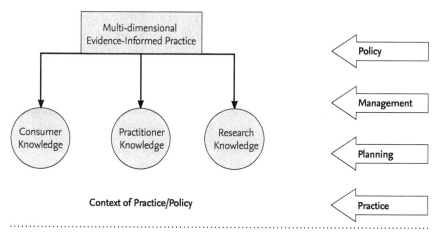

Figure 1.1

Perspectives on Evidence-Informed Practice, participants held challenging conversations related to the evolution of evidence-informed practice. The goal of the event was to strengthen and further develop a network of like-minded organizations, who, although working on their own in isolation, saw the potential to work together to overcome geographical barriers, and to collaborate and develop state-of-the-art thinking and implementation related to evidence-informed practice. The following outcomes were derived from this first international conference:

- Creation of international linkages and partnerships between like-minded human service organizations and academics
- Generation of innovative ideas for linking research to practice in order to improve services for vulnerable children and families
- Dissemination of state-of-the-art information and strategies on knowledge generation
- Linking of research to practice
- Promotion of evidence-informed practice that included: organizational change, implementation strategies, transfer of learning, and strategies to influence policy and practice initiatives

The founding organizers of the event, RiP and RiPfA, chose Canada to host the second biennial event. Practice and Research Together (PART: www.partontario.org), and its partner organization, the Child and Youth Mental Health Information Network (Network: www.onthepoint.ca/index_e.htm), are Canadian knowledge-broker organizations committed to providing practitioners within the fields of child welfare and children's mental health, respectively, accessible information to improve practice and achieve the best outcomes for vulnerable children and families. Together, these two organizations hosted the second international invitational conference from April 18 to 21, 2010, *Connecting the Dots: Making Evidence-Informed Practice a Practical Reality,* The overarching objective of this conference was to share international best practices in the implementation of evidence-informed practice and to recognize the complexity of the role that knowledge-brokers play within organizations that serve vulnerable children and families. A total of 14 teams from the UK, Scotland, Ireland, Finland, Sweden, Australia, the US, and Canada participated in this international event. In order to participate in the conference, all teams were required to first submit a paper.

The formal structure of the second conference led to a more in-depth discussion and understanding of evidence-informed practice and its application within the real world. This outcome had the effect of deepening international relationships among these leading-edge colleagues. Individual practitioners and colleagues were no longer working in isolation. Despite the limits of geography, we realized that we were all working on the same challenges of linking research to practice. This network of colleagues has the potential of spanning across time and geographical borders to the next event being planned in Ireland in 2012. The papers presented at the Ontario event were revised, using new insights the authors had gained from attending the conference. The papers were then resubmitted as chapter contributions for this book.

DEFICIT OF KNOWLEDGE ON EVIDENCE-INFORMED PRACTICE

Much of the literature on Evidence-Informed Practice (EIP) in the human services is conceptual and only deals with the challenges of implementation in a limited way. This book is seen as an important contribution since it provides detailed case examples of the utilization and implementation of evidence-informed practice in a number of different countries. It also attempts to capture a number of cross-cutting themes and challenges for the future. The specific objectives of this book are to:

- share best practices in implementing EIP;
- capture the creative ideas and new innovations related to EIP;
- document the ever-evolving conceptualizations of EIP;
- identify cross cutting themes and challenges in moving EIP forward.

The experiences that are captured in this book emerge from world-renowned authors and leaders in this substantive area. A major focus of the conference presentations and subsequent book chapters was to provide a description and analysis of those factors that facilitate or impede the implementation of EIP. The authors also discuss the methods and initiatives that have been employed to respond to these barriers to implementation. This new knowledge will be invaluable to others attempting similar efforts in human service organizations.

THE BOOK IS DIVIDED INTO FOUR SEPARATE SECTIONS TO CAPTURE DIFFERENT DIMENSIONS OF EIP:

- Section One: Conceptualizing Evidence-Informed Practice
- Section Two: Strategies for Promoting the Use of Evidence-Informed Practice
- Section Three: Systemic Level Efforts to Improve the Use of Evidence-Informed Practice
- Section Four: Multilevel Initiatives in the Implementation of Evidence-Informed Practice

Within each of these sections, authors from a range of countries provide detailed case examples of the design, implementation, and evaluation of an evidence-informed initiative.

Section One: Conceptualizing Evidence-Informed Practice

The chapters in this section provide a broad range of perspectives related to the field's emerging understanding of evidence-informed practice. The papers discuss traditional approaches to evidence-based thinking, the importance of practice wisdom and client knowledge, and multi-level approaches, and identify emerging future directions in the development of evidence-informed practice. The first chapter in this section, by Dill and Shera, explores the creation and implementation of Practice and Research Together, an Ontario, Canada–based knowledge exchange initiative for child welfare practitioners. The second chapter by Julian and Pryor from Research in Practice for Adults (RiPfA) explores the context of the learning organization with particular emphasis on tacit knowledge and its epistemological value as evidence. Shlonsky and Ballan of Canada explore the concepts of Evidence-Based Practice (EBP) and EIP and then trace their origins in social welfare. They discuss some of the most salient challenges facing the implementation of EBP/EIP in social work and child welfare, and conclude with some recommended strategies for overcoming these challenges to implement EBP/EIP in a meaningful and systematic way in child protection settings.

Section Two: Strategies for Promoting the Use of Evidence-Informed Practice

The chapters in this section provide a range of examples of efforts to implement evidence-informed practice, primarily at the direct service level. These initiatives include working with multi-professional teams, engaging a range of stakeholders, and the creative use of technology. Bowyer and Moore from Research in Practice (RiPfA, U.K.), draw on theories of knowledge production and exchange and reflect upon their organization's contribution to innovation and participatory action models and the creation of published material in this area. Buchanan and his colleagues examine social networking strategies and their application for knowledge mobilization, review new research that examines learning preferences in knowledge recipients, and discuss the use of technology in knowledge mobilization. Watson, O'Neil, and Petch at the Institute for Research and Innovation in Social Services (IRISS), Scotland, demonstrate how the potential of web 2.0 technologies is being harnessed by IRISS to provide a range of resources for those involved in supporting children. In addition to a range of multimedia learning resources, communities of practice and web portals, the potential of *Confidence though Evidence* (a toolkit for accessing and using research which seeks to assist both with knowledge mobilization and the creation of social learning network) are examined.

Section Three: Systemic-Level Efforts to Improve the Use of Evidence-Informed Practice

The chapters in this section of the book provide an excellent range of examples of how to use evidence-informed approaches in policy development, interagency collaboration, research unit development, and the operation and creation of outcome-driven systems for decision-makers. The first chapter in this section, by Humphreys and colleagues from Australia, explores the challenge of informing policy with evidence and provides case studies of how EIP can shift or fail to improve policy development within their national context. Canavan and his colleagues from the Republic of Ireland and Northern Ireland employ a case-study method that examines the interface between child welfare and child mental health systems. The authors explore the key interface challenges and examine the potential for evidence-informed frameworks and approaches to meet these challenges with the ultimate aim of better meeting the needs of children and young people. Goldman and her colleagues from the Georgetown University Center for Child and Human Development in Washington, D.C., outline the key decisions leaders are required to consider when building a sustainable infrastructure for an outcomes-driven system, including a performance measurement system to support evidence-informed practice in the long-term. In Sweden, nationally, regionally, and locally based organizations are making significant efforts to promote evidence-based practice, including such professionals as social workers. Alexanderson and her colleagues address how professionals within their country are implementing and exploring the use of evidence-based or informed practice.

They also describe the use of a conceptual framework for understanding evidence-based practice in an organizational context.

Section Four: Multi-level Initiatives in the Implementation of Evidence-Informed Practice

The chapters in this section move beyond the use of evidence-informed practice at a single level to instead focus on what the authors have found to be some of the best examples of the implementation of multi-level practices. The authors focus on participatory, multi-professional partnerships as critical to the implementation of evidence-informed practice. The first chapter in this section is by Mildon and her Australian colleagues. The authors examine two knowledge translation/knowledge exchange strategies that utilize participatory approaches to enhance the use of evidence in a specific practice context. Our Finnish contributors, Högnabba and her colleagues, explore a multi-professional approach to engaging the voices of children in an effort to broaden our understanding of evidence-informed practice within child welfare. The next chapter in this section is a contribution by Courtney and Keating from Partners for our Children in Seattle, Washington. Through the use of a case study analysis, these authors examine the successes and challenges of a university-based public-private partnership devoted to using research, demonstration, and workforce development to improve outcomes for children and families involved in a US state child welfare system. The final chapter in this section is by Fixsen and his colleagues from the National Implementation Research Network in North Carolina. This chapter focuses on the lessons learned in the implementation of evidence-based practices at a systemic level. They identify a number of best practices in ensuring fidelity of the implementation of policies and programs.

The concluding chapter by Dill and Shera identifies major themes and conceptual issues that emerge from all of the chapters. They also generate a list of lessons learned and describe an agenda for international collaborative research. A particular focus of this chapter is on the challenges encountered in the implementation of evidence-informed practice and the types of innovative solutions that have been developed in responding to them.

References

Aarons, G., & Palinkas, L. (2007). Implementation of evidence-based practice in child welfare: Service provider perspectives. *Administration and Policy in Mental Health, 34*, 411–419.

Barth, R.P. (2008). The move to evidence based practice: How well does it fit child welfare services? *Journal of Public Child Welfare, 2*, 145–171.

Briggs, H.E., & McBeath, B. (2009). Evidence-based management: Origins, challenges, and implications for social service administration. *Administration in Social Work, 33*, 242–261.

Chaffin, M., & Friedrich, B. (2004). Evidence-based treatments in child abuse and neglect. *Children and Youth Services Review, 26*, 1097–1113.

Dill, K., & Shera, W. (2009). Designing for success: The development of a child welfare research utilization initiative. *Evidence and Policy: A Journal of Research and Debate, 5*, 155–166.

Dill, K., & Shera, W. (2010). Connecting the dots: Making evidence-informed practice a reality in child welfare. *American Humane Society, 25*(1), 86–98.

Johnson, M., & Austin, M.J. (2006). Evidence-based practice in the social services. *Administration in Social Work, 30*, 75–104.

Kindler, H. (2008). Developing evidence-based child protection practice: A view from Germany. *Research on Social Work Practice, 18*, 319–324.

Petch, A. (2009). Editorial. *Evidence & Policy, 5*, 117–126.

Petr, C.G. (2009). Multidimensional evidence-based practice. In C.G. Petr (Ed.), *Multidimensional evidence-based practice: Synthesizing knowledge, research, and values.* New York: Routledge.

Stevens, M., Liabo, K., Frost, S., & Roberts, H. (2005). Using research in practice: A research information service for social care practitioners. *Child and Family Social Work, 10*, 67–75.

Torrey, W., Rapp, C., Van Tosh, L., McNabb, C., & Ralph, R. (2005). Recovery principles and evidence-based practice: Essential ingredients of service improvement. *Community Mental Health Journal, 43*(1), 91–100.

CONCEPTUALIZING EVIDENCE-INFORMED PRACTICE

CHAPTER 2

PUSHING THE ENVELOPE:
FUTURE DIRECTIONS FOR
EVIDENCE-INFORMED PRACTICE

KATHARINE DILL, PH.D., *Factor-Inwentash Faculty of Social Work, University of Toronto; Executive Director, PART Ontario*

WES SHERA, PH.D., *Professor and Dean Emeritus, Factor-Inwentash School of Social Work; Professor, Department of Psychiatry, Faculty of Medicine, University of Toronto*

ABSTRACT

Practice and Research Together (PART) [1] is an Ontario-based knowledge dissemination and exchange initiative, with a mandate to distill and disseminate practice-relevant research findings to child welfare practitioners. This chapter explores the following key points: (1) the conceptual foundations of evidence-informed practice; (2) the successes and challenges of implementing evidence-informed practice; (3) the essential components of the PART program design; (4) the critical factors in implementation and (5) the areas for future development and research.

FOUNDATIONS AND CONCEPTUALIZATIONS OF EVIDENCE-INFORMED PRACTICE

Evidence-based practice (EBP) refers to a decision-making model in which practitioners competently use interventions that have been proven to be effective by rigorous research studies. Over the past decade, the concept of evidence-informed practice (EIP) has expanded our understanding of EBP to include practice wisdom, client perspectives, and organizational and cultural contexts (Chaffin & Friedrich, 2004; Dill & Shera, 2009; Petch, 2009). This shift toward the use of research evidence in practice has marked an important turning point in a field in which practitioners have traditionally been separated from academic research. Practitioners have historically implemented interventions based on traditional practices as opposed to what has been demonstrated to be effective within the research literature (Chaffin & Friedrich, 2004). EIP has been promoted as a way of encouraging future research initiatives, improving links to policy, and creating an organizational learning culture that supports critical thinking and practice that is firmly rooted in sound evidence (Trocmé, Belanger, & Roy, 2008). An emphasis on research utilization by child welfare practitioners and agencies promotes the development of human service professionals who are able to critically appraise research outcomes and identify the actions that are required to generate better outcomes for children and families (Aarons & Palinkas, 2007). Child welfare practitioners have typically relied upon best practice literature for selecting effective intervention models for clients and/or families (Kessler, Gira, & Poetner, 2005). The limitation of best practice models is they often lack the integration of research evidence. The goal of the PART program and of other knowledge utilization initiatives is to move the fields of social work and child welfare away from a primary focus on "best practices" toward EIP—a model that emphasizes the systematic use of evidence that also includes research from practitioners, and clients (Ferguson, 2001; Kessler et al., 2005). As PART continues to evolve, so too does our understanding and knowledge of EIP. PART highlights the importance of translating theory into practice by implementing the concepts of EIP in the everyday working lives of child welfare practitioners.

Petr's (2009) multi-dimensional evidence-based practice model is congruent with the concept of EIP and includes knowledge from research and from the perspectives of different stakeholder groups, such as consumers/clients and professionals. This model, which is much more congruent with the values and practice of social work, includes systematic criteria for the assessment of knowledge from all three perspectives: research, professional practice, and the views of service users. PART's member agencies have grown in their respect and understanding of EIP and, in so doing, have become more critically reflective of existing knowledge. They increasingly seek to complement this knowledge by incorporating the wisdom of professionals and the voices of vulnerable children and families.

Hall (2008) echoes Petr's (2009) conceptualization by exploring how EBP is constructed within the 'real world' of practice. The limitations of EBP, as outlined by Hall, include a linear construction of problems that in the practice world are not always so 'black and white.' He challenges researchers to take into account the complexities of the context in which practice-based issues are located. Hall concurs with Petr in regards to the need to contextualize research and to include the practice and consumer perspectives that are so often excluded in traditional evidence-based approaches.

PART's current conceptualization of multi-dimensional evidence-informed practice embraces a systematic appreciation of the professional and consumer practice literatures and values professional and client perspectives. Embracing empirical reviews and published, peer-reviewed literature is essential but not sufficient for improving practice in child welfare. Professional and client knowledge must be included in our emerging and deepening understanding of EIP. PART has embraced this notion of multi-dimensional evidence-informed practice by promoting the belief that different "ways of knowing" contribute alternative sources of valuable information for improving practice (Dill & Shera, 2009).

Implementing PART: Successes and Challenges

One of the major goals of PART is to stay on the leading edge of innovation by creating high-impact results with each and every aspect of its program. The PART program design is composed of several key components that include large-scale conferences, webinars, literature reviews, an electronic library that currently contains peer-reviewed journals and will soon be expanded to include electronic texts, agency-based representatives, and a web-site portal that encompasses all elements of the program design.

PART was first developed in 2006, when a group of child welfare leaders went to the UK to visit Research in Practice (RiP)[2], a world-renowned knowledge translation organization located at Dartington Hall, Totnes. RiP assists with the implementation of EIP in social service organizations that work with vulnerable children and families. The site visit examined whether the RiP model could be replicated within the Ontario child welfare system. The visiting child welfare leaders concurred that the UK model had significant potential to create change within the Ontario system, and this marked the genesis for the PART model. PART opened for business on September 24, 2007, beginning with a modest membership of 18 out of a total of 53 child welfare agencies in Ontario. PART now has a current membership roster of 41 child welfare organizations. This represents 75 percent of the province's child welfare organizations. This membership roster has remained intact despite significant provincial cutbacks.

The original fee schedule for membership in PART involved a "one size fits all" fee structure whereby each member organization paid $15,300. This model was revised following feedback from smaller member organizations that they considered it inequitable that they should pay the same fee as larger organizations. Now there is a sliding scale for small-, medium-, and large-sized organizations. The membership fee includes all costs related to PART activities, including attendance at the large conferences. Organizations sign a membership agreement and make a commitment to remain within the program for a period of two years. The PART infrastructure is small, and includes three full-time staff members and one part-time employee. By minimizing its infrastructure costs, PART is able to channel a significant portion of its revenues into creative program design elements for its member agencies.

The implementation process, in large part, has been a process of trial and error. The program unfolded in a way that took into account the degree of organizational readiness of member agencies, practitioner feedback, and cost-containment challenges. The following section outlines the core program components and describes the implementation challenges and successes related to each component. The goal of PART is to provide high-impact, high-quality materials and experiences that resonate with practitioners and organizations and contribute toward improved outcomes for recipients of child welfare services.

PART Program Components

Conferences

The cornerstone of the PART program is the use of conferences as a way of disseminating critical research findings. These large-scale conferences include presentations by distinguished academics and policy-makers on child welfare topics. These events are professionally produced learning opportunities that are provided to all member agencies. The events are simultaneously web-cast so that member agencies located at a distance from the event can attend virtually. Discussion questions can be posed to the presenters via the Internet, allowing remote participants to interact with the presenters in real time. On-site and virtual participation exceeds over 400 participants per event. The split between on-site attendance and virtual participation runs about 50 percent on-site and 50 percent via web-cast, with increasingly more organizations moving toward the use of this innovative technology.

These conferences are events that bring academics and practitioners together to dialogue about challenging practice-related issues. Topics have included kinship care, outcomes for children in care, research related to siblings, substance misuse, linking evidence to child welfare supervision, and improving educational outcomes for children and youth in care. All of the conferences focus on substantive practice-related issues, and the topics are chosen by child welfare practitioners. The conferences are always very well subscribed. In November 2009, the impact of the economic downturn began to be felt, and many agencies failed to send staff members to the event because of the accommodation and travel-related costs. The PART director heard from many agency representatives that, although the events represent a significant turning point for the integration of research into practice, there remained a need to find a way to disseminate research findings without increasing the financial burden of membership by adding additional training and travel costs. This implementation challenge led to the development of a webinar series.

Webinars

During a webinar, PowerPoint slides are visually broadcast on each participant's computer screen, while the telephone line is used to transmit the audio portion of the presentation. This innovative use of technology allows PART to engage world-renowned academics to present on substantive topics right from the comfort of their offices. Webinars allow hundreds of practitioners to become engaged with the research topic from their agency without ever having to leave their desks. Agencies have reported a good, enthusiastic level of participation with these events because the sessions are only one hour and do not require long periods of time away from practice. This limited time frame and easy accessibility provides staff members with the opportunity to engage in a valuable learning opportunity that can be easily incorporated into a busy child welfare professional's schedule. The uptake for these sessions has been significant. Since November 2009 over 8,000 staff members have participated in these sessions, and the participation rate continues to grow. Many organizations invite partner agencies to observe and watch the sessions with child welfare staff members. At one agency, they invited children's mental health partners to dialogue about the issues emerging from the webinars:

> We have identified the webinar series as an opportunity for collabora-
> tion with key partners such as children's mental health, youth justice
> and our foster parents. Response from our community partners has
> been positive. As an outcome of this opportunity to share this resource
> with our partners we anticipate increased local networking and further
> collaboration in our day-to-day work as well as at our community plan-
> ning tables. (personal communication, Director of Service)

One of the implementation challenges related to this program area is the need to make use of low-cost computer technology that is user-friendly. We have developed a system that ensures that academics who are presenting via webinars are comfortable with the technology and that participants receive high-quality audio. Academics that are comfortable using a webcam are encouraged to do so as a further method of enhancing their overall engagement with their virtual audience. As PART continues to have success with this method of disseminating information, future webinar sessions can focus on different substantive areas of practice that will include teamwork, supervision, and community outreach, and on specialized areas of practice such as domestic violence, substance misuse, and children's mental health research. Child welfare executives and managers are asking for webinars specifically related to evidence-based management on substantive topics that include organizational change and effective leadership styles.

Literature Reviews

Another substantive service that PART provides to practitioners is literature reviews called "PARTicles." These literature reviews provide practitioners with access to up-to-date research on substantive topic areas. PARTicles are then used by child welfare practitioners during case conferences, individual supervision, and team meetings. One pioneering organization posts the PARTicles in high-traffic areas that are visible to staff members on a daily basis. As PART publishes new editions of PARTicles, these publications are then rotated to provide new and emerging information to staff members. Most agencies have embraced the dissemination of research materials in innovative ways that include weblinks to PARTicles. These reviews are expected to capture the consumer, practitioner, and academic perspectives. This multi-dimensional perspective provides front-line practitioners with a richer understanding of the complex issues being reviewed in the literature.

Guidebooks

Drawing on research in the area of clinical supervision in child welfare practice (Bogo & Dill, 2008; Dill & Bogo, 2009), the PART program has worked with a team of agency partners to create a guidebook of resources for child welfare supervisors. This guidebook, entitled *Broadening Horizons: Linking Evidence-Informed Practice to Child Welfare Supervision* (Hallberg & Dill, 2011) includes video clips and other resources for integrating research into daily practice. This material is interactive and accessible on the PART website as an e-learning module. The publication is enhanced with several videos that explore the use of evidence in supervision from the perspective of front-line practitioners, supervisors, senior managers, and researchers. A professional videographer was hired to film and capture essential messages that are further reinforced in the publication.

The process of developing this resource has created a parallel process of layered learning for those participating in the evolution of this first large-scale PART publication. The creation of the guidebook appeared to resonate with the needs of the field, but when we ventured into the development of the product, we quickly realized that the foundational learning related to social work supervision was missing. Hence, the publication had to include a comprehensive framework for supervision, then move "up the ladder," so to speak, and increase middle managers' capacity to promote a more evidence-informed approach to practice. The development of this guidebook is similar to the Change Project framework that has been pioneered by the RiP program (Bowyer & Moore, 2010).

Website

A substantial component of the PART model is the website portal. This colourful, user-friendly website provides practitioners with ready access to all of the archived learning event materials and PARTicles. Webinar and web-cast material can be accessed through the website portal for review at any time. Supervisors have been encouraged to use this material in team meetings and retreat days. The value of this technology is that all the materials can be accessed on demand by busy child welfare professionals and caregiver populations such as foster parents. The website is currently being redesigned based on significant feedback from practitioners that the site has become more difficult to navigate. The website must be easy to use or practitioners will cease accessing these important materials.

Link PARTners

Perhaps the most important ingredient for success with the PART model has been the creation of Link PARTners—representatives from the member agencies who work in partnership with the PART program. Link PARTners work with various levels of their member organization to create and promote practice change related to EIP. Each organization that joins PART must assign an individual Link PARTner to work with the PART program. All of these individuals take on the Link PARTner role in addition to their normal duties and assignments. The challenge for PART is to keep these agency representatives engaged and interested in the ongoing development of EIP and best practice initiatives. PART works with the Link PARTners to create program materials and provide feedback on how to engage practitioners in the evolutionary development of the program design. The role of the Link PARTner is invaluable in the overall success of PART and its ability to connect with member organizations. They are, in fact, the "ambassadors" for creating organizational change within child welfare organizations. These individuals bring new research information back to the organizations through mechanisms such as: distribution via staff listservs; discussions at staff and team meetings; and updates on agencies' intranet sites.

The organization and development of the Link PARTner system has created both successes and some of the greatest challenges in the implementation of the PART program. It has become clear that the Link PARTner is the essential "linchpin" in the promotion of a culture of EIP. This group of individuals comprises quality assurance, directors of service, and some mid-level supervisors.

Interestingly enough, the individual person's qualifications are not as essential as his or her commitment to creating and promoting a learning culture, and marketing PART through various venues such as committees, senior management meetings, and presentations at staff meetings. Link PARTners are asked to undertake their duties related to PART on top of their existing responsibilities. Therefore, it is essential that PART provide "perks" that promote continued engagement with this role within the organization. The program achieves this goal through various initiatives that include Link PARTner Retreats and Zone-Based Meetings. Once a year, PART provides an opportunity for all Link PARTners to come together and generate ideas for promoting organizational and systemic change related to evidence-informed practice. Link PARTners, in the most recent program evaluation, expressed a desire to move toward more face-to-face zoned-based meetings. These meetings provide Link PARTners with the opportunity to network, share best practice initiatives, and focus on key elements of organizational change related to evidence-informed practice.

E-Library

A more recent addition to the PART program design has been the implementation of an e-library system. By purchasing access to the SocIndex database, child welfare practitioners have access to over 800 journals, conference papers, and abstracts. Giving child welfare practitioners access to electronic publications empowers these professionals to access evidence in a way that was not possible in previous years. The plan is to move toward downloading key social work/child welfare texts and providing a wider array of electronic publications for use by all member organizations.

Evidence-Informed Practice (EIP) Teams

One mid-sized child welfare organization chose to move toward the implementation of an evidence-informed practice team. This team includes representatives from all levels of the organization, including senior managers, supervisors, and foster parents. The purpose of this team is to facilitate the organization's engagement with PART and other related EIP materials. The team has already committed to facilitating discussion sessions following every webinar session. The ultimate goal of the team is to bolster the organization's integration of EIP into the daily complexity of child welfare decision-making. This team is comprised of the Link PARTner, a front-line worker, supervisors, senior managers, and two foster parents. This same group created an organizational "buzz" when they launched a PART awareness campaign that included a scavenger hunt on the website, a "web-fest" of archived webinar materials, and the dissemination of PARTicles on a daily basis. These types of events ensure organizational buy-in at all levels of the organization. A number of other child welfare organizations have since replicated this model of promoting organizational buy-in for evidence-informed practice by implementing a team-based structure.

Critical Factors in Implementation

International Collaboration

Various factors have created the synergy for PART's initial organizational and systemic successes in Ontario. The link to the RiP program in the UK has been critical. This working partnership, which surpasses the geographical boundaries of Canada and Britain, has been invaluable. From the beginning, the RiP team has offered hands-on technical assistance, guidance, and support in building and creating the PART program.

Recently PART hosted an international conference on the implementation of EIP during which papers from many different countries were presented. The organization and execution of this international invitational workshop has benefited PART in significant ways that include collaboration with key partners in the children's mental health community, interaction with leading-edge academics and professionals working in the area of EIP, and the creation of new knowledge through writing papers and publishing on the evolution of the PART model. The results of this international event should influence the strategic direction of PART for years to come.

PART Image

The PART brand and logo is recognized by child welfare agencies and practitioners throughout the Province of Ontario. In travelling the province, the PART Director has viewed the PART image posted on agency billboards, on intranet sites, and on various agency communications. The colour and resolution of the PART image promotes excitement and interest in what might otherwise be considered by some practitioners a rather dull topic—linking research to practice.

Communication Strategy

Every quarter, PART generates a widely disseminated newsletter for key stakeholders such as academics, child welfare leaders, and policy-makers. This newsletter carries three to four stories that explore various implementation strategies within member organizations. The newsletter is distributed to key professionals within Canada and around the world and has resulted in significant interest from a wider international community that includes organizations from the US, Sweden, Ireland, and Australia.

Role of Child Welfare Leadership

From PART's inception, the executive directors of several child welfare organizations have facilitated and led the development and creation of this innovative program. Through their leadership, the model came to fruition and was embraced by its members. Without their support in the initial phase of the program design and implementation, PART would not have become a reality. These executive directors continue to support the ongoing development and sustainability of the program. Nine executive directors sit on a council that provides board governance and oversight for the program. Through this engagement of senior-level executives, PART has been able to gain momentum and have an impact within the child welfare field in a unique and comprehensive manner.

At the beginning of our recent economic crisis, some agency directors considered terminating their PART membership as a cost-cutting initiative. The PART board members took it upon themselves to challenge these directors to reconsider their position on discontinuing their membership in PART. In early 2010, PART was looking at the possibility of losing from five to ten member agencies. The leadership of executive directors in the child welfare community has created, sustained, and developed much of the thinking and implementation of this important initiative.

Limited Resources

One of the important challenges of operating this initiative is the lack of financial resources to fully implement its mission. The program requires a minimum of five full-time staff members to adequately carry out the core components of the program and grow the model. The current membership model does not allow for the hiring of more than three full-time staff members. As a way of expanding its revenue source, PART is considering associate memberships from other like-minded organizations that include faculties of social work, children's mental health organizations, centres of excellence, and child welfare organizations in other provinces and territories across Canada. Diversification of the funding base would include generating revenues from these associate member organizations and universities and seeking private contributions.

Program Design and Evaluation

In spring 2010, PART launched a program evaluation strategy to measure the impact of PART's activities on child welfare practice in Ontario. This evaluation strategy focused on three key areas: (1) the responsiveness of PART to practitioners and organizations; (2) satisfaction with the PART model and its components; and (3) engagement in EIP. As an organization dedicated to promoting EIP, PART is committed to modelling how evidence can be integrated to guide program development. The evaluation used already existing feedback from ongoing monitoring systems and a variety of other methods of data collection to collect information from various stakeholder groups. Feedback was solicited through online surveys, focus group discussions, and key informant interviews.

While it is clearly beyond the scope of this chapter to provide details of the recently completed evaluation, a few key findings do shed light on the challenges of implementing evidence-informed practice. The evaluation found that (1) front-line workers were not as aware of PART's activities as had been hoped for; (2) Link PARTners did not feel like they were getting sufficient support to change organizational culture; (3) managers and supervisors are aware and supportive of EIP but need more support/resources to move forward; (4) executive directors (child welfare leaders) are generally supportive but they themselves require assistance in translating these ideas into concrete actions that promote a lasting change within the context of busy child welfare organizations.

Efficient Use of Resources

From the beginning, PART has been challenged to make do with limited resources. This lack of staff and financial resources did not impede the program's ability to disseminate high-quality materials for minimal costs. Our ability to deliver these creative and important research messages to staff members in a timely and effective manner has resulted in high expectations from the field for us to continue to provide high-quality materials at the same low-cost membership fee. There is no desire to raise membership fees at this time, and so in a way, we are the "victims of our own success." We have built a highly engaging knowledge exchange infrastructure for limited costs, and so in turn, we are mandated to continue to provide this level of service for a minimal cost. The lesson learned here is that there needs to be a blueprint for developing this type of program design that includes a comprehensive understanding of the staffing and financial resources that are needed to deliver such a program. After four years we have realized that more resources are needed to fully achieve the mission.

Organizational and Systemic Change Needs Participation and Time

Creating change within the context of 40 child welfare agencies is challenging. At first, the PART Director felt responsible for creating this movement toward EIP, but as the initiative developed, it became evident that the best efforts of

PART staff and the Link PARTners was not enough. Creating large-scale change requires the commitment and dedication of senior leaders and engagement at the supervisory and front-line levels. Creating a lasting momentum for change requires a concerted effort on the part of all child welfare leaders and practitioners. PART has been in place for four years and to date has only had a modest impact. In reality, this type of large-scale change requires a minimum of a decade. The lesson learned here is that organizational and systemic change requires both extensive participation and a significant amount of time.

Engaging Practitioners in Evidence-Informed Dialogue

It is evident, after four years of experience, that some academics lack the skill and ability to transform their important research messages into key deliverables that can be easily transferred into practice. We are changing our approach to the delivery of these presentations and plan to provide more in-depth coaching and exemplars of presentations that were previously successful models of practitioner-based presentations. These exemplars can become the framework for helping selected academics present in a way that is meaningful for practitioners.

PART is also moving toward more collaborative presentations that expand our understanding of how practitioners learn. Front-line practitioners complained that webinars, in particular, were too academically focused. PART is moving toward a model that would include academics, practitioners, and client feedback and dialogue about the findings of the studies presented in webinars and other presentations. This new format will create a richer dialogue regarding how research messages can be more effectively infused into practice.

PUSHING THE ENVELOPE AND IDENTIFYING FUTURE DIRECTIONS

Implementation of Evidence-Informed Practice

As described in the previous section, PART has had both its successes and its challenges in the process of implementation. The literature on implementation is growing and has been very instructive in responding to its challenges. Austin and Claassen (2008) conducted a comprehensive review of literature addressing the organizational factors needed to introduce EBP into human service agencies and concluded that "EBP requires special attention to the processes of organizational change, the understanding of organizational culture, and the specialized expertise to promote the successful dissemination and utilization of research" (p. 274). These findings are also echoed in the analysis done by RiP and led to the development of two excellent resources: *Firm Foundations: A Practical Guide to Organizational Support for the Use of Research Evidence* (Barratt & Hodson, 2006) and *Leading Evidence-Informed Practice: A Handbook* (Hodson & Cooke, 2007). Austin and Claassen (2008) contend that the central components of organizational culture that promote EBP are leadership, the involvement of stakeholders at all levels, the nurturing of cohesive teams, organizational resources, and the readiness to become a learning organization.

Hodson (2003) conceptualizes three different approaches to change: individual, systems, and combined. The individual approach focuses on changing the attitudes and practices of direct service practitioners. An example of a systems-level change initiative is the National Implementing Evidence-Based Practice Project in the United States that involved the implementation of a set of EBPs for persons with mental illness (Torrey & Gorman, 2005). The project involved 53 sites in eight states with each mental health centre implementing one of a range of EBPs, including supported employment, integrated dual diagnosis treatment, family psycho-education, illness self-management, or assertive community treatment. A qualitative investigation of the implementation of supported employment and integrated dual diagnosis treatment in Kansas found that the following were critical to the successful implementation of EBPs: (1) instituting expectations; upper level championing of EBP; (2) making supportive structural and policy changes; creating intra-agency synergy (through leadership teams, work teams, and supervision); (3) systematic use of information to monitor and evaluate fidelity and outcomes of interventions; (4) and the provision of training and consultation (Rapp et al., 2008). This combined approach includes increasing the capacity of individual practitioners and making modifications in organizational processes and procedures to integrate EBP into the daily operation of agencies (Austin & Claassen, 2008).

The majority of the research and thinking thus far around EBP and EIP has focused on developing and implementing these concepts with practitioners in front-line work with clients (Briggs & McBeath, 2009). Some systemic-level efforts have been undertaken but combined approaches have been limited. Two additional observations of the current state of affairs of evidence-informed practice warrant comment. While we are encouraged to promote EIP through supervision, teamwork, and continuing professional development, these processes themselves are rarely the subject of EIP. There is in fact significant useful evidence in the area of leadership (Homberg, Fridell, Arnesson & Backvall, 2008), supervision (Dill & Bogo, 2009), teamwork (Abramson & Bronstein, 2006), and other processes that contribute to the effectiveness of working with clients. Secondly, while much of the focus has been on implementation of EIP at the direct practice level, other levels of an organization can lead the way by modelling, rather than just supporting, EIP at the direct practice level. There is a growing literature on evidence-based policy-making (Tomlinson, 2005), evidence-based management (Briggs

& McBeath, 2009), and evidence-based macro practice (Roberts-DeGennaro, 2008). Modelling EIP at these other levels of practice would accelerate the rate of change in an organization's culture and demonstrate that all levels of the organization are committed to EIP.

Evidence-Informed Management

Recently, there has been an increasing focus on EBP at the managerial level, predominantly in the health care, medical, and business sectors (Briggs & McBeath, 2009). This practice has been referred to as evidence-based management. Evidence-based management has been defined by Kovner, Elton, and Billings (2000) as "the conscientious, explicit, and judicious use of current best reasoning and experience in making decisions about strategic interventions" (p. 10). This trend, much like EBP, began as a result of calls for increased accountability and cost-effectiveness (Kovner et al., 2000; Shortell, 2006).

Evidence-based management is a concept meant to assist managers by providing a method with which to use research information to make strategic decisions and, in turn, improve the quality of their decisions and problem-solving (Briggs & McBeath, 2009). Managers can also play a critical role in identifying researchable questions, gathering and reviewing evidence, and choosing and implementing appropriate interventions (Briggs & McBeath, 2009). The RiP guidebook entitled *Firm Foundations* (Barratt & Hodson, 2006) provides an understanding of how to create a managerial agenda that is focused on integrating research into practice. Key suggestions include supporting senior leadership, linking quality assurance initiatives to EIP, promoting EIP in job descriptions and performance evaluations, creating policies and procedures that embed research messages into practice, and providing incentives for staff to remain evidence-informed in their practice.

Evidence-based policy-making has a longer history in the private sector but has also had some exposure in public policy-making, often at the provincial or federal level of government decision making. It has less of a history in human service organizations but there is certainly a rationale and a multitude of opportunities to implement it. One current example from the Province of Ontario does illustrate the complexity of this approach to policy-making. A recent shortfall in provincial budget allocations has led to serious discussions about how to absorb the anticipated cuts. In some agencies there has been significant consideration given to reducing or removing kinship specialization teams. This is an area of EBP that has been successful, but nevertheless decisions have been taken to absorb the cuts in this area. This example illustrates that the evidence-based alternative is not always possible, or the easiest decision to make. Other factors such as seniority, human relations policies, union rules, and/or politics may in fact influence the decision-making process.

Evidence-based macro practice can be fruitfully employed in intervening in organizations, inter-agency networks, communities, and in work with client organizations. All of these new developments are exciting and yet somewhat over-whelming. Resources and time for the implementation of EIP are limited. Making decisions about strategic investments to produce positive outcomes for clients remains a significant challenge. We believe that PART is one example of a "value for money" best practice that moves us in this important direction.

Endnotes

1. Further information about PART is available at www.partontario.org.
2. Further information on Research in Practice is available at www.rip.org.uk.

References

Aarons, G., & Palinkas, L. (2007). Implementation of evidence-based practice in child welfare: Service provider perspectives. *Administration and Policy in Mental Health, 34*, 411–419.

Abramson, J., & Bronstein, L. (2006). Group processes and skills in interdisciplinary teamwork. In C.D. Garvin, L.M. Gutierrez, & M. J. Galinsky (Eds.), *Handbook of Social Work with Groups.* New York: Guilford Press.

Austin, M.J., & Claassen, J. (2008). Implementing evidence based practices in human services organizations: Preliminary lessons from the front-lines. *Journal of Evidence Based Social Work, 5*, 271–293.

Barratt, M., & Hodson, R. (2006). *Firm foundations: A practical guide to organisational support for the use of research evidence.* Totnes, UK: Research in Practice.

Bogo, M., & Dill, K. (2008). Walking the tightrope: Using power and authority in child welfare supervision. *Child Welfare, 87*, 141–157.

Bowyer, S., & Moore, S. (2011). Interactive strategies in evidence-informed practice: Working in collaboration with a multi-professional children's workforce. In K. Dill & W. Shera (Eds.), Implementing evidenced-informed practice: International perspectives. Toronto: Canadian Scholars' Press.

Briggs, H.E., & McBeath, B. (2009). Evidence-based management: Origins, challenges, and implications for social service administration. *Administration in Social Work, 33*, 242–261.

Chaffin, M., & Friedrich, B. (2004) Evidence-based treatments in child abuse and neglect. *Children and Youth Services Review, 26*, 1097–1113.

Dill, K., & Bogo, M. (2009). Moving beyond the administrative: Supervisors' perspectives on clinical supervision in child welfare. *Journal of Public Child Welfare, 3*, 87–105.

Dill, K., & Shera, W. (2009). Designing for success: The development of a child welfare research utilization initiative. *Evidence and Policy: A Journal of Research and Debate, 5*, 155–166.

Ferguson, H. (2001). Promoting child protection, welfare and healing: The case for developing best practice. *Child and Family Social Work, 6*, 1–12.

Hallberg, R., & Dill, K. (in press). *What's My PART: Linking Evidence to Child Welfare Supervision.* PART.

Hallberg, R., & Dill, K. (2011) Broadening Horizons: Linking Evidence to Child Welfare Supervision. Toronto, On: Practive and Research Together.

Hall, J.C. (2008). A practitioner's application and deconstruction of evidence-based practice. *Families in Society: The Journal of Contemporary Human Services, 89*, 385–393.

Hodson, R. (2003). *Leading the drive for evidence based practices for children and families: Summary report of a study conducted by Research in Practice.* Totnes, UK: Research in Practice.

Hodson, R., & Cooke, E. (2007). *Leading evidence-informed practice: A handbook.* Dartington, England: Research in Practice.

Holmberg, R., Fridell, M., Arnesson, P., & Backwall, M. (2008). Leadership and implementation of evidence-based practices. Leadership in Health Services, 21(3), 168–184.

Kessler, M., Gira, E., & Poetner, J. (2005). Moving best practice to evidence-based practice in child welfare. *Families in Society: The Journal of Contemporary Human Services, 86,* 244–250.

Kovner, A.R., Elton, J.J., & Billings, J. (2000). Evidence-based management. *Frontiers of Health Services Management, 16,* 3–46.

Petch, A. (2009). Guest editorial. *Evidence & Policy, 5,* 117–126.

Petr, C.G. (2009). *Multidimensional evidence based practice: Synthesizing knowledge, research, and values.* New York: Routledge.

Rapp, C.A., Etzel-Wisel, D., Marty, D., Coffman, M., Carlson, L., Asher, D., et al. (2008). Evidence-based practice implementation strategies: Results of a qualitative study. *Community Mental Health Journal, 44,* 213–224.

Roberts-DeGennaro, M. (2008). Introduction to the developmental, evolving practice paradigm of evidence based practice. *Journal of Evidence Based Social Work, 5,* 395–406.

Shortell, S.M. (2006). Promoting EBM. *Frontiers of Health Services Management, 22,* 23–29.

Tomlinson, B. (2005). Using evidence-based knowledge to improve policies and practices in child welfare: Current thinking and continuing challenges. *Research on Social Work Practice, 15,* 321–322.

Torrey, W.C., & Gorman, P.G. (2005). Closing the gap between what services are and what they could be. In R.E. Drake, M.R. Merrans, & D.W. Lynde (Eds.), *Evidence-based mental health practice* (pp. 167–188). New York: W.W. Norton.

Trocmé, N., Belanger, S., & Roy, C. (2008). *Knowledge mobilization in child welfare.* Retrieved November 23, 2010, from www.mcgill.ca/files/crcf/Knowledge_Mobilization_Chapter.pdf

TACIT KNOWLEDGE AS EVIDENCE: THE ROLE OF CONVERSATION AND STORIES IN THE VALIDATION OF PRACTICE WISDOM

GEORGE JULIAN, *Director, and* TODOR PROYKOV, *Research and Development Officer, Research in Practice for Adults (UK)*

ABSTRACT

The information blizzard, together with rapid organizational change, are current challenges in promoting evidence-informed social care. The notion of the learning organization is explored with particular emphasis on tacit knowledge and its epistemological value as evidence. Structured storytelling and communities of practice are suggested solutions to the above challenge.

EVIDENCE-INFORMED PRACTICE AND NEW CHALLENGES

The notion of evidence-based practice emerged in the field of medicine and focused on the "conscientious, explicit, and judicious use of current best evidence in making decisions about the care of individual patients" (Sackett et al. as cited in Mullen, Bledsoe, & Bellamy, 2008). Evidence in this instance referred to clinical interventions and was defined in the form of knowledge gained from clinical trials or controlled experiments.

Stemming from the Enlightenment notion of the power of reason and science, and the ethos that patients deserved the best medical care, evidence-based practice was summoned to assure that practice is based on proven facts of "what works" and that it will not become "rapidly out of date, to the detriment of patients" (Sackett et al., 1996).

While evidence-based practice undoubtedly dominates the domains of medicine and of health care in general, its implementation and reception in the realm of social work has not been straightforward. Questions are being asked of its validity (Webb, 2001), mechanistic approach (McNeill, 2006), and of what setting and practice works to promote its use (Nutley, Walter, & Davies, 2009).

In response to this, a range of solutions have been proposed for the adoption of evidence-based practice in social work and social care. For example, Petr (2008) proposes a model of multi-dimensional evidence-based practice (MEBP) that combines research findings with consumer and professional perspective, and values criteria to appraise best practice models.

In recent years, evidence-informed practice is increasingly prominent in social care. It has been defined as "the practice of a range of professionals whose decisions are grounded in a sound knowledge of the needs of service users. This knowledge is informed by the best available evidence of what is effective, the practice wisdom of professionals and the experience and views of service users" (Atherton, Barratt, & Hodson, 2005, p. 14).

The traditional notion of a hierarchy of evidence (Evans, 2003) is not a central tenet of multi-dimensional evidence-based practice or evidence-informed practice. Instead, both approaches seek to provide pragmatic ways in which different types of evidence (including practice experience and customer/client perspectives) can complement each other to improve practice.

This chapter seeks to address two current challenges in promoting evidence-informed social care. Firstly, the constantly accelerating pace of change in social care at a central government and local practice level. This results in a pressure to transform services while also making it difficult for research and evaluation to keep pace and provide evidence to inform decision-making through the changes. Secondly, the accompanying rapid increase in policy and practice processes, alongside new approaches to electronic media, is contributing to the information blizzard. Organizations, managers, and practitioners now have to cope with vast amounts of information on a daily basis. The apparent importance of all this data and the need to keep pace with it leads to what some call "information anxiety" (Wurman, 1989).

We propose that these challenges can be tackled, at least partially, by utilizing the practice knowledge available within organizations. The provision of opportunities and structures to share and develop practice knowledge, particularly through story-telling and social media, is discussed. This is based on the premise that for an organization to adapt to a changing environment such as the one described above, it needs to "learn how to learn" and to create a culture in which both learning and knowledge creation happens at all organizational levels (Senge et al., 1994).

THE NATURE OF PRACTICE WISDOM AND TACIT KNOWLEDGE AS EVIDENCE

The notion of tacit knowledge originated in knowledge management theory developed in the corporate world (Nonaka, 1994) in contrast with the evidence-informed

Box 3.1

A Story—Part I

To illustrate the argument put forward in the current text, the authors will tell the story of a research officer working for an organization called "research in practice *for adults*" (rip*fa*). Although some details in the story are changed, it is based on the real experience of the authors and it takes place in a very real organization.

Research in practice *for adults* is a partnership of 50 adult social care agencies from England, and its mission is to support the use of best evidence of what works in adult social care.

The research officer in question was approached a year ago by one of the partner agencies with a request to find out what research says about the impact of a new governmental policy on re-ablement schemes. The request included preparing and submitting written evidence on the subject matter. As part of the routine process, the research officer scoped for written material through the available online databases and literature. Not surprisingly, he found out that research in this area was close to non-existent. Additionally, there was very little written about what local authorities did in practice to tackle the consequences of this change. So, the research officer was contemplating the idea of calling the agency in question and sincerely apologizing for not being in a position to fulfill their request.

However, maybe because he did not want to give up, or maybe because he was inspired by other knowledge-sharing initiatives in his organization, the research officer had another idea. He called the agency and suggested that instead of writing up a literature evidence review, rip*fa* set up and facilitate a virtual group of representatives from different agencies with experience in the subject area. The idea was enthusiastically accepted, and a telephone conference lasting 90 minutes was planned and facilitated at an agreed time, allowing the participants to share their experience and the challenges to date. The person requesting the support and all other participants found the process helpful.

The research officer became aware that, with the rapid policy and practice changes taking place, his organization was likely to increasingly receive similar requests. The classic scoping for published evidence was not likely to produce the desired results and so a focus on finding evidence through knowledge exchange was required. However, this new approach challenged his established view of what evidence-informed practice was. He was a bit uneasy, asking himself if sharing between professionals was really sufficient evidence to inform decisions about improving practice. (To be continued…)

practice heritage discussed above. An essential element of knowledge management theory is the distinction between knowledge and information. "Information is a flow of messages, while knowledge is created and organized by the very flow of information, anchored on the commitment and beliefs of its holder" (Nonaka, 1994, p. 15). Thus knowledge creation and the use of knowledge is inseparable from the existing organizational setting and organizational culture.

Leung (2009) proposes an extended continuum of knowledge in social services organizations, with knowledge as object at one end and knowledge as process at the other. Figure 3.1 demonstrates an adaptation of this model.

Knowledge-as-object ◄——————————————————► Knowledge-as-process		
Guidelines Policy Research Theory	*Examples*	Intervention between service user and practitioner Supervision — individual or group
Policy and Research Knowledge	*Source*	Practitioners, service users, organization as community
Explicit knowledge	*Mode*	Tacit knowledge
Recapping	*How shared or used*	Co-constructing

Figure 3.1

The "source" element of Leung's (2009) model looks similar to Atherton et al.'s (2005) definition of evidence-informed practice sources. However, a distinction needs to be kept in mind; for example, service user views could be exemplified as explicit knowledge (left-hand column) through customer satisfaction research, which is different from the process of service users participating directly in the co-creation of the organization's tacit knowledge (right-hand column).

The notion of tacit knowledge was first introduced by Polanyi, who pointed to the understanding that we know more than we can tell. It helps to show the limitations of relying solely on traditional approaches to the dissemination of evidence such as publications, briefings, and other forms of codified (explicit) knowledge. As Reddy and McCarthy (2006) claim:

> Much of best practice knowledge is tacit—held in people's heads and not always easy to document. Therefore, most best practice programmes combine two key elements: explicit knowledge such as best practices database (connecting people with information) and methods for sharing

tacit knowledge such as communities of practice (connecting people with people) (Reddy & McCarthy, 2006, p. 595)

The use of tacit knowledge to make decisions about best practice is particularly important when, due to the speed of change of policies in the realm of social care, research knowledge is scarce. One possible solution is to rely on an exchange of experience between network members. The role of knowledge sharing within the context of the UK government's Beacon scheme for local authorities has demonstrated the value put on the transfer of tacit knowledge (Hartley & Bennington, 2006; Rashman, Downe, & Hartley, 2005).

Some learning network members aimed to acquire knowledge (mainly tacit local knowledge) through *site visits* to a Beacon council: "Managers valued tacit knowledge, obtained through observation of organizational practices and talking with counterpart managers" (Rashman et al., 2005, p. 692).

THE TRANSFER OF TACIT KNOWLEDGE THROUGH CONVERSATION

However, the very nature of tacit knowledge can make it difficult to transfer and replicate as practice. Bowman (2001) states: "tacit knowledge cannot quickly migrate, i.e. it cannot be transported to other firms, because the knowledge depends upon specific [idiosyncratic] relationships (between colleagues, customers, etc.)" (p. 813).

Tacit knowledge and practice wisdom[1] play such a critical role in knowledge exchange that organizations looking to support the use of evidence in practice need to identify a methodology to facilitate and spread this learning. If we acknowledge the value of tacit and practice knowledge, and concede that the world in which this knowledge is formed is "quite different from the research-about-practice world" (Petr, 2008, p. 25), then it follows that we need a different approach to collecting and validating this knowledge.

The standard approach is for policy-makers and organizations to assume that strategies for transferring explicit knowledge and standardizing practice will also be applicable to the transfer of tacit knowledge. However, tacit knowledge by definition defies easy codification and exemplifying in written form that can be then transferred in a larger scale. It is transferred through the very process of communication: staff meetings, supervision, mentoring, site visits, conversations with peer professionals during coffee breaks at events, and so on. This transfer more often than not happens through spoken discourse or conversation.

The notion of conversational exchange is not new; indeed it is core to learning processes within organizations. However, simply acknowledging the value of conversations in the transfer of tacit knowledge is not enough. We need to consider what conditions or structures optimize the opportunities and impact of conversational exchange. Structured conversations are required to entail the learning and transfer of tacit knowledge.

Consequently any effort to create knowledge sharing within an organization needs to plan for structure, whether the sharing is done through online forums, group or individual supervision, usage of a community of practice, or other initiatives (Callahan, 2009). This structure is what enables tacit knowledge to be considered legitimate evidence for improving practice. It is also vital to ensuring reflections on local practice move the organization forward, rather than falling into hearsay and prejudice, something that evidence-informed practice came into existence to challenge, as discussed earlier.

Box 3.2

A Story—Part II

Our research officer from the story was still pondering about the value of knowledge sharing as "sufficient evidence" when a new challenge in his work emerged. A couple of months after the telephone conference he was asked to work with a group of social workers from a local authority who had undergone a training course for the implementation of the new governmental policy on self-directed support. According to the initial request, in spite of the very detailed training process, the social workers were feeling unconvinced about the benefits of the new practice.

After a period of consultation with the agency, he became aware that no amount of new "information" would address the workers' concerns; he had familiarized himself with the contents of their prior training and it looked robust enough. He decided instead to carry out a workshop with the practitioners, structured around the discussion of particular cases from their practice. The workshop started with a person presenting a case in the form of an interview. After that, the group had the opportunity to ask further clarifying questions. This was followed by a definition of a problem to be addressed by the group and a solution-focused discussion during which the person presented the case was encouraged to listen with an open mind.

One particular case presented to the group led to people having the "a-ha" experience of what the new self-directed support practice could achieve. An elderly woman had moved to the UK 30 years ago and very recently lost her circle of support. Thanks to the new policy, the social worker was able to provide her with a laptop, webcam, broadband, and Skype, enabling her to have daily contact with the extended family from her country of origin, and in this way changing her life for better.

> The group was very positive about the use of this case discussion method and subsequently met twice more using a similar format. At present, the research officer is setting up an online facility that will further facilitate the peer practice group.

Robust organizational mechanisms through which knowledge sharing naturally flows and practitioner's conversations are encouraged serve as a self-regulating system, ensuring that the best working tacit knowledge is sustained by people questioning, sharing, criticizing, and finding commonalities and differences in their professional experience.

Senge (2006) defined three core capabilities of a learning organization:

1. Aspiration—which fuels the passion for learning
2. Conversation—building a shared vision is always a conversational process
3. Understanding complexity

Speculating on the above principles, the following suggestions for enabling organizational knowledge sharing can be made:

- The professional conversation needs to be encouraged *at all levels*: including staff meetings and peer or individual supervision.
- A community of practice should be nothing more than an extended version of what is already happening between people in the organization.
- People are invited to present cases at meetings and supervision sessions and learn from the feedback. Then the community of practice or other knowledge-sharing initiatives will not be perceived as different but as a logical continuation of what people already naturally do.
- Workers are not afraid of "complexity" per se. In their daily interaction with service users and decision making, they often are pressed to make decisions that are too complex even for the most elaborate set of policies. These decisions are often made on the basis of tacit knowledge; reflection through conversations about how these decisions were made can encourage people's aspiration to further learn or reveal that they are more creative than they have originally thought they were.

Using Social Media to Share Tacit Knowledge

There are many approaches to social media but the key characteristic in all of them is a focus on social interaction. This interaction is ideally placed to support the collection, development, and dissemination of tacit knowledge.

Box 3.3

Social Media Tools for Conversation

Twitter is a real-time information network powered by people around the world that lets you share and discover what's happening now.
www.twitter.com/about

A wiki is a website that allows the easy creation and editing of any number of interlinked web pages via a web browser.
www.wikipedia.org/wiki/Wiki

A blog is a type of website, usually maintained by an individual with regular entries of commentary, descriptions of events, or other material such as graphics or video.
www.wikipedia.org/wiki/Blog

Box 3.4

Social Media Tools for Logging and Sharing Primary Data

YouTube allows people to easily upload and share video clips across the Internet through websites, mobile devices, blogs, and email.
www.youtube.com/t/fact_sheet

Flickr makes it easy to get photos or video from one person to another in whatever way they want.
www.flickr.com/about/

Those working in social care, or receiving support from social care, can freely access any of the tools mentioned in Box 3.3 and 3.4. They are one way of offering structure to knowledge sharing, while also providing a platform for discussion and reflection.

Twitter is an ideal platform for individual reflection; the sum of all tweets is what combines to create a narrative. A blog provides an opportunity for individual reflection between one person or an extended group, with each blog post having its own narrative. A wiki allows for a more collaborative and collective approach to reflection with the development of a consensus narrative.

Box 3.5

A Story—Part III

We come back to the story of our rip*fa* research officer who was asked to work on a new request. This time it was a partner agency that wanted to improve the use of their Evidence Bank. The Evidence Bank was a corporate intranet library where the practitioners were encouraged to tell their stories of good, successful practice and what they had learned from it. It was meant to be used by other professionals within the organization and also during external inspections. The two big questions that the agency had were the following: how do we encourage people to share stories from practice and, on the other hand, how do we encourage people to read what is already there?

The research officer did a scoping study on the subject and what he found out was that these two issues were not in any way unique to the aforementioned local authority. Other similar initiatives had faced exactly the same challenge of how to encourage supposedly busy professionals to use these "good practice" libraries.

After studying the subject carefully, one suggestion that the research officer gave to the partner agency was for them to have a closer look at how the stories were told: were they inspiring enough change to make the practitioners consider changing their practice?

Stories as a Narrative Form to Share Tacit Knowledge

In addition to the organizational prerequisites or social media approaches to supporting interaction, the other important aspect to consider is how narrative is structured to optimize the transfer of tacit knowledge. There is an increasing body of literature discussing the use of stories and storytelling for stimulating organizational change (Denning, 2000; Girard & Lambert, 2007; Simmons, 2001).

Denning (2000) describes the difficult process of conveying his vision for the future of the World Bank:

> What is amazing to me is that the success in communicating the idea
> of knowledge sharing … and in re-energizing a huge group of people
> comes not from crafting a superior chart but rather from throwing the
> chart aside and simply telling a story. (p. 51)

In addition to the organizational change element of storytelling demonstrated by Denning (2000), stories are an ideal approach to sharing tacit knowledge (Snowden, 1999). This is due to the nature of the story as a complete piece of narrative that has the potential to contain very complex meaning and dilemmas, much like real life. According to Denning (2000), when listening to a story, the audience are not passive recipients; they relate themselves to the story and actively reorganize their [tacit] knowledge while doing so, thus learning on a deeper level and leading them to the experience of "getting it."

Box 3.6

A Story—Part IV

Here the story of our research officer ends ... for now. He was asked to prepare a presentation about his organization and about evidence-informed practice, for a diverse audience of gardeners, artists, caterers, finance, and fundraising officers, as part of an organization-wide induction day. This endeavour had always proven to be a challenge in the past, sometimes leaving people confused about what evidence-informed practice actually meant.

Inspired by Denning's writing, the research officer decided to show the audience a short film instead. The film highlights the dangers of not using evidence in practice. It was about the final days of King Charles II, during which the poor King had to bear a series of "interventions" ranging from regular bloodlettings to the administering of "a drink made of 40 drops of extract from human skull of a man who had met violent death," and the reported puzzlement of his doctors that the treatment was not working. The film was followed by a discussion, and the reward for the research officer came when someone from the audience approached him and said, "I was always wondering what you lot in the building down there do, but now I understand."

Chartier, Lapointe, and Bonner (2007) define a number of key elements to a good knowledge-sharing story:

- Be brief and simple
- Be told from the perspective of a single character
- Describe a dilemma that is familiar to the audience
- Have a degree of strangeness or peculiarity to capture the audience's interest and stimulate the imagination
- Be at the same time plausible and oddly familiar
- Be true
- Have a happy ending (or give hope)
- Be told with a bit of flair and passion

However, we should be cautious too. Sole and Wilson (2002) discuss a potential trap in the improper use of stories in what they call their potential seductiveness and single point of view.

A possible answer is provided by Haines and Livesley (2008). They suggest a structured approach to a story that they use with their students. The structure is based on Labov's narrative theory and includes:

- (A) abstract, which communicates the substance of the narrative
- (O) orientation that sets the scene and introduces key characters, place and time
- (CA) complicating actions, which detail the sequence of event
- (E) evaluation that communicates the significance and meaning of the action for the narrator
- (R) resolution that communicates what finally happened
- (C) coda that represent the returning to the present

What differentiates the use of evidence stories to transfer tacit knowledge as opposed to practice based on hearsay, customary practice, and prejudice is the *level of consciousness* through which this process is carried out. Storytelling as sharing evidence needs to be the product of a disciplined method, with consideration of its best relevance and awareness of the potential traps. Nevertheless, more research is needed in order to develop models of storytelling that address both the epistemological and ethical concerns of using stories as evidence in practice.

CONCLUSION

Knowledge-sharing practices that tap into the existing tacit knowledge and practice wisdom can help contemporary social services organizations to steer their way through rapid policy change and information overload. An organization with a learning culture is far more likely to survive major changes in their environment (Senge, 2006). Reddy and McCarthy point out the importance of people's pride of owning and authoring the learning:

> If there is a 'not invented here' culture, then good practices will be slow to emerge and spread, as each part of the organisation will defend its own way of doing things rather than learning from, and sharing with others. Where people are generally encouraged to seek out knowledge and learning, best practices are more likely to emerge and spread. (Reddy & McCarthy, 2006, p. 597)

Authoring the knowledge at all levels is what can help people perceive themselves as cathedral builders rather than as bricklayers.

Box 3.7
....

A Different Story

A man came upon a construction site where three people were working. He asked the first, What are you doing? and the man answered, I am laying bricks. He asked the second, What are you doing? and the man answered, I am building a wall. He walked up to the third man, who was humming a tune as he worked and asked, What are you doing? and the man stood up and smiled and said, I am building a cathedral. (Simmons, 2001, 16)

ENDNOTES

1. For the purpose of the current text "tacit knowledge" and "practice wisdom" are used interchangeably.

REFERENCES

Atherton, C., Barratt, M., & Hodson, R. (2005). *Teamwise, Using research evidence: A practical guide for teams.* Dartington, England: Research in Practice.

Bowman, C. (2001). Tacit knowledge: Some suggestions for operationalization. *Journal of Management Studies, 38,* 811–829.

Callahan, S. (2009). Want to manage tacit knowledge? Communities of practice offer a versatile solution. Whitepaper retrieved March 1, 2010 from Anecdote.com.au.

Chartier, B., Lapointe, S., & Bonner, K. (2007). *Get real: The art and power of storytelling in workplace communities.* Ottawa, ON: National Managers' Community.

Denning, S. (2000). *The springboard: How storytelling ignites action in knowledge-era organizations.* Woburn, MA: Butterworth-Heinemann.

Evans, D. (2003). Hierarchy of evidence: A framework for ranking evidence evaluating healthcare interventions. *Journal of Clinical Nursing, 12,* 77–84.

Girard, J.P., & Lambert, S. (2007). The story of knowledge: Writing stories that guide organisations into the future. *The Electronic Journal of Knowledge Management, 5,* 161–172.

Haines, C., & Livesley, J. (2008). Telling tales: Using storytelling to explore and model critical reflective practice in integrated children's services. *Learning in Health and Social Care, 7,* 227–234.

Hartley, J., & Bennington, J. (2006). Copy and paste, or graft and transplant? Knowledge sharing through inter-organizational networks. *Public Money & Management, 26,* 101–108.

Leung, Z. (2009). Knowledge management is social work: Types and processes of knowledge sharing in social service organizations. *British Journal of Social Work, 39,* 693–709.

McNeill, T. (2006). Evidence-based practice in an age of relativism: Toward a model for practice. *Social Work, 51,* 147–156.

Mullen, E., Bledsoe, S., & Bellamy, J. (2008). Implementing evidence-based social work practice. *Research on Social Work Practice, 18,* 325–338.

Nonaka, I. (1994). A dynamic theory of organizational knowledge creation. *Organizational Science, 5,* 14–37.

Nutley, S., Walter, I., & Davies, H. (2009). Promoting evidence-based practice: Models and mechanisms from cross-sector review. *Research on Social Work Practice, 19,* 552–559.

Petr, C. (2008). *Multidimensional evidence-based practice: Synthesizing knowledge, research and values.* London: Routledge.

Rashman, L., Downe, J., & Hartley, J. (2005). Knowledge creation and transfer in the beacon scheme:

Improving services through sharing good practice. *Local Government Studies, 31,* 683–700.

Reddy, W., & McCarthy, S. (2006). Sharing best practice. *International Journal of Health Care, 19,* 594–598.

Sackett, D., Rosenberg, W., Gray, J.A., Haynes, R.B., & Richardson, W.S. (1996). Evidence based medicine: What it is and what it isn't. *British Medical Journal, 312,* 71–72.

Senge, P., Ross, R., Smith, B., Roberts, C., & Kleiner, A. (1994). *The fifth discipline fieldbook: Strategies and tools for building a learning organisation.* New York: Nicholas Brealey Publishing.

Senge, P. (2006). *The fifth discipline: The art & practice of the learning organisation* (2nd ed.). New York: Doubleday Currency.

Simmons, A. (2001). *The story factor: Inspiration, influence, and persuasion through the art of storytelling.* New York: Basic Books.

Sole, D., & Wilson, D. (2002). Storytelling in organizations: The power and traps of using stories to share knowledge in organizations. *Learning Innovations Laboratories.* Cambridge, MA: Harvard Graduate School of Education.

Snowden, D. (1999). Story telling: An old skill in a new context. *Business Information Review, 16,* 30–37.

Webb, S. (2001). Some considerations on the validity of evidence-based practice in social work. *British Journal of Social Work, 31,* 57–79.

Wurman, R. (1989). *Information anxiety.* New York: Bantam Doubleday Dell Publishing Group.

CHAPTER 4

Evidence-Informed Practice in Child Protection

*Aron Shlonsky, Associate Professor, Factor-Inwentash
Faculty of Social Work, University of Toronto*

*Michelle Ballan, Assistant Professor, School of Social Work,
Columbia University*

Abstract

Child protection services have been continually reshaped and challenged since their inception in response to internal and external forces. Over the last decade, arguably the most significant of these forces has been the evidence-based practice movement. This new "wave" of practice involves the use of effective services to improve outcomes. Evidence-informed practice (EIP) asks us to think critically about the research, identify what is known and unknown, accurately assess clients and/or systems, weigh the evidence with respect to client context, and make the best decision(s) possible given the limitations of each of these steps. Child welfare presents challenges similar to other disciplines with respect to the implementation of EIP, as well as its own set of unique theoretical and practical difficulties. This chapter begins by introducing the concepts of evidence-based practice (EBP) and EIP and then traces their origins in social welfare. Next, an in-depth discussion of some of the most salient challenges facing the implementation of EBP/EIP in social work and child welfare is presented. The chapter concludes with some recommended strategies for overcoming these challenges in order to implement EBP/EIP in a meaningful and systematic way in child protection settings.

Unearthing the Roots of Evidence-Based Practice in Social Work

The term "evidence-based practice" (EBP) began its formal usage in the early 1990s with the advent of "evidence-based medicine" or EBM (Guyatt, 1991). EBP was then translated from medicine more broadly into the helping professions

(Gibbs, 2003). Using evidence in social care has gained traction over the last decade since first being introduced by Eileen Gambrill (1999). Originally developed in medicine by Sackett and colleagues (1997), EBP consists of both an underlying model and a set of specific steps. The original model envisions three concentric circles that overlap in the middle. The circles represent best evidence, practitioner expertise, and client values and expectations. EBP is the union, or overlap, of these three constructs (Gibbs, 2003; Sackett et al., 1997). A later modification by Haynes, Devereaux, and Guyatt (2002) frames clinical expertise as the optimal integration of current best evidence, client preferences and actions, and client clinical state and circumstances, with the overlap conceptualized as clinical expertise (Figure 4.1). That is, clinical expertise only occurs when these three constructs are optimally combined. In some cases, evidence may be strong and perhaps it is weighted accordingly with respect to decisions. In other cases, there may be little or no valid evidence and strong client preferences, in which case these would figure more prominently in decisions.

Figure 4.1

This underlying philosophy translates into a series of specific, practical steps to ensure that each element of the model is systematically implemented (Table 4.1). While the process of EBP has been described elsewhere (Gibbs, 2003; Shlonsky & Gibbs, 2004), the general progression requires individual practitioners to pose a question in a way that a scholarly database can be used to answer it, locate and appraise the evidence found, try to establish its applicability with respect to client context, and evaluate whether the intervention was helpful for this particular client. Some scholars claim that the term "evidence-based" is somewhat

Table 4.1. Steps of Evidence-Based Practice

- Become motivated to apply EBP
- Convert information need (prevention, assessment, treatment, risk) into an answerable question
- Track down the best evidence to answer the question
- Critically appraise the evidence for its validity (closeness to the truth) impact (size of the effect) and applicability (usefulness in our practice)
- Integrate critical appraisal with our practice experience, client's strengths, values circumstances
- Evaluate effectiveness and efficiency in exercising steps 1-4 and seek ways to improve them next time
- Teach others to follow the same process

Source: Gibbs, L.E. (2003). *Evidence-based practice for the helping professions: A practical guide with integrated multimedia.* Pacific Grove, CA: Brooks/Cole-Thomson Learning.

misleading, instead preferring the term "evidence-informed" (Chalmers, 2005; Gambrill, 2010). In reality, while the names EBP and EIP differ by one word, the terms refer to the same exact set of steps and processes for integrating current best evidence with client context.

THE FALSE DICHOTOMY: EVIDENCE-BASED AND EVIDENCE-INFORMED PRACTICE

Building on decades of practice and scholarship in medicine, Chalmers (2005) proposes that "evidence-informed practice" is a better description of the process of systematically using evidence in practice (both in medicine and social care). For at least 35 years, Chalmers has been an outspoken advocate for the proper understanding and use of evidence, having always maintained that the unique circumstances faced by individuals require a far more thoughtful approach than simply finding a study or two and deciding what to do "based" on these results (Shlonsky, Noonan, Littell, & Montgomery, in press). The term "evidence-informed" was first used in the peer-reviewed medical literature by Entwistle, Sheldon, Sowden, and Watt (1998) when they used the term "evidence-informed patient choice." The first use of the term "evidence-informed medicine" found in our searches was made by Schriger (2001). Like Chalmers, he argued that "informed" is a better word than "based." In the social sciences, the first use of the term "evidence-informed practice" (EIP) appears to come from education (Hargreaves, 1999) and refers back to the original Sackett et al. (1997) book in medicine; the term is now seeing more widespread use in the social sciences (see, for example, Gambrill, 2008; 2010).

Thus, "evidence-informed" rather than "evidence-based" better conveys that decisions are guided or informed by evidence rather than based solely upon it, and that clients themselves are informed consumers of services. EIP is not a practice model that differs from EBP. Rather, EIP can be seen as a more fitting name for the same process. These not-so-subtle distinctions are important, given that one of the myths of EBP that has been perpetuated in the literature is that EBP consists of simply using random controlled trials to dictate (not inform) what is done with clients (see, for example, Webb, 2001). In all fairness, there is reason for concern. The terms EBP and EIP are in constant use but rarely refer to the philosophy and steps outlined here. There have been, and continue to be, other movements that associate the use of empirically supported treatments with EBP, or that promote the use of practice guidelines as a ready substitute due to concerns that social workers are unable or unwilling to find and use current best evidence (Rosen & Proctor, 2003). The critics of EBP have actually served a useful purpose in that they highlight the incorrect use of the term and all of the problems inherent with these other approaches. Yet many of the arguments against EBP use a false or partial definition of EBP, and then deconstruct what amounts to a false idol (for an excellent article outlining such arguments and offering strong rebuttals, many of which are used in this paper, please see Gibbs & Gambrill, 2002). Whether called EBP or EIP, if these do not include the original steps outlined in Sackett et al.'s (1997) seminal work, whatever process is being described is neither EBP nor EIP.

EVIDENCE-INFORMED PRACTICE IN CHILD PROTECTION

As in many other disciplines within social care, child protection has moved toward including more and better sources of evidence with which to make practice and policy decisions. Many government agencies are insisting on "evidence-based" approaches in order to qualify for funding (for example, the state government of the State of Oregon). A simple Google search of the terms "child welfare" and "evidence based" yielded over 550,000 hits (search conducted on October 31, 2010), indicating widespread use of this combination of terms across a wide spectrum of published and unpublished sources. Yet, while the seeds have been sown, it is unlikely that EIP in its pure form has been fully implemented and systematically evaluated in very many jurisdictions. For the most part, it remains an ideal rather than an accomplishment. The innovation is still quite new and faces serious challenges, not the least of which is the difficult nature of child protection services.

Child protection workers must make decisions about how to assess families and, ultimately, about whether and how children are to remain with their birth parents. While the same determinations are repeatedly made (e.g., decisions to investigate, substantiate, take children into care, provide in-home services, return children) and similar sets of problems are invariably encountered (e.g., poor parenting, substance misuse), there is little indication that these decisions and problems are approached in a systematic way that integrates evidence with basic social work skills. It seems that child welfare, and perhaps the social work profession, struggles with a perceived disconnect between a scientific approach and a more intuitive, artistic endeavour (Cash, 2001). Gambrill and Gibbs (1999) revealed this conflict by asking caseworkers to rate the types of evidence they would consider when making casework decisions, and then asking them to rate the same types of evidence for a medical decision. Almost invariably, social work students completing this task rated intuitive and traditional approaches higher for casework than they did for doctors making medical decisions, ranking evidence from clinical trials and the research literature much higher in the latter. Why are we satisfied with less than would be required of doctors? After all, the stakes are every bit as high in child welfare. Child welfare workers have the power to take children away from their parents, sometimes for life, or allow children to remain in homes where they face potentially life-threatening situations. As such, child welfare workers and the child welfare system bear a great burden of responsibility for the decisions they make about how to intervene in the lives of the families they encounter. The proper use of knowledge can, and has been, framed as a social justice issue (see, for example, Gambrill, 2008). Clients have a right to the very best services social workers have to offer or, minimally, to receive an honest appraisal of the likelihood that such services will help them to accomplish their goals. Anything less is simply unethical.

The question is whether, as a profession, we are holding ourselves to a high enough standard of care. Our assertion is that, if practice is not evidence-informed, then we are falling short of providing the highest quality of care. Yet establishing and maintaining such a high standard presents considerable challenges. How can child welfare workers be responsible for acquiring and using detailed and accurate information when they do not necessarily have the time, resources, or training to do so? How can we tell good evidence from bad? How do we know which sources to trust? How do we stay abreast of a constantly changing knowledge base? How do we ensure that, once we are aware of the evidence, that we are able to deliver high-quality, effective services? These are the types of questions to be grappled with if we have any hope of improving child welfare services.

These hurdles to implementing EIP centre around the changing nature of knowledge, the complex context in which decisions are made in child protection, and the inherent difficulty of bridging the gap between evidence and context.

CHALLENGES TO IMPLEMENTING EBP IN CHILD WELFARE

Overwhelming and Unreliable Information

The information revolution is a double-edged sword. While it is welcome in the sense that information is more widely available than at any time in our history, this has resulted in an overwhelming number of information sources, many of them of dubious quality. In addition, knowledge is a moving target. That is, what we believe to be effective today might, over the course of time, turn out to be ineffective or even harmful. Newer, more effective interventions may also become available but there is no guarantee that they will be adopted (e.g., they may not adhere to what we have been taught to do or what we feel comfortable employing). As with any type of human services, the potential to do harm is ever-present. There may also be limited opportunities to provide clients with services at a time when they are, perhaps, more amenable to receiving them. Thus the opportunity cost of providing ineffective services is probably quite large.

Lack of Evidence

One of the main critiques levelled at EBP/EIP is that there is simply not enough evidence in social work to make such a process worthwhile. While it is true that there is less evidence than we would like, such statements ignore the fact that we have very strong evidence about many areas of practice. Furthermore, the rate of high-quality studies conducted across disciplines has been increasing dramatically for years (Shlonsky & Gibbs, 2004). Groups like the Campbell and Cochrane Collaborations[1] are producing an ever-increasing number of systematic reviews across a wide range of topic areas. The EBP/EIP model also contends with the lack of evidence in some areas by relying more on the client preferences/values and clinical state/circumstances in such cases.

Limited Access to Articles

Another critique is that access to databases is limited, especially with respect to full-text articles. This is a serious problem, and one we will have to contend with as a discipline. It does us little good to promote EBP/EIP in schools of social work and then fail to provide graduating social workers with access to the literature when they enter the workforce. As a field, we must pressure publishers to allow alumni *full* access to the research holdings at their former schools, and for a reasonable price. The financial incentive for these publishers is monumental, and they are short-sighted if they do not take advantage of this opportunity. Similar to the recording industry, if the academic publishing industry wishes to avoid collapsing in the wake of unprecedented pirating or publishing in open source journals, they would be wise to find a lucrative but non-exploitive way of providing these resources to those who are willing to pay a reasonable price. This is an advocacy issue.

Resource Limitations

Yet another challenge to implementing EIP in child protection involves the claim that social workers do not have time to pose questions and conduct literature searches—that their time is better spent with clients. There are many strategies for minimizing the time for searches (see, for example, Shlonsky, Baker, & Fuller-Thomson, in press) and plain language instructions for the evaluation of evidence[2], but the reality is that it must become a sanctioned and, indeed, required part of what we do. In supervision, does anybody ask whether a search was conducted and, if so, what was found? If not, why not? Are our clients worth less than, say, patients at a hospital (in fact, our clients may well be patients at a hospital)? Agencies must find creative ways to provide the time and resources for workers to search the literature if EBP/EIP is to be a reality. Perhaps if clients receive better services as a result, there will be lower caseloads.

THE COMPLEXITY OF SOCIAL SERVICES AND CLIENT SITUATIONS

Another hurdle to implementing EIP/EBP involves the complexity of social services and the impossibility of finding a study that perfectly fits an individual client. Related to this is the reality that many interventions may not translate well into different contexts (e.g., a parenting program in the US might not have application in Sweden or sub-Saharan Africa). Again, if EIP referred only to taking the findings from random controlled trials, or even systematic reviews, and trying to apply the results without considering context, this would be a valid criticism. But such an approach would not be EBP/EIP, which would require us to know the evidence and to carefully consider its relevance in specific situations. Considerable training will be necessary to help practitioners navigate their way through the EBP/EIP process.

THE DIFFICULTY OF THE DECISION-MAKING CONTEXT

A barrier that is often not addressed is the difficulty of making decisions in an uncertain world. Gambrill (2005; 2007) is one of the few scholars in social work who addresses the cognitive barriers to making informed decisions (i.e., heuristic biases). Yet less often considered is the fact that the myriad of problems faced by our clients means that, often times, our interventions will not work or may only address one of the issues for which they are seeking treatment. Decision making in an uncertain world is difficult at best, and it is made that much more difficult by this complexity. Perhaps for this very reason, the systematic use of evidence may appear to practitioners to be next to impossible. Try as we might, perhaps we, as social workers, find it difficult to consider the possibility that some of the work we do may not be all that helpful. Perhaps this reality prompts cognitive dissonance (Festinger, 1957) in some. That is, we make the commitment to social work and its generally poor pay and long hours because we want to make a difference. We want our work to matter. The notion that we may not be helping may be intolerable. And yet, this is the truth. Our best option is to try to find what works for whom and in what circumstances. And there is no manual for doing this. The EBP literature is replete with information about how to search (Gibbs, 2003; Shlonsky & Gibbs, 2004) but is fairly sparse with respect to how to combine evidence with context.

The Relationship between Evidence and Context

Rather than seeing evidence as giving a definite answer or providing absolute certainty with respect to a particular intervention, EIP asks to consider the evidence with respect to client context. As with any form of evidence in any discipline, knowledge is constantly updated and its meaning is not static across contexts. Theories are born and discarded, resurrected and changed, applied in different ways and in different contexts. A level of uncertainty will always exist in all that we do. The first step is acknowledging that evidence is not deterministic. That is, it cannot generally tell us exactly what to do in most circumstances. As suggested by the model, evidence is used as a decision aid rather than as the final word. EIP is a systematic process that is also inclusive of different types of evidence, is critical of both evidence and the process of its generation, and is flexible with respect to incorporating other pieces of information (e.g., issues of culture, class, gender, co-morbidity, structural deficits).

The use of evidence in practice requires the proper blend of social work skills and evidence, providing the structure within which the complex array of clinical information can be understood, organized, and acted upon in systematic ways that have the highest possible probability of successful outcomes (Sexton & van Dam, 2010). As part of EIP, we must determine what skills are necessary to help social workers increase the chances of successful delivery of empirically supported interventions. To help us think about these skills, one can examine the relationship between worker and client, the therapeutic alliance, which has been demonstrated to have significant influence on outcomes across studies (Norcross & Lambert, 2006; Wampold, 2002). While such skills as building rapport and developing trust and empathy have long been regarded as hallmarks for engaging clients, how best to teach and assess communication skills is a challenge across disciplines in higher education (Boud, 1999; McDowell & Sambell, 2003), and these include health and social care (Cartney, 2006). Teasing this apart even further, there is little agreement regarding how to define difficult terms such as empathy (and if it should be operationally defined in a rigorous way), effective methods for teaching empathy, and how best to assess or evaluate one's ability to use empathy effectively with clients (Lu, Dane, & Gellman, 2005).

The profession of social work needs to examine engagement and assessment components in both our delivery of pedagogy in the classroom and in field education. Although many of our core values have been translated into actions to be taken with clients, there is limited evidence about their effectiveness and still less evidence about the best way to practice them. There is a growing body of literature suggesting that common factors are just the beginning. For example, many of the empirically supported treatments share a common theoretical base and their manuals are comprised of what has been termed "common elements" (Chorpita, Daleiden, & Weisz, 2005). These are specific actions within manualized, empirically supported treatments (e.g., time out) that have been used to contend with an array of problems within specific populations (e.g., disruptive child behaviour). Manualized interventions tend to require substantial training, can be very costly, and are not always available. Although there is still a great deal of work to do in this area, training social workers to deliver some of the key elements that are commonly used in many of the most effective interventions makes a good deal of sense.

Some next steps might be as suggested by Howard, Allen-Meares, and Ruffolo (2007) and Bogo (2010), to utilize simulated clients to help train students to deliver appropriate care, and to reduce professional errors (Mangan, 2006), and employ competency tests to ensure that social workers have the ability to perform basic professional functions prior to graduation and licensing. Howard et al. (2007) further suggest that student-practitioners should be prepared to provide a description of the scientific rationale and weight of the evidence in support of any practice recommendation they make to clients. There needs to be a radical overhaul of social work education both in the classroom and field for social workers to deliver empirically supported interventions in the context of EIP. The structure of EIP consists not only of being able to locate and appraise the evidence, but includes advanced assessment skills, the ability to deliver complex interventions (or refer clients to those who can), and the knowledge to evaluate the specific criteria needed to monitor effectiveness.

Despite the challenges of implementing EIP in practice, recently there have been some promising advances. First, the electronic revolution is proceeding at an exponential pace. The increasing availability of relevant search tools, valid decision-making aids (Baird & Wagner, 2000), critical appraisal guides (Equator

Network, 2009), and efficient search strategies (Shlonsky, Baker, et al., in press) will translate into a more rapid process. Second, the pace of publication of rigorous studies has been rising in recent years across disciplines. A search in various disciplinary databases using a methodological filter designed to find random controlled trials (Figure 4.2) indicates an exponential increase, across disciplines, in articles containing such terms.

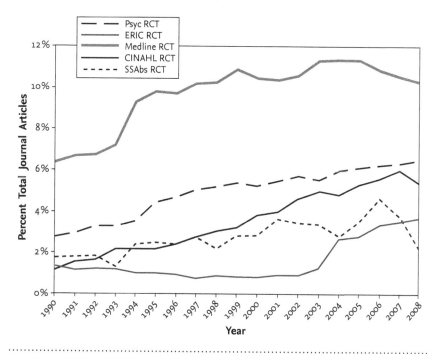

Figure 4.2

While still a relatively small proportion of overall current publications, the likelihood of being able to find high-quality studies of effectiveness is increasing annually. Moving forward, there are several strategies that can improve the uptake of EIP. Chief among these are improving training in critical thinking, investing in systematic reviews, and utilizing child welfare information systems to generate evidence.

STRATEGIES FOR IMPLEMENTING EIP IN CHILD WELFARE AND SOCIAL CARE

Training in Critical Thinking: The Cornerstone of EBP/EIP

The key to using evidence in practice is training helping professionals and students to think critically (Gambrill, 2007). Only by incorporating cogent independent thought can the basics of EBP/EIP be realized. While there are many definitions of critical thinking, one such definition comes from Gambrill (2005). She states:

> Critical thinking is a unique kind of purposeful thinking in which we use standards such as clarity and fairness. It involves the careful examination and evaluation of beliefs and actions in order to arrive at well reasoned decisions. It involves clearly describing and carefully evaluating our claims and arguments, no matter how cherished and considering alternative views when needed to arrive at decisions that do more good than harm. Critical thinking encourages us to examine the context in which problems occur, to view questions from different points of view, to identify and question our assumptions, and to consider the possible consequences of different beliefs or actions. (Gambrill, 2005, pp. 11–12)

Table 4.2. Eight Critical-Thinking Guidelines

1. Ask questions: Be willing to wonder
2. Define your terms: This is the key to research
3. Examine the evidence
4. Analyze assumptions and biases
5. Avoid emotional reasoning
6. Don't oversimplify
7. Consider other interpretations
8. Tolerate uncertainty

Source: Wade, C., & Tavris, C. (2000). *Psychology* (6th ed.). Upper Saddle River, NJ: Prentice-Hall.

The guiding principles of critical thinking appear to be constant questioning, a willingness to ponder and a willingness to be incorrect (Table 4.2). Critical thinking also includes a flexibility of thought that allows one to come to the best possible conclusion at a given moment, yet be able to consider alternatives if the evidence suggests that this is necessary. Examples of child welfare practice abound where such an approach was not the case. For instance, Munro's (1999) investigations of child deaths as a result of maltreatment consistently find a pattern of ignoring alternative evidence and stubbornly sticking to original assessments (e.g., she is a good mother who is just under a lot of stress. She will not harm her child). But these principles will do little good if they are not part of how child welfare practices are routinely executed. In particular, an environment that embraces a critical stance is an imperative, and this means that supervisors and managers must be willing to be questioned and allocate the time to advance reasoned arguments with a set of critical-thinking employees. The environment that social workers find themselves in is sometimes less than supportive of such a critical stance, and this may be especially the case in child protection where the stakes are extremely high (Regehr et al., 2004). In fact, some jurisdictions may be moving away from such critical approaches (Munro, 2009), and this does not bode well for EIP. If a workforce is created whereby the only tasks accomplished are the completion of forms and adherence to rigid procedures, whether valid measures are utilized or not, the indispensable use of clinical skills to integrate evidence and context will become exceedingly difficult.

Investing in Systematic Reviews

Systematic reviews are a major component of the evolving set of tools available to social workers and other helping professionals. Currently, the Campbell (social science) and Cochrane (health) Collaborations (see note 1) are the premier sources of high-quality systematic reviews for social intervention topics world-wide (Shlonsky, Noonan, et al., in press). Systematic reviews are syntheses of studies, gathered systematically in an unbiased fashion, according to explicit and transparent guidelines that are decided upon prior to undertaking extensive literature searches that also include unpublished studies. Systematic reviews from these collaborations allow consumers to obtain a critical and inclusive assessment of the effectiveness of specific interventions, and Campbell reviews are available, free of charge, on the Web (Cochrane reviews are available through most university libraries in the US, many high-income countries have paid for a national subscription (e.g., Norway, Denmark, England), and they are available free of charge in low- and middle-income countries). While the collaborations have, to this point, mostly focused on reviews of the effectiveness of interventions, more recent reviews include questions involving diagnosis, prognosis, and economics.

One only has to look at poorly conducted (i.e., biased) reviews and meta-analyses to understand the importance of these collaborations to the process of EIP. Littell, Popa, and Forsythe (2005) produced a review of Multisystemic Therapy (MST), a program designed to decrease juvenile justice involvement and improve mental health outcomes for high-risk youth. While dozens of literature reviews of the program found beneficial effects (Littell, 2008), the less biased Cochrane review found no treatment effect for the program. While the intervention does not appear to be harmful, administrators and policy-makers might want to rethink committing millions of dollars to a program that does not clearly show a positive effect. The search process of EIP is also important in this context. Government and other "official" websites touting the effectiveness of various programs still include MST[3], even though there are substantial questions with respect to its effectiveness. If governmental agencies are going to make a statement about what is effective, perhaps they should base their recommendations on systematic reviews rather than haphazard reviews.

Another useful strategy for implementing EIP involves the generation and use of child welfare administrative (i.e., management information system) data as part of the array of evidence used in making critical decisions. Such information has been a key component of many innovations in child welfare (Lindsey & Shlonsky, 2008) and will often be the only "best evidence" available for specific localities. Administrative data systems must be capable of producing longitudinal data so that the complex movements of families and children, in and out of the child welfare system, can be monitored and responded to over time. It is foolhardy to pursue empirically supported treatments without first understanding the population being served (i.e., their number, demographic characteristics, previous history, etc.). In addition, the effectiveness of service interventions can only be gathered, long term, if these are being documented over time. For many years, child welfare agencies have simply rolled out interventions to the entire population without first testing them to an adequate degree (e.g., family preservation, family group conferencing, wraparound services). Once these interventions are implemented across entire populations being served, it becomes more difficult to rigorously evaluate their effectiveness (i.e., using a differently treated or non-treated comparison). Instead, service interventions should be carefully considered and implemented in the context of a rigorous evaluation.

Discussion

While EIP (posing a question of relevance, systematically searching for an answer, evaluating the evidence, applying it to client context, and evaluating its effect) is an involved and, some would say complex process, it is the one approach developed in recent years that has withstood the various theoretical challenges levelled at it from a spectrum of epistemological stances. The difficult pathway ahead involves its implementation in social work.

Probably the first step in implementation is to begin teaching the process of EIP and critical thinking in schools of social work. At the University of Toronto and some of the top schools in the US (Columbia University, Washington University in St. Louis), traditional research and other classes have been modified to teach these concepts. Rather than teaching students how to conduct research, these classes focus on helping students understand study design and statistics in ways that allow them to interpret research and apply it in clinical, administrative, and policy contexts (Shlonsky & Stern, 2007). In addition, North America and the rest of the world would be well advised to fund systematic reviews across a range of questions, both practice- and policy-oriented. The process of searching can be time-consuming and is necessarily incomplete. Finding a systematic review is like finding a gold mine. Unlike guidelines, systematic reviews allow the reader to judge the merit and applicability of the research found without imposing a decontextualized intervention plan. A focus on increasing the number of systematic reviews in child welfare and related fields will uncover areas where more primary research is needed, filling in the gaps in research over time and in a targeted manner.

A useful approach for training helping professionals in the identification and implementation of effective practices is to create expertise among students and child welfare workers in common factors (key practice components commonly associated with positive treatment effects across a range of problems) and common elements (specific practices commonly found in empirically supported treatments for a given problem). There is a growing body of evidence indicating that effective practice includes several essential factors (Hubble, Duncan, & Miller, 1999; Wampold, 2002) and it would appear that manualized interventions contain a good number of common elements (Chorpita et al., 2005). For instance, social learning theory underpins several parenting programs that have shown substantial effects (e.g., Incredible Years, Triple P, Multidimensional Treatment Foster Care), and these can easily be integrated into social work training (Shlonsky & Stern, 2007). Of course, little will be accomplished if social work students and those working in child welfare are unable or unwilling to use critical thinking. Critical thinking is the glue that holds the EIP endeavour together, allowing practitioners and policy-makers to move between current best evidence, clinical state and circumstances, and preferences and values. Critical thinking facilitates practitioner expertise.

CONCLUSION

The theoretical basis for EIP has been fairly well established, as have the beginning steps of the process. What has been less well developed is its implementation in specific service contexts such as child welfare. If EIP is to become a reality in child protection, we need to improve the training of social workers in the basic building blocks of EIP (e.g., search, retrieval, and evaluative skills), common factors and common elements, and the critical thinking skills that are necessary for making optimal decisions in the context of uncertainty that is sure to define child welfare services for the foreseeable future.

Implementing evidence-informed practice in a meaningful and systematic way in child welfare is an enormous task, but the cost of not doing so is even more overwhelming. And there has been progress. The evolution of evidence-based practice in social work over the last decade indicates that its philosophical under-pinnings can withstand substantial critiques, and the approach's most important shortcomings tend to be practical in nature rather than theoretical.

Seldom is it enough to simply find evidence, even systematically, and apply it to a client. Careful consideration must be given to the state of the evidence, particularly with respect to the limits of our knowledge. Being honest and trans-parent about the uncertainty of our decisions is difficult but essential if we are to adapt as a profession to the ever-changing state of knowledge.

ACKNOWLEDGEMENTS

We would like to thank Liz Lambert for her contributions to this chapter.

ENDNOTES

1. Further information on Campbell and Cochrane Collaborations is available at www.campbellcol-labortion.org and www.cochrane.org respectively.
2. See, for example, www.medicine.ox.ac.uk/bandolier/learnzone.html.
3. See, for example, www.nrepp.samhsa.gov.

REFERENCES

Baird, C., & Wagner, D. (2000). The relative validity of actuarial and consensus-based risk assess-ment systems. *Children and Youth Services Review, 22*, 839–871.

Bogo, M. (2010). *Achieving competence in social work through field education.* Toronto, ON: University of Toronto Press.

Boud, D. (1999). Avoiding the traps: Seeking good practice in the use of self assessment and reflec-tion in professional courses. *Social Work Education, 18*, 121–131.

Cartney, P. (2006). Using video interviewing in the assessment of social work communication skills. *British Journal of Social Work, 36*, 827–844.

Cash, S.J. (2001). Risk assessment in child welfare: The art and science. *Children and Youth Services Review, 23*, 811–830.

Chalmers, I. (2005). If evidence-informed policy works in practice, does it matter if it doesn't work in theory? *Evidence & Policy, 1*, 227–242.

Chorpita, B.F., Daleiden E., & Weisz, J.R. (2005). Identifying and selecting the common elements of evidence based interventions: A distillation and matching model. *Mental Health Services Research, 7*, 5–20.

Entwistle, V.A., Sheldon, T.A., Sowden, A., & Watt, I.S. (1998). Evidence-informed patient choice. Practical issues of involving patients in decisions about health care technologies. *International Journal of Technology Assessment in Health Care, 14*, 212–225.

Equator Network. (2009). *Enhancing the quality and transparency of health research.* Retrieved November 3, 2010, from http://www.equator-network.org/

Festinger, L. (1957). *A theory of cognitive dissonance.* Stanford, CA: Stanford University Press.

Gambrill, E. (1999). Evidence-based practice: An alternative to authority-based practice. *Families in Society, 80*, 341–350.

Gambrill, E. (2005). *Critical thinking in clinical practice: Improving the quality of judgments and deci-sions* (2nd ed.). Hoboken, NJ: John Wiley and Sons.

Gambrill, E. (2007). *Social work practice: A critical thinkers guide* (2nd ed.). New York: Oxford University Press.

Gambrill, E. (2008). Informed consent: Options and challenges. In M.C. Calder (Ed.), *The carrot or the stick* (pp. 37–55). Lyme Regis, England: Russell House Publishing.

Gambrill, E. (2010). Evidence-informed practice: Antidote to propaganda in the helping professions? *Research on Social Work Practice, 20*, 302–320.

Gibbs, L., & Gambrill, E. (1999). *Critical thinking for social workers: Exercises for the helping professions.* Thousand Oaks, CA: Pine Forge Press.

Gibbs, L.E., & Gambrill, E. (2002). Evidence-based practice: Counterarguments to objections. *Research on Social Work Practice, 12*, 452–476.

Gibbs, L.E. (2003). *Evidence-based practice for the helping professions: A practical guide with integrated multimedia.* Pacific Grove, CA: Brooks/Cole-Thomson Learning.

Guyatt, G.H. (1999). Editorial: Evidence-based medicine. *ACP Journal Club, 14*, A-16.

Hargreaves, D.H. (1999). Revitalising educational research: Lessons from the past and proposals for the future. *Cambridge Journal of Education, 29*, 239–249.

Haynes, R.B., Devereaux, P.J., & Guyatt, G.H. (2002, March/April). Clinical expertise in the era of evidence-based medicine and patient choice. *ACP Journal Club, 136*, A11–A14.

Howard, M.O., Allen-Meares, P., & Ruffolo, M.C. (2007). Teaching evidence-based practice: Strategic and pedagogical recommendations for schools of social work. *Research on Social Work Practice, 17*, 561–568.

Hubble, M., Duncan, B., & Miller, S. (1999). *The heart and soul of change: What works in therapy.* Washington, DC: American Psychological Association.

Lindsey, D., & Shlonsky, A. (Eds.). (2008). *Child welfare research.* Oxford, England: Oxford University Press.

Littell, J. (2008). Evidence-based or biased? The quality of published reviews of evidence-based practices. *Children and Youth Services Review, 30*, 1299–1317.

Littell, J., Popa, M., & Forsythe, B. (2005). Multisystemic therapy for social, emotional, and behavioral problems in youth aged 10–17. *Cochrane Systematic Reviews, 4*. doi: 10.4073/csr.2005.1

Lu, Y.E., Dane, B., & Gellman, A. (2005). An experiential model: Teaching empathy and cultural sensitivity. *Journal of Teaching in Social Work, 25*, 89–103.

Mangan, K. (2006, September 15). Acting sick: At medical schools, actors help teach doctors how to 'fess up to mistakes—and how to avoid them. *Chronicle of Higher Education*, A10–A12.

McDowell, L., & Sambell, K. (2003). The experience of innovative assessment: Student perspectives. In S. Brown & A. Glasner (Eds.), *Assessment matters in higher education: Choosing and using diverse approaches* (pp. 71–82). Buckingham, England: Open University Press.

Munro, E. (1999). Common errors of reasoning in child protection work. *Child Abuse & Neglect, 23*, 745–758.

Munro, E. (2009). Managing societal and institutional risk in child protection. *Risk Analysis, 29*, 1015–1023.

Norcross, J.C., & Lambert, M.J. (2006). The therapy relationship. In J.C. Norcross, L.E. Beutler, & R.F. Levant (Eds.), *Evidence based practices in mental health: Debate and dialogue on the fundamental questions* (pp. 208–217). Washington, DC: American Psychological Association.

Regehr, C., Hemsworth, D., Leslie, B., Howe, P., & Chau, S. (2004). Predictors of traumatic response in child welfare workers. *Children and Youth Services Review, 26*, 331–346.

Rosen, A., & Proctor, E. (Eds.). (2003). *Developing practice guidelines for social work intervention: Issues, methods, and research agenda.* New York: Columbia University Press.

Sackett, D.L., Richardson, W.S., Rosenberg, W., & Haynes, R.B. (1997). *Evidence-based medicine: How to practice and teach EBM.* New York: Churchill Livingstone.

Schriger, D.L. (2001). Analyzing the relationship of exercise and health: Methods, assumptions, and limitations. *Medicine & Science in Sports & Exercise, 33*, 359–363.

Sexton, T.L., & van Dam, A.E. (2010). Creativity within the structure: Clinical expertise and evidence-based treatments. *Journal of Contemporary Psychotherapy, 40*, 175–180.

Shlonsky, A., & Gibbs, L. (2004). Will the real evidence-based practice please step forward: Teaching the process of EBP to the helping professions. *Journal of Brief Therapy and Crisis Intervention, 4*, 137–153.

Shlonsky, A., & Stern, S. (2007). Reflections on the teaching of EBP. *Research on Social Work Practice, 17*, 612–618.

Shlonsky, A., Baker, T., & Fuller-Thomson, E. (in press). Using methodological search filters to facilitate evidence-based social work practice. *Clinical Social Work Journal.*

Shlonsky, A., Noonan, E., Littell, J., & Montgomory, P. (in press). The role of systematic reviews and the Campbell Collaboration in the realization of evidence-informed practice. *Journal of Clinical Social Work.*

Wade, C., & Tavris, C. (2000). *Psychology* (6th ed.). Upper Saddle River, NJ: Prentice- Hall.

Wampold, B. (2002). An examination of the bases of evidence-based interventions. *School Psychology Quarterly, 17*, 500–507.

Webb, S. (2001). Some considerations on the validity of evidence-based practice in social work. *British Journal of Social Work, 31*, 57–79.

Strategies for Promoting the Use of Evidence-Informed Practice

CHAPTER 5

INTERACTIVE STRATEGIES IN EVIDENCE-INFORMED PRACTICE:
WORKING IN COLLABORATION WITH A MULTI-PROFESSIONAL CHILDREN'S WORKFORCE

SUSANNAH BOWYER, *Research and Development Manager: Resources, Research in Practice, Totnes, Devon, United Kingdom.*

SARAH MOORE, *Team Leader, Research in Practice, Sheffield, United Kingdom.*

ABSTRACT

The paper draws on theories of knowledge production and exchange to reflect on our organization's experience in the co-production of evidence-informed resources. Examples include the development of learning events in collaboration with our partnership network; the Change Project method of collaborative enquiry; and our facilitation of a children's services research consortium.

INTRODUCTION

Systematic reviews of interventions to promote research utilization have made evident the relative ineffectiveness of "passive dissemination" interventions, and suggest that the most effective strategies are multi-faceted and take into account "local circumstances that mediate implementation strategies" (Nutley, Walter, & Davies, 2002, p. 11). Research in Practice employs a multi-faceted approach to research dissemination and utilization across its partnership network of local authorities and national organizations delivering services to children, young people, and families. Our position as an intermediary organization facilitating knowledge exchange has allowed us to create innovative methods for research utilization, for generating primary research, and for building research capacity in partner agencies. This chapter reflects upon aspects of this multi-component approach.

A cross-sector review of what works to promote evidence-based practice conducted by the team at the Research Unit for Research Utilisation (RURU) at the

University of St. Andrews provides a useful conceptual structure for thinking through work in this field (Nutley, Walter, & Davies, 2009). Our discussion here is framed by reference to the five key mechanisms underlying research use strategies identified by the RURU team:

- Dissemination
- Interaction
- Social influence
- Facilitation
- Incentives and reinforcement

The RURU review concluded that of these five, interactive approaches showed most promise in improving practice use of research evidence. Interactive approaches are defined as those that develop collaboration between research and policy or practice communities, creating and supporting a two-way flow of information "so that researchers are better able to orient their work to users' needs and research users are enabled to adapt and negotiate research findings in the context of the use" (Nutley et al., 2009, p. 554). Such interactive strategies can range from "enabling greater discussion of findings by practitioners at presentations, through local collaborations between researchers and research users to test out the findings from research, to formal, ongoing, large scale partnerships that support better connections between research and practice over the longer term" (Nutley et al., 2009, p. 554).

The work of research in practice overall enacts one such large-scale partnership within which we utilize combinations of the first four of these mechanisms in our service delivery and resource production. This chapter considers two elements of our work—Change Projects and the work of the Local Authorities' Research Consortium (LARC)—which provide well-developed examples of an interactive approach in action. We go on to discuss work we are doing to develop interactive mechanisms in the context of the program of dissemination events that we run every year.

CHANGE PROJECTS: COLLABORATIVE ENQUIRY

Change Projects bring together participants from partner agencies to work with a facilitator with research expertise in the topic area of focus, and a research-in-practice facilitator with expertise in the principles of evidence-informed practice. The group meets over a number of months to develop the project, one outcome of which is the production of new resources to inform practice or policy. Most often these have been handbook publications, which typically include a set of tools (practical exercises, audits, checklists) to help put the materials into practice; resources and practice examples generated by agencies in the research-in-practice network; links for "digging deeper" into information on particular topics; and often a disc with DVD film resources. Other Change Projects have resulted in electronic outputs. At their best, Change Projects may be argued to enact a dialogical process "in which new and contextualized understandings are created from an accommodation between practitioner-based knowledge and values on the one hand, and research-based findings and ways of thinking on the other" (Social Dimensions of Health Institute, 2009).

The Change Projects enact what Gibbons et al. (1994) termed "Mode 2 knowledge production." This is defined in contrast to Mode 1 knowledge production—which is an objective investigation conducted by academics in a university setting to advance thinking within a single academic discipline. Mode 2 knowledge production takes place in the context of its application, through work focused on questions developed in that applied setting. Production is through collaborative interaction between stakeholders from across disciplinary backgrounds and is carried out in non-hierarchical and essentially transient settings, with outputs intended to be useful in practice from the start. While this opposition between Modes 1 and 2 creates a somewhat simplistic dichotomy, it nevertheless provides a useful context for thinking through the changing imperatives and circumstances in which research knowledge is produced and used.

The Change Project process involves practitioners in developing problem-solving knowledge, testing out research evidence, sharing practitioner experience and tacit knowledge, and developing resources tailored to support evidence-informed practice. The resources are then formally evaluated across the partnership network in contexts in which practice relevance becomes a core "quality marker for knowledge" (Marsh & Fisher, 2008, p. 974).

CHANGE PROJECT CYCLE

The first three Change Projects (1999–2006) addressed the development of evidence-informed practice itself and produced handbooks designed for use in teams at a strategic level and across a large organization (Atherton, Barratt, & Hodson, 2005; Barratt & Hodson, 2006; Hodson & Cooke, 2007). More recent Change Projects have applied evidence-informed approaches to topics identified through consultation with the partnership network and through our engagement with academic researchers. For example, a research review we commissioned on integrated working (Frost, 2005) identified a lack of resources addressing integrated practice among front-line workers. This provided the starting point for a Change Project that resulted in a handbook and tool kit of resources for front-line staff (Garrett & Lodge, 2009). Another commissioned review (Morris & Pullen, 2007) addressed educational disengagement at Key Stage 3 (ages 11–14) and provided the starting point for a Change Project with staff who work with young people at this critical transitional period in their educational journey (Cooke & Barnes, 2010).

A current Change Project addresses a core area of social work practice—raising the quality of analysis and critical thinking in social workers' assessments. The need for professional development in this area became evident in the course of an earlier Change Project described in *Evidence Matters: Social Work Expertise in the Family Court* (Eccles & Erlen, 2008). The quality of analysis in social workers' assessments submitted to court is frequently criticized in inspection reports and in the comments of legal professionals and of other experts submitting evidence in court. Assessment quality is "highly variable," with some "sophisticated pieces of work," but was also said to be "very, very poor, often very process oriented with little or no analysis" (Brophy, 2006, p. 42). The Change Project on analysis and critical thinking in assessment began with a literature review (Turney, 2009), and an expert knowledge exchange (see Figure 5.1) to map areas of inquiry the project might usefully address. Nine agency teams are participating in the development group meetings facilitated by one of our research officers, a senior lecturer from the School for Policy Studies at Bristol University, and an independent consultant (both of whom have experience as social workers). A pilot version of the resources will be produced in late 2010 with the final version scheduled for publication in 2011. The group uses a wiki as a "virtual community of practice" (Wenger, 1998; Wenger, White, & Smith, 2009) to facilitate sharing resources and building social relationships. Participants upload project plans and resources from their own agencies and comment on each other's plans online, and the wiki provides a means for capturing learning from the face-to-face meetings, the individual agencies, and the online discussions in one place.

These Change Project examples illustrate how we are able to maximize on the "virtuous feedback loops" generated by our role as a knowledge exchange organization. Ongoing cycles of consultation with partner agencies inform the commissioning of research reviews from academic researchers, which help us to identify areas of policy or practice in need of development. Recruiting partner agency staff alongside researchers to Change Project groups allows us to develop resources that address identified needs. We can then go on to assess their relevance by piloting these within the network and then produce a final set of resources, the relevance of which reflects this cycle of co-production.

Facilitated interaction is at the core of the Change Project process and our experience with this method endorses what is recognised in the literature—that

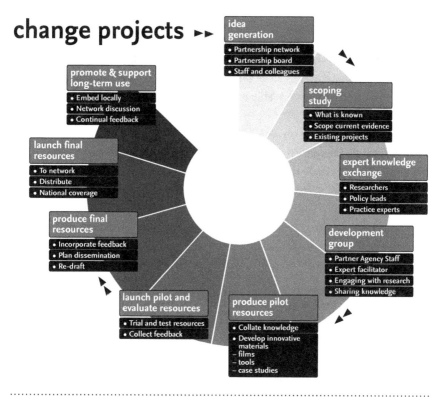

change projects

idea generation
• Partnership network
• Partnership board
• Staff and colleagues

scoping study
• What is known
• Scope current evidence
• Existing projects

expert knowledge exchange
• Researchers
• Policy leads
• Practice experts

development group
• Partner Agency Staff
• Expert facilitator
• Engaging with research
• Sharing knowledge

produce pilot resources
• Collate knowledge
• Develop innovative materials
  – films
  – tools
  – case studies

launch pilot and evaluate resources
• Trial and test resources
• Collect feedback

produce final resources
• Incorporate feedback
• Plan dissemination
• Re-draft

launch final resources
• To network
• Distribute
• National coverage

promote & support long-term use
• Embed locally
• Network discussion
• Continual feedback

Figure 5.1

interaction is key to the flow and uptake of research in policy and practice environments (Mullen, Bledsoe, & Bellamy, 2008; Nutley, Walter, & Davies, 2007; Walter, Nutley, & Davies, 2005; Yorks, 2005; Zeira et al., 2008). Yorks' article on practitioner-based collaborative action inquiry places a good deal of emphasis on the creation of a "generative social space within which intense dialogue and knowledge creation can take place" (Yorks, 2005, p. 1211). It is certainly our experience that skilled facilitation of the social processes of the group work stage of a Change Project is essential, and that interaction between practitioner-peers from different agencies, and between those professionals and academic researchers, can be the basis of generative exchange. Facilitators aim to draw upon the skills and experience within the group, create a space in which participants can inquire into issues without predetermined goals, and shape the group process and delivery of relevant, practical resources. The group process encourages critical thinking, tests and substantiates research messages through practical application, and externalizes tacit knowledge through dialogue and collective reflection (Nonaka & Takeuchi, 1995). Reflective processes are developed through learning logs and by being encouraged to challenge each others' analyses, question underlying assumptions, and offer alternative perspectives. This climate of active questioning and continuous learning is the culture needed if evidence-informed practice is to thrive within an organization. By rehearsing and modelling these approaches, participants are able to champion and spread this way of working within their agencies.

The Change Project on analysis and critical thinking in assessment also encouraged participants to develop their own individual mini-projects. These were based on an issue linked to the topic of assessment that they had found particularly pertinent for their team and ran throughout the six-month period of the formal meetings. Supported by the facilitators, participants developed project plans, carried out the relevant data collection, and gave feedback at each group meeting. Many participants initially felt that their projects needed to be full academic studies. They were therefore surprised at their own capacity to incorporate research presented by the facilitators at the formal face-to-face group meetings and comment on each others' projects with authority; the development of the wiki was central to cultivating constructive relationships that enabled participants to adopt a questioning approach to the individual projects. The group members said that these individual projects were key to making the learning from the Change Project more relevant to their own practice. The impact of this approach to learning was clearly significant, as all participants developed proposals about how they were going to disseminate this work or replicate the projects with other teams in their organization beyond the life of the Change Project.

The iterative nature of this process presents challenges when it comes to evaluation, and we are currently piloting improved methods for evaluating the outcomes of Change Project development groups. Participants will use a pre- and post-assessment to gauge their knowledge and confidence in generic skills related to evidence-informed practice (such as finding and evaluating research) and their familiarity with and understanding of the research base in relation to the Change Project topic. At the end of the meeting cycle, participants also rate the contribution their participation has made toward their individual professional development and to activity at their home agency. The intention is to design an evaluation approach that will capture both the capacity-building aspect of participation—in that the group are skilled in taking an evidence-informed approach that can be applied to any practice challenge—and to assess specific learning outcomes in relation to the topic at hand. The evaluation pilot also uses a case study approach to assess the impact of participants' involvement in the Change Project on work in their home agency. A generic case study template has been developed, informed by the approach to assessing the impact of academic research as part of the Research Excellence Framework currently being implemented in the UK. The "outputs" of the Change Project development group—the pilot resources—are formally tested and evaluated by agencies recruited from the partnership network.

THE LOCAL AUTHORITIES RESEARCH CONSORTIUM: COLLABORATIVE PRIMARY RESEARCH

Change Projects maximize on the network structure of research in practice, bridging peer-to-peer collaborations between staff within the practice agencies themselves, and between the practice agencies and primary research organizations and individual academics.[1] The Local Authorities Research Consortium (LARC) takes collaborative knowledge production a step further by bringing together local authorities and researchers in large-scale, primary research projects. Developing a culture of evidence-informed policy-making and practice requires commitment across an organization. Participation in the consortium ensures this kind of commitment in requiring the active participation of strategic directors in framing the direction of the research and of front-line staff in carrying out the research. Participation results in both research findings and capacity building for evidence-informed practice.

LARC was set up in 2007 as a collaboration between local authorities, the National Foundation for Educational Research (NFER), EMIE (NFER's information service for local government), research in practice, and the Improvement and Development Agency for local government (IDeA).[2] LARC has now completed two rounds of research designed to investigate the impact of integrated working in children's services.[3] Strategic leaders of local authorities in the consortium agree on the research focus and NFER's research team works closely with practitioner-researchers to design and carry out the research. By drawing together individual projects around a single research question, LARC authorities benefit from the knowledge gained locally and gain an understanding of how local findings fit within a wider national context. Economies of scale are achieved by sharing the financial costs of the project across the consortium.

LARC 1 (2007–2008) involved 14 local authorities in exploring the early impact of integrated working on three key groups of children and young people.[4] Research was mainly interview-based, capturing the views of directors, service managers, practitioners, children and young people, and their parents and caregivers. Twenty-five local authorities were involved in LARC 2 (2009), which examined practice around the Common Assessment Framework (CAF).[5] Directors identified the research questions ("Does the CAF process support the achievement of better outcomes for children and young people?" and "What are the key factors that promote the effectiveness of CAF in different contexts?"), and again, three specific groups of young people were the focus of the research.[6] There was an increased emphasis on practitioner-led research in LARC 2. Each authority received five days of research support from NFER to help structure their projects and carry out their fieldwork. Participants exchanged ideas in a series of workshops, and NFER also provided individual guidance on designing interview questions, questionnaires, and analysis.

The Local Government Association funded an evaluation of LARC 2 to examine the perceived benefits and challenges of being involved in practitioner-led research (Southcott & Easton, 2010).[7] Participation in LARC 2 was seen to inform improved delivery and planning, to provide managers with insights into local front-line practice, and to provide evidence of the impact of integrated working on outcomes for children and families. Participants particularly liked the fact that LARC 2 allowed them to contribute to a national project while tailoring individual projects to local needs and priorities.

There was wide variation in organizational cultures of practitioner-led research in participating authorities, with just under a third of participating authorities saying there had been little or no practitioner-led research in their agency prior to involvement in the LARC project. Participants felt that developing knowledge and expertise in doing local research demonstrated the authorities' value of their front-line staff. Challenges associated with practitioner-led research were related to the insufficient allocation of time, capacity, and resources, and to the low confidence and skill set of participating practitioners. However, there was a strong and consistent view among the participating authorities that taking part in LARC had helped to build local evidence-informed cultures through developing research capacity, raising the profile of and interest in research across the agency, and creating a context of ownership within which the findings were more likely to have an impact. Indeed, one participant stated:

> Research can be a bit buried in local authorities and goes on over there in the corner.... With LARC, it has caught people's attention at all different levels of the authority really and that means that there is commitment to resources being put in, people will listen and act on the findings a lot easier.

The findings of the evaluation will feed into the development of the LARC 3 process. For example, participants emphasized the benefits of an initial meeting with the NFER researchers to explain the commitment and resources needed for the project. As a result, this meeting will be mandatory for all authorities involved in the third round, enabling participants to take ownership of their project and speed up the planning process. The evaluation clearly shows that for participants in LARC 2, the benefits far outweighed the challenges. As one participant put it:

> I don't get very many opportunities to interact with other researchers, so working on the LARC projects, for me it's a "double whammy"—I get to share knowledge and understanding, and network with local authority contacts who are carrying out research.

The LARC program's iterative process for identifying research questions, the collaborative nature of the consortium, and the methods for pulling together local findings to produce national results are innovative. Active strategic commitment and participation, and the engagement of practitioners in the primary research process contribute to both individual professional development and the development of organizational cultures of evidence-informed practice.

EVENTS AND E-LEARNING: COLLABORATIVE LEARNING

Our work in developing and delivering learning events utilizes a combination of dissemination, facilitation, and social influence approaches. We mobilize the mechanism of social influence at events in various ways. Through facilitating peer-to-peer discussion of new information and providing opportunities for social networking, we provide the means for participants to reach consensus about the relevance and significance of the research presented and to shape its use in a practice context. Our conferences and workshops are dissemination opportunities, but also allow for a more discursive approach through exchange between practitioners and researchers. This provides the opportunity to translate research for application in local practice or policy contexts so that dissemination "shades into a more interactive and collaborative approach" (Walter, Nutley, & Davies, 2003, p. 6).

Recent research has highlighted the importance of using a range of approaches to enhance the learning experience. Cooner and Hickman's (2008) concept of blended learning emphasizes that learners do not wish to simply receive knowledge from an "expert" in the field. They want to engage with knowledge, critically reflect on it, and investigate on how it can be applied to their own practice; learning is emergent rather than provided or discovered (Cooner & Hickman, 2008; Walter et al., 2003). All participants bring their own personal history, knowledge, and experiences to the learning process, and it is through the sharing of these experiences that new knowledge emerges. These theories have led to increased interest in so-called "problem-based learning," which encourages teamworking skills and critical thinking through discussion and debate around issues that occur in practice settings (Payler, Meyer, & Humphris, 2008, p. 67).

As a result, educators have had to be more inventive about the methods they use to engage learners. This can still include face-to-face training and learning events, but also introduces new technologies and focuses on interaction and discussion between the facilitator and delegates, rather than following a traditional lecture-style format. These methods help to address Honey and Mumford's (1986) widely accepted model of learning, which identifies four different learning styles (activists, reflectors, theorists, and pragmatists). Effective training will incorporate as many of these learning styles as possible, combining discussion, reflection, presentation, and networking, as well as time to plan how to take the learning back into practice and to encourage delegates to take ownership of their own learning.

One particular approach we use here is "case study workshops" for up to 10 participants. Each participant brings an anonymized case study, which the facilitator leads the group in discussing in detail. This facilitative approach "stresses the importance of giving practical assistance for individuals and groups to change" (Nutley et al., 2009, p. 554). The peer-to-peer sharing of practice information provides a non-threatening environment that encourages delegates to share their experiences, and creates a more equal approach between the participants and the facilitator (Nixon & Murr, 2006). Not only does this generate new knowledge from other perspectives about how each case could be approached, but the use of "real" cases highlights the strengths and weaknesses of research implementation. A case study workshop around social work assessments, for example, would look at two aspects of research in the assessment brought by the delegates: how to find and use research appropriately to back up their decisions; and how delegates could utilize wider evidence-informed approaches and resources (such as supervision policies or assessment frameworks) to improve the quality of their individual assessment. The format of these workshops therefore means that delegates are able to discuss the use of evidence-informed practice skills and peer reviewing methods when facing complex problems. Feedback from these workshops shows that participants valued the case study approach, as well as the opportunity to generate new knowledge through sharing experiences.

Generating knowledge that is relevant to local context and meets local learning needs is important to both front-line practitioners and managers (Beddoe, 2009), and we are currently developing individualized training for our partner agencies that is designed to build local capacity and commitment to evidence-informed practice. We will be providing training from a menu of topics, which will be delivered as interactive in-house workshops. Initially, this menu will be based on building research skills capacity. In future years, we will work in collaboration with partner agencies to focus on local priorities, for example, topic-based sessions on neglect or domestic violence. These workshops will be offered across the network from October 2010.

There has been an increasing focus on multi-agency working in England in recent years. With this focus has come an associated need for training so that the knowledge generated around the benefits of multi-agency working can be put into practice effectively. The *2020 Children and Young People's Workforce Strategy* outlines the government's strategy to provide all staff who come into contact with children with the skills and knowledge to ensure positive outcomes for the young people they work with, and emphasizes the importance of

> [s]upporting people in the workforce to develop the skills and behaviours they need to work effectively in *partnership with children, young people and parents, and with each other*, in ways that help secure better outcomes. (Department for Children, Schools, and Families, 2008, p. 7)

There are many advantages for professionals from different disciplines in participating in multi-agency training, particularly in terms of improving professional relationships (Bowyer, 2008; Barr, 2002). Learning designed to bring professionals together can help to address issues such as failed communication, stereotyping, and misconceptions of the roles and responsibilities of colleagues. Carpenter, Hackett, Patsios, and Szilassy (2010) recently researched the outcomes of inter-agency safeguarding training. Their research showed the potential of inter-agency training to not only build shared knowledge across disciplines but to enact multi-agency work. This thereby allows for the kind of shared communication and understanding of colleagues' roles that are essential to effective multi-agency practice. Research into the issue of professional identity within multi-agency teams highlights the dangers of professionals (particularly social workers) feeling that their identity is threatened or lost. Smith and Anderson (2008) have shown that multi-agency teams are less effective if they merely dilute the roles and values of the professions within them. It is also important to create a non-threatening environment in which participants are enabled to share experience without fear of recrimination (Payler et al., 2008). Without this, the opportunities for maximum knowledge generation will be stifled.

We have therefore developed a series of learning events designed to bring together a range of professionals around issues such as the mental health of looked after children (children in care), safeguarding, and transitions for young people with learning disabilities. The workforce development literature highlights that participants feel more positive about workers from other professions, and more confident about their own professional identity when they have been involved in multi-agency training (Smith & Anderson, 2008). Through innovative training that incorporates Nutley et al.'s (2009) mechanisms of interaction and social influence, as well as dissemination, professionals from different agencies are encouraged to work together and share experiences, which can have a significant impact on the way they work in practice. The social influence aspect of this training, generated through discussions and networking, serves to create greater understanding among different professionals and an improved sense of how their identity contributes to the work of the whole team.

This approach can be extended to cover work at the intersection between services for children and adults, for example, through our workshops around transitions for young people with learning disabilities. This series of workshops aimed to encourage professionals working in both of these service areas to discuss effective strategies for ensuring that transitions are coherent and structured so that young people feel adequately supported through this difficult period of change. Delegates were encouraged to develop strategies for using the research messages around transition to improve their own local procedures, shared good practice from their own agencies, and heard from a service user who had been through the process. These workshops demonstrated how effective facilitation can, as Nutley et al. (2009) suggest, provide practical assistance in putting research messages into practice through the assimilation of both the knowledge of the facilitator and the experiences of peers.

There is also increasing focus on the role of digital technology in promoting learning (Cook-Craig & Sabah, 2009; Cooner & Hickman, 2008). The term "e-learning" refers broadly to the use of digital technology to enhance learning and facilitate knowledge exchange, and it can include traditional teaching modules, as well as more innovative approaches, such as discussion forums or wikis. Our e-learning modules are designed to enhance other aspects of the learning process, such as learning events or case study groups, rather than to replace them. We have found that e-learning has to be very carefully designed to ensure that it provides an engaging experience for the learner so that they come away having learned something that they can then apply effectively to their practice. This means that is has to take on the role of Nutley et al.'s (2009) facilitator, enabling the use of research to contribute to changes in practice, rather than simply consisting of a series of facts on a page. Our e-learning around alcohol and offending, for example, includes an introductory "myths and facts" quiz designed to challenge presumptions around this topic. It also offers an interactive section that asks participants to take on the role of a professional talking to a young person who has committed an offence when drunk and identify the questions that they would ask the young person. This role-play technique has often been used with social work students, and has been found to be very effective in helping them to apply their learning to a practice context (Lam, 2009).

Alternatively, a mixed-method approach that uses a range of different methods that can engage learners on a variety of levels may be particularly effective. For example, the key messages from our *Integrated Practice on the Front Line* handbook have been incorporated into a one hour e-learning module. When combined with the handbook and research review, as well as with a previous learning event around this topic, the module provides a complete suite of materials tailored to different learning styles that help to disseminate key messages about partnership working to front-line staff.

Although e-learning may seem like a solitary method of learning, when applied effectively, it can be a successful way of implementing interaction, social influence, and facilitation approaches in a way that allows the user to take ownership of the project. As mentioned above, "e-learning" encompasses any use of digital technology to further learning. The development of online "virtual communities of practice" shows how learning techniques and digital technologies can generate new knowledge through interaction and social influence. These virtual communities tend to focus on a particular topic, rather than a geographical context, and can therefore bring together practitioners, policy-makers, and researchers around common interests (Cook-Craig & Sabah, 2009). They will often consist of discussion forums or online web-chat facilities that allow participants to share their experiences. It is through this peer discussion and review that new approaches to practice can be created, developed, piloted, and implemented.

As mentioned above, the development group for the Change Project on the analysis and critical thinking in assessment use a wiki as a virtual community of practice. Similarly, as part of our Change Project on growing digital, we developed a forum to encourage delegates who had attended learning events to continue to network, share experiences, and create new ideas through online discussions. Delegates are set up as members on the forum, and are informed during the workshop about how the forum can be used. They are provided with the URL for the forum and are encouraged to log on once they get back to their office. This process is still in its early stages, but is currently being tried with delegates from one of our workshops around the mental health of looked-after children.

Conclusions

The RURU team's analysis of the mechanisms underlying research use strategies provides a strong conceptual framework for reflecting upon our work in collaboration with partner agencies and research professionals. The interactive approach of our Change Projects and LARC demonstrate how collaboration between researchers and staff working in children's services can lead to the development of new, relevant knowledge at both local and national levels. The case study workshops demonstrate how effective facilitation encourages participants to share experiences and discuss evidence-informed interventions to generate new ways of using research in complex situations. Innovative resources such as the Change Project wiki and post-event discussion forums help to facilitate further collaborative discussion among participants, encouraging them to develop, pilot, and implement new ideas and evidence-informed ways of working to improve outcomes for children, young people, and their families.

Acknowledgements

Thanks to Jane Lewis and Colleen Eccles for their comments on earlier drafts of this paper.

Endnotes

1. Local government in England and Wales is delivered through 174 local authorities. Each authority has a Directorate of Children's Services, 106 of which are partners in the research in practice network. In recent years, children's service departments have worked with other services (police, health, schools, etc.) in a Children's Trust arrangement to deliver integrated services to children and families.
2. NFER is the UK's largest independent provider of research, assessment, and information services for education, training, and children's services. They undertake around 200 research projects every year across the sector (www.nfer.ac.uk). EMIE is NFER's information service for local authorities on education and children's services. IDEA is part of the Local Government Association (LGA), a membership body funded by subscription by authorities in England and Wales. LGA lobbies and campaigns for changes in policy and legislation on behalf of its member councils. IDEA supports improvement and innovation in local government (www.idea.gov.uk).
3. The Every Child Matters (ECM) policy initiative developed in the wake of the abuse and murder of a child, Victoria Climbié, in 2000. The ECM Green paper was published in 2003, and informed the Children Act 2004. The Act brought all local government functions (child welfare and education) under the statutory authority of local Directors of Children's Services (DCS), with a view to developing more effective integrated working across the sector. The ECM outcomes framework and the requirement for multi-agency partnership working to achieve those outcomes provide the overall framework for work with children and families in the UK. LARC developed out of DCS's interest in commissioning research to identify the impact on outcomes for children and families of these major restructuring initiatives.
4. Looked after children; children and young people with autistic spectrum disorder; and young people with over 20 percent absence from school at key stage 3.
5. The Common Assessment Framework is a key element in delivering integrated front-line services. The aim is to identify a child's or young person's additional needs that are not being met by the universal services they are receiving, and provide timely and coordinated support to meet those needs. The CAF was initiated in 2005–2006. All local authorities were expected to implement the CAF between 2006–2008. While the CAF is a standardized approach to conducting assessments of children's additional needs, local authorities have largely developed their own procedures for the use of the CAF.

6. Early years; school non-attenders; and children and young people at risk of negative outcomes.
7. With a random sample of 15 of the 25 authorities.

REFERENCES

Atherton, C., Barratt, M., & Hodson, R. (2005). *Teamwise: Using research evidence, a practical guide for teams.* Dartington, England: Research in Practice.

Barr, H. (2002). Interprofessional education: Today, yesterday, and tomorrow, The Learning and Teaching Support Network for Health Sciences and Practice, London.

Barratt, M., & Hodson, R. (2006). *Firm foundations: A practical guide to organisational support for the use of research evidence.* Dartington, England: Research in Practice.

Beddoe, L. (2009). Creating continuous conversations: Social workers and learning organizations. *Social Work Education, 28,* 722–736.

Bowyer, S. (2008). Multi-professional working: Distinct professional identities in multi-professional teams. In S. Bowyer (Ed.), *Prompt topic briefings.* Dartington, England: Research in Practice.

Brophy, J. (2006). *Research review: Child care proceedings under the Children Act 1989.* London: Department for Constitutional Affairs.

Carpenter, J., Hackett, S., Patsios, D., & Szilassy, E. (2010). Outcomes of interagency training to safeguard children. Bristol, England: University of Bristol.

Cook-Craig, P., & Sabah, Y. (2009). The role of virtual communities of practice in supporting collaborative learning among social workers. *British Journal of Social Work, 39,* 725–739.

Cooke, E., & Barnes, T. (2010). *Engagement and re-engagement at key stage 3.* Dartington, England: Research in Practice.

Cooner, T., & Hickman, G. (2008). Child protection teaching: Student's experiences of a blended learning design. *Social Work Education, 27,* 649–657.

Department for Children, Schools, and Families. (2008). *2020 children and young people's workforce strategy.* London: Author.

Eccles, C., & Erlen, N. (2008). *Evidence matters: Social work expertise in the family court.* Dartington, England: Research in Practice.

Frost, N. (2005). *Professionalism, partnership and joined-up thinking: A research review of front-line working with children and families.* Dartington, England: Research in Practice.

Garrett, L., & Lodge, S. (2009). *Integrated practice on the front line: A handbook.* Dartington, England: Research in Practice.

Gibbons, M., Limoges, H., Nowotny, H., Schwartzman, S., Scott, P., & Trow, M. (1994). *The new production of knowledge: The dynamics of science and research in contemporary societies.* London: Sage.

Hodson, R., & Cooke, E. (2007). *Leading evidence-informed practice: A handbook.* Dartington, England: Research in Practice.

Honey, P., & Mumford, A. (1986). *A manual of learning styles.* Maidenhead, England: Peter Mumford.

Lam, D. (2009). Impact of problem-based learning on social work students: Growths and limits. *British Journal of Social Work, 39,* 1499–1517.

Marsh, P., & Fisher, M. (2008). The development of problem-solving knowledge for social care practice. *British Journal of Social Work, 38,* 971–987.

Morris, M., & Pullen, C. (2007). *Disengagement and re-engagement of young people in learning at key stage 3.* Dartington, England: Research in Practice.

Mullen, E.J., Bledsoe, S.E., & Bellamy, J.L.. (2008). Implementing evidence-based social work practice. *Research on Social Work Practice, 18,* 325–338.

Nixon, S., & Murr, A. (2006). Practice learning and the development of professional practice. *Social Work Education, 25,* 798–811.

Nonaka, I., & Takeuchi, H. (1995). The knowledge-creating company: How Japanese companies create the dynamics of innovation. New York: Oxford University Press.

Nutley, S., Walter, I., & Davies, H. (2002). *From knowing to doing: A framework for understanding the evidence-into-practice agenda.* St. Andrews, Scotland: Research Unit for Research Utilisation, University of St. Andrews.

Nutley, S., Walter, I., & Davies, H. (2009). Promoting evidence-based practice: Models and mechanisms from cross-sector review. *Research on Social Work Practice, 19*, 552–559.

Nutley, S.M., Walter, I., & Davies, H. (2007). *Using evidence: How research can inform public services.* Bristol, England: The Policy Press.

Payler, J., Meyer, E., & Humphris, D. (2008). Pedagogy for interprofessional education: What do we know and how can we evaluate it? *Learning in Health and Social Care, 7*, 64–78.

Smith, R., & Anderson, L. (2008). Interprofessional learning: Aspiration or achievement? *Social Work Education, 27*, 759–776.

Social Dimensions of Health Institute. (2009). *Making sense of knowledge production. Seminar 2: Co-producing knowledge.* St. Andrews, Scotland: Universities of Dundee and St. Andrews.

Southcott, C., & Easton, C. (2010). *Supporting local authorities to develop their research capacity.* London: Local Government Association and National Foundation for Educational Research.

Turney, D. (2009). *Analysis and critical thinking in assessment.* Dartington, England: Research in Practice.

Walter, I., Nutley, S., & Davies, H. (2003). *Developing a taxonomy of interventions used to increase the impact of research.* St. Andrews, Scotland: Research Unit for Research Utilisation, University of St. Andrews.

Walter, I., Nutley, S., & Davies, H. (2005). What works to promote evidence-based practice? A cross-sector review. *Evidence & Policy: A Journal of Research, Debate and Practice, 1*, 335–364.

Wenger, E. (1998). *Communities of practice.* Cambridge, England: Cambridge University Press.

Wenger, E., White, N., & Smith, J. (2009). *Digital habitats: Stewarding technology for communities.* Portland, OR: CPsquare.

Yorks, L. (2005). Adult learning and the generation of new knowledge and meaning: Creating liberating spaces for fostering adult learning through practitioner-based collaborative action inquiry. *The Teachers College Record, 107*, 1217–1244.

Zeira, A., Canali, C., Vecchiato, T., Jergeby, U., Thoburn, J., & Neve, E. (2008). Evidence-based social work practice with children and families: A cross national perspective. *European Journal of Social Work, 11*, 57–72.

CHAPTER 6

METHODS FOR ENGAGING KEY STAKEHOLDERS IN CHILD AND YOUTH MENTAL HEALTH

MELANIE BARWICK, Learning Institute/Research Institute, The Hospital for Sick Children, University of Toronto, Toronto, ON

DON BUCHANAN, Offord Centre for Child Studies, McMaster University and McMaster Children's Hospital, Hamilton, ON

MICHAEL CHENG, Children's Hospital of Eastern Ontario, Ottawa, ON

IAN MANION, Provincial Centre of Excellence for Child and Youth Mental Health, Children's Hospital of Eastern Ontario, University of Ottawa, Ottawa, ON

FRANCES RUFFOLO, Children's Mental Health Ontario, Toronto, ON

KATHY SHORT, Evidence-Based Education and Services Team (E-BEST), Hamilton-Wentworth District School Board, Hamilton, ON

ABSTRACT

Moving research findings into practice has been shown to be difficult across a number of fields and disciplines. This has led researchers to try innovative strategies to determine if they will lead to improved knowledge translation (KT). This chapter briefly reviews strategies that have been used in KT in child and youth mental health in Canada; with practitioners, allied professionals, and the public at large. The influence of scientific findings in the area of social networking strategies, communities of practice, learning preferences, and the use of technology as a platform of knowledge mobilization are examined. Promising directions for knowledge mobilization in child and youth mental health, including research and evaluation strategies required to move this work forward, are described.

INTRODUCING THE CHILD AND YOUTH MENTAL HEALTH INFORMATION NETWORK

The Child and Youth Mental Health Information Network (CYMHIN) is a loosely-structured co-operative among several large organizations that provide information about children's mental health problems in the Province of Ontario. These organizations include Children's Mental Health Ontario, a membership organization of mental health service providers; the Offord Centre for Child Studies and the Hospital for Sick Children's Community Health Resource Group, two university and hospital-based research centres; the Evidence-Based Education Services Team (E-BEST) at a major school board; and the Provincial Centre of Excellence for Child and Youth Mental Health, a government-funded centre with a broad mandate to improve mental health services delivered across Ontario.

These organizations meet on a regular basis, either by teleconference or in person, to share ideas and work together on projects of common interest. The network has produced two documents, both directed at a parent audience, which provide guidance on seeking mental health services and on what parents can expect when they receive those services.[1]

While the member organizations share common projects and goals, each organization acts independently in exploring new and innovative ways to move evidence into practice. Some of the organizations conduct research activities in knowledge translation and implementation science, and others are more focused on the practicalities of how to move new knowledge directly into the field. This chapter provides an overview of selected projects from these partners.

ENGAGING STAKEHOLDERS IN RESEARCH USE

There is an emerging science related to bridging the worlds of research and practice. Many terms are used to describe the strategies used to move research into practice; for example, knowledge translation, knowledge exchange, and knowledge mobilization (see Mitton et al., 2007, for a review of these terms). While there may be slight differences in intent, these terms can largely be used interchangeably to describe the process that extends from research generation and synthesis to access, adoption, and sustained uptake. In this chapter, the term knowledge translation (KT) will be used to describe this range of techniques and the associated science.

A central understanding among network members is that, to engage stakeholders in research use, KT strategies need to be tailored for specific audiences with whom we engage in knowledge sharing. Studies led by the Offord Centre for Child Studies using a marketing technique, consumer preference modelling, suggest that even within broad audiences for mental health information (e.g., parents of children with mental health problems), there are segments that prefer certain formats over others (Cunningham et al., 2008). Moreover, KT best practice dictates that targeted messages are more effective in achieving knowledge-sharing aims, such as increasing awareness, knowledge, and/or changing practice or behaviour (Goering, Ross, Jacobsen, & Butterill 2006). Similarly, the specific aims or goals for knowledge translation must be considered when selecting strategies (Goering et al., 2006). That is, sharing basic mental health literacy information with a goal of awareness building would suggest different knowledge translation strategies than would a project to develop or incorporate new behaviours with respect to a particular treatment strategy.

CYMHIN members work with a range of audiences. The breadth of activities and foci across sites has provided a rich opportunity to share ideas and approaches that may be adaptable to new settings. This chapter will provide an overview of selected projects focusing on three target audiences: (1) practitioners in children's mental health services, (2) allied professionals who work with children and youth, and (3) the public at large.

Practitioners in Children's Mental Health Services

There is increasing emphasis in the field of child and youth mental health on the implementation of evidence-based practices (Garland, Kruse, & Aarons, 2003). Practitioners and leadership in provider organizations are coming to terms with the need to ensure services are of the best quality and backed by science. In Ontario, the last decade has seen extensive implementation and change in outcome measurement, such that we now have a common metric in place for assessing outcomes as the result of services in 114 provider organizations across the province. Although there continues to be some measure of variability in how well service providers are using aggregate outcome data for service planning, some are making efforts to examine the services they have on offer and whether these represent the most scientifically sound for the clients they are seeing.

The establishment of an outcome measurement system is but the first of many building blocks needed to move the field toward evidence-based practice. Providers need processes, tools, and facilitation to assist them in considering which evidence-based practices are best for their client populations, and to engage in the often complex and extensive process of implementation. At present, the existing inventory of implementation frameworks is limited, and the effectiveness of many KT strategies remain untested in the Child and Youth Mental Health (CYMH) field (Barwick et al., in press).

The field must engage in further research on KT strategy effectiveness and implementation processes and frameworks, but the pool of strategies and frameworks must also evolve. For several years now, the Community Health Systems Resource Group at the Hospital for Sick Children has been exploring how social media—specifically wikis, can support practice change and implementation of evidence-based practice.

Leveraging Practice Change with Social Media

Implementation science has long identified the role of social interaction in practice change and scale-up efforts. Social media supports the human need for social interaction, using Web-based technologies, and provides the medium to transform knowledge exchange from one to many into collaborative dialogues, or many to many. For social media to support practice change, practitioners need to appreciate the value added for their work and patients, and a central way to do this is through storytelling and building connections.

Exploratory work using a wiki to support clinician practice change has been ongoing related to our support and oversight for Ontario's outcome measurement initiative. In Ontario, 114 CYMH organizations comprising over 6,000 practitioners have been mandated since 2000 to adopt an electronic version of a standardized outcome measurement tool to monitor client response to treatment and measure service outcomes. The Child and Adolescent Functional Assessment Scale (CAFAS) (Hodges, 2003) is a clinician-rated global measure of functional impairment in children aged 6–18 years who have or may have emotional, behavioural, substance use, psychiatric, or psychological problems. An overview of its use in Ontario is provided elsewhere (Barwick, Boydell, Cunningham, & Ferguson, 2004).

Nine years of CAFAS training and implementation have identified a pressing need to develop practitioners' knowledge beyond that which is imparted during training to rate the tool. Recognizing that what is needed is a range of KT and educational supports, our team developed an implementation support infrastructure (Barwick, Boydell, & Omrin, 2002) that includes reliability and software training; Web, wiki, email, and telephone supports; site visits for individualized consultation; and regional face-to-face communities of practice. Recently published research has documented that communities of practice can lead to faster uptake of the outcome measurement tool in practice (Barwick, Peters, & Boydell, 2009). The "communi-CAFAS wiki" is a virtual community for provincial CAFAS users that is intended to leverage the regional face-to-face communities of practice by adding a virtual meeting place. It is also a part of our model of implementation support.

Hospitals were the early adopters of social media (Bennett, 2010), with over 871 hospitals using social media tools such as Twitter, Facebook, and YouTube. Our experience with wikis has taught us several valuable lessons, and reiterated how difficult it is to change practice, even when that practice is to visit a wiki, and to make time for reflective practice and continuous learning. Starting with a wiki working group in August 2007, the SickKids team was oriented to the Web

2.0 technology and a relationship with our wiki vendor, Socialtext, was brokered. We had a month-long trial run in January 2008 and began training our CAFAS in Ontario staff in March 2008. Training for practitioners in the field began in May of that year and remains ongoing at each training opportunity.

We have purposefully grown our wiki membership slowly, allowing time to learn, adapt, and train new users. From our earliest tracking accounts in March 2009, we have grown from a membership of 450 to 666 users as of April 2010 (See Figure 6.1).

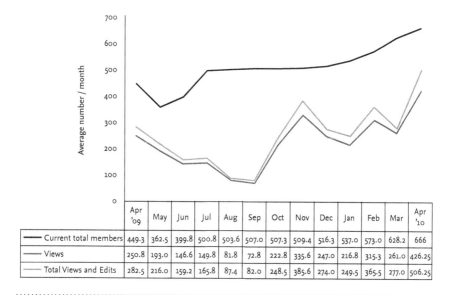

	Apr '09	May	Jun	Jul	Aug	Sep	Oct	Nov	Dec	Jan	Feb	Mar	Apr '10
⎯⎯ Current total members	449.3	362.5	399.8	500.8	503.6	507.0	507.3	509.4	516.3	537.0	573.0	628.2	666
⎯⎯ Views	250.8	193.0	146.6	149.8	81.8	72.8	222.8	335.6	247.0	216.8	315.3	261.0	426.25
⎯⎯ Total Views and Edits	282.5	216.0	159.2	165.8	87.4	82.0	248.5	385.6	274.0	249.5	365.5	277.0	506.25

Figure 6.1

Web 2.0 research suggests that 10% of overall users will visit a wiki site in the first 30 days; 10% will participate in the overall usage of the wiki. According to authors and bloggers Ben McConnell and Jackie Huba, 90% will browse or lurk, essentially viewing content without contributing, while 9% will edit or modify the content, and 1% will create the content (McConnell, 2006).

In our experience, we have been able to accomplish just under 3% of unique content creators/contributors every month (see Figure 6.2). In the course of one week on our Communi-CAFAS wiki (03/2010), we had 2 (0.45%) unique contributors and 22 (3.5%) unique visitors out of a membership of 621 practitioners. A collaborativeness score of 9 represents the number of unique contributors as a percent of unique visitors.

Surprisingly, it is our lack of success in engaging clinicians more quickly and in more active participation that is the main message of our learning to date.

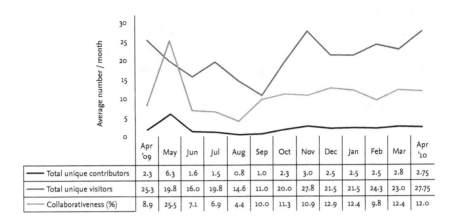

	Apr '09	May	Jun	Jul	Aug	Sep	Oct	Nov	Dec	Jan	Feb	Mar	Apr '10
—— Total unique contributors	2.3	6.3	1.6	1.5	0.8	1.0	2.3	3.0	2.5	2.5	2.5	2.8	2.75
—— Total unique visitors	25.3	19.8	16.0	19.8	14.6	11.0	20.0	27.8	21.5	21.5	24.3	23.0	27.75
----- Collaborativeness (%)	8.9	25.5	7.1	6.9	4.4	10.0	11.3	10.9	12.9	12.4	9.8	12.4	12.0

Figure 6.2

Recently, a group think tank opportunity we led at the National Institutes of Health (NIH) 3rd Annual Conference on Dissemination and Implementation provided an opportunity to share our experiences with others. Group thinking led to the following reflective propositions and tips:

- Users need freedom to share their ideas within the context of a safe environment.
- The motivation and desire to share ideas is a better indicator of wiki use than is a user's age.
- Collaboration makes you competitive: as such, considerations for academic promotion and tenure must look beyond conventional academic activities.
- Clinicians need to see clearly and succinctly how they can contribute and make use of wikis; too many options can lead to decision paralysis.
- Clinicians need to see and understand how the wiki will improve their professional lives. This, however, is not often apparent in the early stages of use, leading to the question of how this initial barrier can be addressed.
- Incorporating wiki use into daily activity promotes comfort with the tool.
- Monitoring the level of accuracy of the information shared on wiki sites is important, other users' comments and critiques help with this tremendously.
- Charging one person as web weaver on the wiki site is important to handle administrative tasks, monitor site activity, and promote engagement.
- Privacy issues and strict quality assurance procedures often present a barrier to wiki collaboration.
- Take small incremental steps to create comfort around issues of privacy and comfort with the tool.

- Managerial-level buy-in is essential; a cultural shift within the workplace is required for change.
- Leaders can become champions of wiki use.
- Tapping in to other social media (e.g., Twitter) could help to drive traffic.
- Give-aways can serve as incentives to promote wiki use.
- Engaging reminder emails can act as a bridge between emails and user groups.
- Including contributors/topics of the week/month piques interest and increases traffic.
- Inviting a high-profile person to the group can attract community and entice participation.
- Give wiki user groups an opportunity to meet face to face periodically.

We continue to invite more practitioners to our wiki space, and to discover new active methods for engaging them. In time, we will look for funding opportunities to examine our efforts with greater rigour and to document the impact of this knowledge translation strategy.

Developing Virtual Communities of Practice (VCoPS)

Children's Mental Health Ontario (CMHO) undertook a very pragmatic and participatory process with its membership of 85 child- and youth-serving agencies in developing communities of practice (CoPs). Initially, CMHO envisioned launching several regional CoPs across the province where members would meet face to face or by teleconference to discuss evidence-based practices (EBPs). By engaging stakeholders early on and incorporating their feedback throughout the process, the notion of regional communities gave way to the development of six Web-based virtual CoPs (VCoPs). Their evolution is outlined below.

During the exploration and planning stage, staff from member agencies as well as representatives from community stakeholders were asked about their interest in cultivating regional CoPs. Although there was interest in and recognition of the value of CoPs, the reality was that the majority of agencies lacked the capacity and human resources necessary to successfully carry out their development. Consequently, when it came time to nominate "champions" to lead a CoP or for regions to set up and host a CoP, individuals were hesitant to take on leadership roles.

With this knowledge in hand, CMHO decided to host and resource the VCoPs. We began by customizing an online platform using free open source software. Various methods were employed to identify topics of interest from which to form CoPs: for example, members were polled, CMHO was approached by specific groups requesting technical and resource support for existing CoPs (e.g., Home-based Services, Reducing Restraints), and CMHO identified areas of need (e.g., Privacy Practices). The VCoPs were formed with the intent to: (1) foster knowledge building and sharing, (2) support networking among member centres across the province, (3) support and showcase existing CoPs, (4) discuss specific evidence-based interventions and implementation practices, and (5) narrow the gap between research to practice. Once the platform was up and running, a multi-stage roll-out of the pilots began.

Currently, CMHO is piloting six virtual communities. They include: EBP Implementation and Outcomes, Reducing Restraints, Accreditation Leads, Home-Based Services, Dialectical Behavioural Therapy, and Privacy Practices. To ensure their success, each VCoP is assigned a moderator who provides both technical and social support (Gray, 2004). Moderator guidelines were created to assist moderators in carrying out their role.

To date, positive knowledge translation/exchange outcomes include: identifying gaps in knowledge, service delivery, and clinical practices; developing, disseminating, and implementing best practice polices addressing identified gaps; hosting peer-led webinars; and compiling e-repositories of tools and resources.

The VCoPs are active to varying degrees. However, participation remains low. Thus far we have a total of 191 members with 133 topics identified and some 299 posts. Challenges in supporting these VCoPs include overcoming barriers due to the level of comfort with and access to technology (Garcia & Dorohovich, 2005), building trust among members, and fostering active participation (McDermott, 1999). That said, it should be noted that we are in the early stages of implementation. Key areas that require further development and attention include providing ongoing support and training to sustain the use of the platform as well as evaluating the VCoPs to determine if they are an effective knowledge exchange strategy. Lessons learned include the need to employ multiple communication modalities including teleconferences, webinars, web-casts, and face-to-face meetings to encourage participation and draw members to the forums, and to rigorously market the VCoPs to engage new members. Overcoming these barriers and applying the lessons learned will increase the likelihood that VCoPs have a place in CMHO's knowledge exchange initiatives.

Engaging Allied Professionals

In the area of child and youth mental health, allied professionals play an important role, but their knowledge needs are significantly different from those of direct service providers (Flaspohler, Anderson-Butcher, & Wandersman, 2008; Rowling, 2009). Educators, for example, are often the first line for identifying students with mental health issues, and for directing them and their families to pathways for care. Research-based mental health literacy is, however, not a part of their usual training.

In recent scans of the practice landscape, it was determined that educators are gravely concerned about student mental health, but feel ill-prepared to respond to the issues they observe in classrooms each day (Intercamhs, 2008; Short, Ferguson, & Santor, 2009). The goals for KT for this audience are: to raise awareness about mental health, to reduce stigmatization, to provide strategies for first response, and to alert educators to programs and techniques that can be applied universally to promote positive student mental health.

In terms of context for delivering KT, it is also important to be aware of the learning preferences of educators. Recent systematic reviews related to educator practice change have demonstrated a solid relationship between high-quality collaborative Continuing Professional Development and Learning (CPDL) and positive outcomes for teacher practice and for student performance (Cordingley, Bell, Rundell, & Evans, 2003; Timperley, 2006). Educator outcomes, such as an enhanced sense of professional efficacy and greater commitment to changing instructional practice to include new evidence-based methods, have been highlighted. At the student level, use of CPDL has been associated with enhanced motivation and confidence, increased participation, increased satisfaction with their work, and improvements in learning and performance. The core features of collaborative Continuing Professional Development and Learning that are linked to these positive outcomes include:

- Use of external expertise linked to school-based activity
- Observation and feedback
- Involving the teachers in applying and refining new knowledge and skills and experimenting with ways of integrating them in their day-to-day practice
- Emphasis on peer support rather than exclusive leadership by supervisors
- Processes to encourage, extend, and structure professional dialogue as well as ongoing collaborative working
- Processes for sustaining the CPDL over time to enable teachers to embed the practices in their own classroom settings
- Working in small groups, which may be more effective than larger discussion groups

The Knowledge Mobilization and Implementation Science Lab at the Hamilton-Wentworth District School Board (KM Lab @ HWDSB), an E-BEST initiative, has been drawing on this literature to create and test knowledge translation and exchange strategies for educators that align with these princi-ples. Two KTE projects currently underway in the Lab, the School-Based Mental Health Learning Forum, and the Making a Difference Educator Resource, illus-trate this connection to the CPDL literature.

Bringing Scientists and Educators into Conversation: The School-Based Mental Health Learning Forum

The School-Based Mental Health (SBMH) Learning Forum aims to link evidence and practice by creating a sustained, structured, and inter-professional dialogue about the mental health of youth in a secondary school setting. It is designed to enhance research-based mental health literacy among educators and, recipro-cally, to foster a deeper understanding among researchers of the realities that make implementation of evidence-based practices challenging in schools. The Forum creates opportunities for face-to-face and electronic dialogue between researchers and education professionals. Three specific KT strategies have been piloted within the forum:

1. Mental Health Speaker and Dialogue Series—Engaging experts in child and youth mental health to lead sessions with all school staff related to topics identified by teachers as most pressing and relevant (e.g., identify-ing symptoms of common mental health problems, talking with students and parents about mental health, navigating local pathways to care).
2. Study Group Sessions—Engaging experts in child and youth mental health to lead and coach small group sessions on a focused topic (e.g., anxiety) with a view to collaboratively selecting evidence-based strategies to imple-ment in the classroom, with opportunity for peer support, observation, and coaching to assist with embedding practices in classroom culture.
3. E-Forum—An online tool to facilitate dialogue between sessions, links to resources, and so forth.

Now in its second year, the SBMH Learning Forum evolved iteratively and collaboratively with school staff and scientists. The KM Lab @ HWDSB is moni-toring the implementation of this platform. Key learnings to date suggest the importance of co-creation of the Forum, the value of intermediaries to bridge the worlds of research and practice (i.e., members of the KM Lab who serve as "go betweens" and coordinate sessions), and the commitment to developing a long-term relationship between researchers and practitioners in education (Davies, Gardner, Parkin, & Short, 2009; Short, Gardner, Eaton, & Buchanan, 2010).

Nurturing Implementation: The Making a Difference Resource

Building on CYMHIN products developed for parents related to child and youth mental health information, network members created a resource for teachers about common mental health issues and how best to respond in the classroom. The resource is meant to offer Bottom-Line Actionable Messages (BLAMs) that resonate with teachers, providing them with user-friendly evidence-based strategies that can be easily embedded into school life. A consulting team of educators, community clinicians, and researchers have helped to shape this resource and are assisting with an implementation pilot across two Ontario school boards. In this pilot, Making a Difference Leads in each school select from an implementation menu and track the use of the resource within the school. Leads work with a coach from the Consultation Team to deepen implementation efforts. The use of coaches has been instrumental in motivating teachers to use and share the resource. Also critical to stimulating uptake has been the deliberate attempt to appeal to both teachers' minds and hearts in delivering the resource. That is, knowing that addressing mental health problems in school using evidence-informed techniques can assist the one in five children who struggle with these issues is important, but knowing they "made a difference to that one" is the driver for moving teachers to embedding this resource into their daily work.

Moving evidence about child and youth mental health into practice in allied settings has unique challenges. Network members are building emerging knowledge about techniques that appear to optimize KT efforts in schools. In addition to conducting original experiments in this area, through E-BEST, the KM Lab @ HWDSB aims to facilitate the work of other scientists with an interest in this area, providing access to educators and the range of services associated with the Lab.

Moving Information and Evidence to Broader Audiences

Providing mental health information to broad audiences can improve mental health literacy, increase help-seeking in families and young people who might not access services otherwise, and may contribute to reducing stigma about mental health problems. While mental health prevention and promotion have long been recognized as important elements in a comprehensive mental health plan, few resources have been directed to these efforts.

YooMagazine (www.yoomagazine.net) is a Web-based interactive health and mental health literacy program designed for youth, parents, and teachers. It gives youth reliable information in a variety of formats while providing schools with timely information about students' health and mental health needs. Students receive monthly "editions" that include articles, polls, quizzes, and interactive games.

This program was developed by psychologist Darcy Santor and psychiatrist Alexa Bagnell, with contributions from experts across the country (Santor, & Bagnell, 2008). YooMagazine is available to schools and community groups throughout Canada. Research informs the material that is shared virtually and captures the impact of this technological approach to knowledge exchange with young people.

A parallel edition is produced for teachers and other school personnel, which includes additional information about the topics in that month's magazine, as well as suggestions for using YooMagazine in the classroom. A similar parallel edition is also available for parents, providing information and help for them to discuss the topics covered in that edition.

Topics include relevant mental health issues such as depression, bullying, date violence, relationships, anxiety, and anger management. Each individual school can "filter out" topics that may conflict with the values and beliefs of that school or school board. For instance, many religious schools filter articles on birth control that conflict with their teaching.

A feature of YooMagazine that is particularly attractive to schools is the ability to provide interactive polls on such subjects as school inclusiveness and climate, problems with bullying, and other issues of importance to students and educators. With the recent emphasis on student engagement as an important predictor of student success, educators can receive regular feedback from their students.

YooMagazine combines high-quality information with an electronic format that is appealing to young people. Usage statistics help identify topics of greater interest, and also show that most young people are accessing the information outside of school hours. Many of the mental health topics are accessed in the early hours.

eMentalHealth.ca (www.ementalhealth.ca) is a web-based resource that combines local knowledge of resources and information with high-quality information about child and youth mental health problems. It also includes a local events calendar, newsworthy items about child and youth mental health, and screening tools for common mental health problems that individuals can access.

eMentalHealth.ca operates under a "distributed workload" model, where local partners supply their knowledge of services and programs while eMentalHealth.ca supplies the open-access software that enables the consistent gathering and display of information from community to community. While much of the information currently available on the site is limited to communities in eastern Ontario, a number of national organizations have expressed interest in becoming information partners.

Much of the general information about child and youth mental health problems has been written by members of the CYMHIN, and is shared under a Creative Commons license that allows others to freely share and reprint information, provided the original source is cited, and it is a not-for-profit venture.

The Community Education Service (www.communityed.ca) uses a similar "distributed workload" method to produce quarterly information flyers about workshops, courses, and groups that are offered in a local community. Each agency can log on to the website for their community, update information about the courses they offer, or add new courses they have developed. Information about the courses offered during a particular time period are then rolled up in an automated report that can be delivered in a print version or electronically.

In one local community, more than 75,000 copies of the flyer are printed, and then distributed through partnerships with local school boards to every parent. This reduces the stigma of a parent being "singled out" as one who needs help with parenting or other problems, and also provides a powerful incentive for agencies to meet the publication deadlines and keep their information up to date.

A common thread running through these projects is the innovative use of traditional health promotion messages and new technologies, such as web-based publishing, distributed work loads, and mass customization. The challenge in providing information in this manner is understanding and responding to a wide range of preferences and clients.

Communicating directly to a broad audience allows for two-way communication that enables refinement and tailoring of messages. This should be accompanied by systematic research into audience preferences, as the audience members who respond may not be representative of the audience as a whole. Social desirability biases and a keen interest on the part of audience members almost always results in requests for more information and detail. The voice of those who "just want a little information they can read in 10 minutes" is seldom heard, although this time constraint is shown consistently in consumer preferences.

SUMMARY

The CYMHIN projects demonstrate a variety of techniques that can enable KT and move evidence into practice. Partner members are experimenting with innovations such as social media, virtual and face-to-face communities of practice, platforms for co-learning, and Web and print resource use. The range of strategies employed speaks to the need for a careful understanding of the specific audience targeted as an exchange partner. Methods that work well with one audience may not work with other audiences.

Moreover, broad audiences, such as mental health practitioners or teachers, are seldom homogeneous. An audience may require a variety of approaches and messages. Detailed research into consumer preferences has long been a standard in marketing new products. A similar approach has begun to be applied to knowledge exchange, with choice-based conjoint techniques allowing a detailed understanding of information preferences within an audience.

Despite the differences across settings, much can be learned from the innovations that are applied for varying audiences. CYMHIN members have found that the knowledge exchange that takes place within the network has inspired the generation of many new resources and practices. By sharing information about projects or approaches that have worked, and techniques that have failed, all members of the network benefit from each other's learning and experimentation. This direct modelling of a "community of practice" in knowledge exchange allows us to understand the challenges and reap the benefits that our audiences and partners in the field are also facing.

ENDNOTE

1. These documents and further background information about the network are available at www. CYMHIN.ca.

REFERENCES

Barwick M.A., Schacter, H.M., Bennett L.M., McGowan J., Ly, M., Wilson A., et al. (in press). Knowledge translation efforts in child and youth mental health: A systematic review. *Implementation Science.*

Barwick M., Peters J., & Boydell, K.M. (2009). Getting to uptake: Do communities of practice support the implementation of evidence-based practice? *Journal of the Canadian Academy of Child and Adolescent Psychiatry, 18,* 16–29.

Barwick, M.A., Boydell, K.M., Cunningham, C.E., & Ferguson, H.B. (2004). Overview of Ontario's screening and outcome measurement initiative in children's mental health. *Canadian Child and Adolescent Psychiatry Review, 13,* 105–109.

Barwick, M.A., Boydell, K.M., & Omrin, C. (2002). *A knowledge transfer infrastructure for children's mental health in Ontario: Building capacity for research and practice.* Toronto, ON: The Hospital for Sick Children. Retrieved October 31, 2010, from www.cafasinontario.ca/downloads/knowledge_transfer.pdf

Bennett, E. (2010, October 19). Hospital social network list. *Social Media Resources for Health Care Professionals.* Retrieved October 25, 2010, from http://ebennett.org/

Cordingley, P., Bell, M., Rundell, B., & Evans, D. (2003). The impact of CPD on classroom teaching and learning. In *Research Evidence in Education Library, Version 1.1.* London: EPPI-Centre, Social Science Research Unit, Institute of Education.

Cunningham, C.E., Deal, K., Rimas, H., Buchanan, D.H., Gold, M., Sdao-Jamie, K., et al. (2008). Modeling the information preferences of parents of children with mental health problems: A discrete choice conjoint experiment. *Journal of Abnormal Child Psychology, 7,* 1123–1138.

Davies, S., Gardner, S., Parkin, C., & Short, K.H. (2009). *School-based mental health learning forum: A feasibility pilot.* Ottawa, ON: Report submitted to the Provincial Centre of Excellence for Child and Youth Mental Health at CHEO.

Flaspohler, D., Anderson-Butcher, D., & Wandersman, A., (2008). Supporting implementation of expanded school mental health services: Application of the interactive systems framework in Ohio. *Advances in School Mental Health Promotion, 1,* 38–48.

Garcia, J., & Dorohovich, M. (2005). The truth about building and maintaining successful communities of practice. *Defense Acquisition Review Journal, 10,* 18–33.

Garland, A.F., Kruse, M., & Aarons, G.A. (2003). Clinicians and outcome measurement: What's the use? *Journal of Behavioral Health Services & Research, 30,* 393–405.

Goering, P., Ross, S., Jacobson, N., & Butterill, D. (2006). *A tool and accompanying guide for assessing health research knowledge translation (KT) plans, in towards more effective peer review of knowledge translation (KT) plans in research grant proposals.* Retrieved October 25, 2010, from http://www.camh.net/hsrcu

Gray, B. (2004). Informal learning in an online community of practice. *Journal of Distance Education, 19,* 20-35.

Hodges, K. (2003). *Child and adolescent functional assessment scale* (3rd ed.). Ypsilanti, MI: Eastern Michigan University.

Intercamhs. (2008). *International survey of principals concerning emotional and mental health and well-being: Report of major findings.* Newton, MA: Educational Development Center, Health and Human Development Programs.

McConnell, B. (2006, May 3). *The 1% rule: Charting citizen participation, Ben McConnell and Church of the Customer blog.* Retrieved May 3, 2006, from www.churchofthecustomer.com/blog/2006/05/charting_wiki_p.html

McDermott, R. (1999). Learning across teams: How to build communities of practice in team organizations. *Knowledge Management Review, 8,* 32–36.

Mitton, C., Adair, C.E., McKenzie, E., Patten, S.B., & Waye Perry, B. (2007). Knowledge transfer and exchange: Review and synthesis of the literature. *Milbank Quarterly, 85,* 729–768.

Rowling, L. (2009). Strengthening "school" in school mental health promotion. *Health Education, 109,* 357–368.

Santor, D.A., & Bagnell, A. (2008). Enhancing the effectiveness and sustainability of school based mental health programs: Maximizing program participation, knowledge uptake and ongoing evaluation using internet based resources. *Advances in School Mental Health Promotion, 1,* 17–28.

Short, K.H., Ferguson, B., & Santor, D. (2009). *Scanning the practice landscape in school-based mental health.* Ottawa, ON: The Provincial Centre of Excellence for Child and Youth Mental Health at CHEO.

Short, K.H., Gardner, S., Eaton, I., & Buchanan, D. H. (2010, February). *The development of a knowledge mobilization lab: What are the best ways to mobilize research knowledge in school board settings?* Poster presented at the Ontario Education Research Symposium, Toronto, ON.

Timperley, H. (2006). Teacher professional learning and development. In J. Brophy (Ed.), *The educational practices series.* Brussels: International Academy of Education & Bureau of Education.

CHAPTER 7

CHANGING LIVES THROUGH TECHNOLOGY AND INNOVATION

IAN WATSON, *Project Manager, Institute for Research and Innovation in Social Services*

AMY O'NEIL, *Project Manager, Institute for Research and Innovation in Social Services*

ALISON PETCH, *Ph.D., Director, Institute for Research and Innovation in Social Services*

ABSTRACT

The *Changing Lives* agenda of the Scottish Executive in Scotland promotes the development of a competent, confident, and valued workforce, focused on the delivery of effective outcomes for people who use services. This chapter will demonstrate how the potential of Web 2.0 technologies is being harnessed by the Institute for Research and Innovation in Social Services (IRISS) to provide a range of resources for those involved in supporting children. In addition to a range of multimedia learning resources, communities of practice, and web portals, the potential of the IRISS tool kit *Confidence through Evidence* will be highlighted. This is a tool kit for accessing and using research that seeks to assist with both knowledge mobilization and the creation of social learning networks.

INTRODUCTION

The particular challenges of achieving evidence-informed practice among the social services workforce have been well documented (e.g., Sheldon & Macdonald, 1999; Stevens, Liabo, Roberts, & Witherspoon, 2009). The baseline survey of practitioners in England by Sheldon and Chilvers (2000) highlighted the relatively low profile of research findings in daily practice, with just over half of the respondents considering that their practice was influenced by research. Marsh (2002) captured the tension between the traditional dissemination of research results through journal articles and books and the preference of many practitioners for "relational knowledge," that is, consultation with colleagues and

supervisors. This was evidenced by Booth, Booth, & Falzon (2003) in their study of attitudes to evidence-based practice, access to information, and training requirements among social care practitioners in five local authorities within the English Trent region. Respondents cited heavy workloads, lack of accessibility to relevant information, and absence of time allocated to finding and reading research. More fundamentally, they queried whether there was a culture that encouraged asking questions and seeking evidence-based solutions. The knowledge and information-seeking habits of social work practice assessors, a particular subset of the workforce, have been reported by Horder (2007). For this group there is much more ready access and use of the Internet; talking to colleagues and other forms of verbal communication remain, however, the most important sources of knowledge.

Most recently the use of different sources of evidence has been detailed in two English local council authorities by Cooke, Bacigalupo, Halladay, & Norwood (2008), who conclude that "making research evidence more available through different formats and multiple sources can improve the use of evidence in practice" (p. 546). Responses from 368 individuals suggested that 69 percent had access to the Internet at work, with two-thirds of these using it; 31 percent had access to journals, and just under a half of these used them; and literature databases were accessible to only 13 percent and research summaries to 21 percent. Access varied significantly by location, highest in central offices and lowest, perhaps surprisingly, in hospital settings. Use of a range of evidence sources was positively correlated with having a post-graduate qualification.

Scotland is fortunate in being able to provide wider access to web-based bibliographic databases and full-text journals through the extension to social services staff of the resources available to National Health Service staff. As yet we do not have comparable usage data although it is hoped that a survey currently being conducted by IRISS will provide this baseline. This article will detail a range of resources that have been developed in an attempt to overcome some of the traditional barriers to evidence-informed practice outlined above, equipping the Scottish social services workforce with the routes to the delivery of effective outcomes.

THE SCOTTISH CONTEXT

> If we are serious about developing social work as a profession and having practitioners able to practise safely and innovatively, then we need to both develop and use evidence to inform practice. (Scottish Executive, 2006, p. 55)

A major review of social work in Scotland was undertaken in 2006. It concluded that doing more of the same won't work, with increasing demand, greater complexity, and rising expectations all contributing to the need for development. *Changing Lives: Report of the 21st Century Social Work Review* (Scottish Executive, 2006) sets out the agenda for building a competent, confident, and valued workforce. This highlights the key role for what they term evidence-based practice and provides a context for much of the work undertaken by IRISS.

> Evidence based practice has a crucial role to play in this area. Workers will need access to up-to-date research findings, evidence of what works, evaluation tools, methods for carrying out quality audits and successful ways of involving people who use services in evaluating them.... These kinds of tools will play a critical role in developing practice which is sharply focused on performance improvement. (Scottish Executive, 2006, p. 71)

Against this backdrop, a specific initiative has emerged in relation to children, *A Guide to Getting It Right for Every Child* (GIRFEC) (Scottish Government, 2008). Building on *For Scotland's Children* (Scottish Executive, 2000) and in line with the UN Convention on the Rights of Children, GIRFEC is a national approach to supporting and working with all children and young people in Scotland. Building on research and practice evidence, it is designed to help practitioners focus on what makes a positive difference for children and young people and act to deliver these improvements. It seeks to achieve a number of objectives:

- Better outcomes for all children
- A common, coordinated framework across all agencies that supports the delivery of appropriate, proportionate, and timely help to all children as they need it
- Streamlined systems and processes, efficient and effective delivery of services focused on the needs of the child
- A common understanding and shared language across all agencies
- A child-centred approach
- Changes in culture, systems, and practice across services for children
- More joined-up policy development with GIRFEC in the delivery mechanism of all policies for children (and policies for adults where children are involved)
- The ambition for Scotland's children is that they are confident individuals, effective contributors, successful learners, and responsible citizens

THE CONTRIBUTION OF IRISS THROUGH TECHNOLOGICAL DEVELOPMENT

The Institute for Research and Innovation in Social Services (IRISS) is a voluntary sector organization, funded to support the social services workforce to deliver positive outcomes for the people who use Scotland's social services. It works through three core programs: evidence-informed practice, innovation and improvement, and knowledge media. Our in-house team combines a range of skills—Web applications analyst, multimedia designer, multimedia developer, knowledge management professionals, and evidence-informed practice specialists—to harness the potential of Web 2.0 technologies.

Web 2.0 is a term coined to describe websites and services that allow users to interact with other users, share and collaborate, or change website content. This contrasts with the first generation of non-interactive websites in which users were limited to the passive viewing of information.[1] Collaborative tools include:

- Social bookmarking services such as Delicious and Diigo
- RSS, which allows the contents of one website to be syndicated, or shared with other websites
- Blogs, which allow the free flow of comment and opinion
- Media-sharing sites such as YouTube for video and Flickr for still images

Before the widespread availability of collaborative sites, the only practical way to distribute video was on hard media such as CD or DVD, which incur tangible creation and distribution costs. YouTube and Flickr have demonstrated how simple it can be to create and share video and still images respectively. In the UK, almost every BBC Radio program is available as a podcast, that is, a series of programs packaged and delivered (or "shared") in a form that can be listened to on MP3 players, such as iTunes.

While many of the developments have been characterized as trivial or simply passing consumer fads, we believe they offer great potential for creating and sharing "bite-sized" learning materials.

LEARNING EXCHANGE

In 2005, the IRISS launched the Learning Exchange, a digital repository of learning objects. The learning objects were catalogued in accordance with international metadata standards[2] to allow interoperability with other systems. In particular, the intention was that multimedia learning objects could be downloaded as IMS[3] packages and uploaded into virtual learning environments in higher education institutions.

The Learning Exchange was built using IntraLibrary software (Intrallect, 2009) and access was restricted to students and staff of the higher educational institutions in Scotland engaged in teaching social work. Access was password-protected using the Athens Eduserve[4] authentication system. Working with National Health Service Education Scotland (NES), we were able to extend access to the entire social services workforce in Scotland, again using Athens Eduserve for password protection. These two initiatives allowed the Learning Exchange to become part of a portfolio of licensed content available to the higher education sector and the entire social services workforce.

In practice, much of the content of the Learning Exchange does not require password protection, partly because in 2008 IRISS adopted a policy of releasing its own content using Creative Commons[5] licensing. As IntraLibrary itself supports information sharing by allowing metadata to be exposed for harvesting by third parties, we decided to create an "open" interface (Institute for Research and Innovation in Social Services, 2010a) that removed the barrier of registering for and remembering passwords.

The ability to allow metadata harvesting by third parties means that Learning Exchange content is automatically searchable by Social Services Knowledge Scotland (SSKS), a portal to social service knowledge and information created by NHS Education Scotland (NES) in partnership with IRISS, Scottish Social Services Learning Networks, and the Social Care Institute for Excellence (Social Services Knowledge Scotland, n.d.).

IRISS Multimedia

Beginning in 2005, IRISS began creating web-based multimedia learning objects based on scenarios devised by social work educators. The scenarios were scripted, professional actors were cast, and then the scenarios were filmed by professional filmmakers.

For example *Children, Families and Child Protection* (Cadman & Cameron, 2009) is a case study focusing on the legal, ethical, and practice issues emerging from a child protection case scenario. Through a series of five short video clips, we see the case from the perspective of the key players: an anonymous caller, social workers, a neighbour, a foster carer, and the 13-year-old girl taken into care. As the case moves from allegations of abuse to planning for permanent care, the learner is asked to interpret and assess an unfolding scenario of complex need.

The Assessment Triangle (IRISS, 2007) is a different kind of learning object, being more text-based. In Scotland, the Assessment Triangle has been adopted within the development of the Integrated Assessment Framework of GIRFEC. This object helps the student understand the key concepts and includes a timeline for a typical child.

The Golden Bridge (IRISS, 2008) represents yet another kind of learning object. It began as a project to "virtualize" an existing social work museum exhibition on the migration of "Home Children" from Scotland to Canada in the late 19th and early 20th centuries (Daly & Ballantyne, 2009).

The exhibition used text, images, video, and a blend of social-historical analyses with witness testimony accounts to describe this complex human story, including the true stories of some Canadian elders in their eighties and nineties. The exhibition included artefacts from Quarriers organization, a major voluntary sector child care agency. These included a selection of "Narratives of Facts," annual reports that detailed stories and images of children who emigrated to Canada. There was also a collection of photographic images from the 1860s depicting children and staff at different stages of the migration journey. The project objectives were:

- To re-establish public access to the exhibition material for research and education
- To repurpose and enhance the exhibition with new digital media
- To preserve the historic artefacts

The Golden Bridge is a unique example of how new media can be harnessed to re-tell and interpret an old story. The rich virtual media approach adds another dimension to the story of the home children. The audio commentary from the virtual curator, the film of adult home children sharing their experiences of migration, and the ability to zoom in to high-resolution images all serve to bring the exhibits to life.

Audio and Video

The convenience of hearing radio programs again has become well established in recent years. We have been recording research seminars and other events since around 2006, and now have a collection of some 160 recordings, a very effective and inexpensive way of capturing and sharing knowledge.

These recordings are available as a podcast (IRISS, 2010b) either direct from our website or from the iTunes Store.[6] Delivery in this medium allows the opportunity to listen, for example, while driving, or to download the recording and edit it for use in teaching. The National Residential Child Care Initiative was launched in December 2009, and we recorded the various presentations. As part of this event, Who Cares? Scotland[7] had gone to some trouble to create a short dramatization in which young people imagine how residential child care might look in 2014. This dramatization would have been lost had we not recorded it.[8]

Video perhaps requires a little more skill to create and is less easily accessible. Generally, we prefer not to record a video of seminar presentations. Instead, we concentrate on capturing participant reaction through short "vox pop" interviews.

For distribution, we use Vimeo, a free video streaming and sharing service (Vimeo, 2010). This allows us to organize clips into albums for different events, and present, for those unable to attend the event, short overviews of the key points. One of the most powerful uses of this technique is illustrated by the stories told at the Forgotten Citizens conference held in Glasgow in 2008 (Vimeo, 2008).

SOCIAL NETWORKING

A social network is formed when a group of people uses web-based services to create a community in which members interact to share information, knowledge, and experience. Well-known social networking services include Facebook and Friends Reunited, but there are other services aimed at enabling people with shared professional interests to form communities that meet their own needs and preferences.

The sharing of knowledge underpins the success of the GIRFEC agenda, and social networks offer a simple and effective way of sharing and communicating (Scottish Government, 2008). The Knowledge Management Strategy for the Social Services—derived from *Changing Lives*—also stresses the importance of a workforce who are confident and competent in the use of the technologies that allow them to access and share knowledge.

The main benefits of a social network is the creation of a collaborative environment that

- encourages the development and sharing of ideas, knowledge, and expertise;
- supports the sharing of documents, video, audio, and other media;
- supports faster problem-solving;
- reduces the number of documents sent by email;
- reduces the need to file documents and keep track of versions.

We worked with the Multi-Agency Resource Service (MARS) to decide on a suitable platform for a network to enable child protection professionals working in various agencies—including police, higher education, and statutory social work—to share information in a secure environment (Multi-Agency Resource Service, 2010). An important requirement was that the network should be simple to set, join, and maintain. We established that Ning would offer enough features to allow the sharing of formal documents as well as tacit knowledge through discussion forums (Ning, 2010).

INFORMATION LITERACY

Although the Web has revolutionized the way in which we search for, find, use, and share information, not everyone is adept at using this new medium. Indeed, it could be argued that the need for information management skills is greater than in the pre-Web days. As the ubiquity of the Web has grown, a new set of skills have been emerging, known collectively as information literacy: "the ability to find, evaluate and use digital information effectively, efficiently and ethically" (Information Literacy, 2009). In collaboration with NES, we first developed a paper-based manual aimed at helping social services practitioners develop their information literacy skills, and we have recently adapted this into a short and simple interactive web-based introductory tutorial (IRISS, 2010c).

Technical Barriers

The effectiveness of Web 2.0 technology has been severely hampered in the public sector by corporate policies that block access to video-sharing sites such as Vimeo and social networking services such as Ming. Out-of-date browsers such as Internet Explorer 6 also limit the user's ability to make use of the functionality offered by Web 2.0 services, yet some public authorities as a matter of policy do not install later versions. In some cases, plug-ins (such as Flash, which allows video to be played within the browser, or javascript, which is sometimes used for display of contextual help or calendars for selecting dates) are installed only on request. In January 2010, the Society of Information Technology Management (SOCITIM) published a report urging public authorities to "embrace social media and not be party to moves to block staff from using these important new tools for business" (Society of Information Technology Management, 2010).

Confidence through Evidence: Making Better Use of Evidence in Social Services

Social services based on the best evidence of effectiveness are more likely to lead to successful outcomes for the people using them. While it is difficult to contest the principle of evidence-based practice, ensuring that service design, management, and delivery are evidence-informed is rarely easy. In the complex world of social care, with its competing priorities and demands on resources, the process of getting research into practice remains fraught with difficulty.

In an effort to support staff to engage more confidently and effectively with research evidence, IRISS has sought to better understand the relationship between social services research and the work of social services practitioners. In part, this has necessitated an understanding of the various theoretical frameworks advanced for promoting and embedding evidence-informed practice. It has also required an understanding of the barriers and challenges faced by staff in attempting to access and use evidence to improve practice.

The *Confidence through Evidence* tool kit has been developed as a result of these collective understandings and is a key example of the way in which IRISS has harnessed Web 2.0 technologies in an effort to enhance both the use and impact of evidence in practice.

EVIDENCING OUR PRACTICE: THE CASE AND CONTEXT FOR CONFIDENCE THROUGH EVIDENCE

> There is an emerging view that strategies and interventions aimed at promoting research use are most effective when underpinned by an appropriate theoretical framework. (Nutley, Walter, & Davies, 2007, p. 155)

The *Confidence through Evidence* tool kit was conceptualized in the IRISS 2009–2010 business plan as a tool that would "promote the use of research and evidence throughout the workforce." As Nutley et al. (2007) have well documented, developing an intervention aimed at improving evidence-based practice is made challenging by the fact that research use is a complex process that is more often conceptual than empirical, leading to subtle changes in processes and outcomes, rather than to direct changes in practice.

Also complicating the development of interventions to promote research use in the social services is the need to understand the numerous barriers and enablers that shape the use of research in the sector. In a range of studies, management, front-line practitioners, and policy staff have identified the following as among the key barriers to evidence-informed practice (Moseley & Tierney, 2005; Nutley, Walter, & Davies, 2003; Walter et al., 2004):

- Lack of time and competing demands
- Limited access to research evidence
- Lack of skills to appraise research
- Lack of research relevance (real or perceived) to practice
- Lack of organizational support
- Local cultural resistance to research and its use

In response to these barriers, strategies have been developed to facilitate research use in the sector. These strategies include: ensuring a relevant research base, improving access to research, making research comprehensible, and developing an organizational culture that supports research use. While all of these strategies help to inform thinking about what interventions may be most successful in promoting and embedding research use, they do not spell out the relative significance of any given strategy, or combination of strategies, in any one context.

The conceptual models developed by the Research Unit for Research Utilisation (RURU) (i.e., the research-based practitioner model, the embedded model, and the organizational excellence model) capture the various ways in which research use has been promoted in the UK social care sector. These models are useful in emphasizing the importance of context for research utilization,[9] as well as the need for combined strategies in promoting research, particularly those that acknowledge research use as a shared responsibility of both individuals and organizations. In terms of practice, however, they have been criticized for bearing little resemblance to social care realities and for offering little in the way of explicit guidance on how to put research findings into practice (Nutley et al., 2007).

Theories on knowledge management and the diffusion of innovations offer further insights on how research use may be promoted, since both are broadly concerned with how knowledge and ideas are acquired, spread, and acted upon. Knowledge management theorists stress the need for organizations to share knowledge in order to embed it and see the use of technology as critical to that end. Conversely, diffusionists argue that the main barriers to evidence use relate more to the knowing-doing gap (where people have knowledge to improve practice, but do not act upon it) than to sharing problems, and point to organizational configurations as heavily influencing evidence use (Pfeffer & Sutton, 2006) as cited in Nutley et al., 2007). According to diffusion theory, organizational cultures and systems need to support an innovation (in this case, evidence) if it is to be adopted.

The literature on implementation science goes a step further in addressing the knowing-doing gap (or science to service gap) by highlighting that, while evidence may support the *adoption* of an intervention, it does not guarantee its *implementation*. In order to successfully implement an evidence-based intervention, Fixsen and colleagues (2005) suggest that several key components are critical. The most basic of these components is that there is an explicit need for the intervention and that the proposed implementation method is the right one for the context (Guldbrandsson, 2008).

Although a relatively new and underdeveloped body of theory, implementation science appears to offer important guidance on how to address some of the most complex barriers known to impede the process of getting evidence into practice. By acknowledging the importance of evaluation in the implementation process, it also provides a useful framework in which to consider how evidence-based interventions can be continually modified for sustained success.

WHAT IS THE TOOLKIT AND HOW DOES IT WORK?

Confidence through Evidence (IRISS, 2010d) is a web-based tool kit aimed at guiding social services staff through the stages of acquiring, interpreting, and implementing evidence in order to improve practice and service outcomes. It is a tool kit that combines both the organizational excellence and research-informed practitioner approaches to research use, seeing research use as dependent on both individual and organizational influences. It also uses technology as a means of sharing evidence, cultivating skills, and building capacity with the key aim of assisting individuals bridge the gap between science and service.

The tool kit is organized into four general areas of guidance: Acquire, Assess, Adapt, and Apply. While these areas follow a logical sequence, they have been designed in a way that allows them to be accessed and navigated independently of each other. We have not assumed, therefore, that research utilization is a linear process, or that individuals using the tool kit will have the same guidance requirements.

Within each of the four steps, individuals are asked a number of reflective questions relating to evidence use, which then serve as guides to existing Web resources. These Web resources are intended to assist users in acquiring skills and confidence in using evidence in practice. The aim is that social services staff will be alerted to key issues and supported in their ability to arrive at solutions relevant to their own practice needs.

Acquire, Assess, and Adapt

The first three steps of the tool kit provide guidance on how to access, assess, and adapt evidence for practice. In each of these steps, individuals are prompted to think about what type of evidence they need, how to access it, how to assess its credibility, and finally how to adapt it to suit their own context. In each case, important barriers to research use are addressed. In Acquire, for example, problems of accessing evidence are alleviated by assisting users to adopt a strategy for finding evidence and by signposting reputable evidence sites, including Social Services Knowledge Scotland (SSKS) and the Learning Exchange. For those seeking evidence related directly to their field of expertise, the tool kit contains several sector-specific evidence sites. For example, those working in children's services are provided with useful shortcuts to sites such as the National Children's Bureau and the Centre for Excellence and Outcomes in Children and Young People's services. In Assess, our focus has been to address concerns that staff often do not have the skills and/or the confidence to determine the credibility of evidence. In this instance, we have provided useful summaries of the key issues that individuals should consider in appraising research and provided a range of useful Web tools to increase capacity in this area. Finally, in Adapt, users are prompted to consider how their practice experiences and local context come to bear on the ways in which evidence is used. In this step, we aim to tackle concerns that research is rarely relevant to practice by increasing the individuals' capacity to adapt evidence to their own practice setting.

Apply

The Apply step of the tool kit is arguably the most original and has been heavily influenced by implementation science. It is a step designed to help staff turn evidence into action by guiding them through the critical steps of identifying not only effective evidence-based interventions, but also successful methods for implementing and evaluating those interventions. Critical in this step is the effort to alert users to the need for system-level change in successful evidence-informed practice. For instance, in pointing to the criteria for implementing a new practice, users are encouraged to consider which groups will be affected by change, which staff or service users should be involved in implementing the change, and what resources may be required to increase the chances of success.

Organizational culture is also highlighted as important to the implementation process, and here individuals are prompted to consider, depending on the scale of the change proposed, whether their organization is ready or able to change in ways that will enable the evidence-based invention to be successfully implemented. To this end, tool kit users are provided with guidance on how to cope with organizational challenges and provided with various audiovisual tools that may be used to facilitate a shift in organizational culture in support of evidence-based change. A podcast illustrating what works in the area of childhood resilience, for example, can be accessed as a means of stimulating best practice. Similarly, the Apply step provides quick and easy access to evidence summaries, such as those published by the Centre for Excellence and Outcomes, that are geared toward stimulating service improvements for children, young people, and families.[10] In these various ways, the Apply step highlights the interactive nature of evidence use and the importance of social influence and culture in determining the nature of research use and impact.

WEB 2.0 TECHNOLOGY AND THE FUTURE OF THE TOOL KIT

Precisely because of the highly social and collective nature of research use, Nutley et al. (2007) suggest that interactive and social influence approaches hold the most promise in terms of advancing our efforts to increase research use within the social service sector. Examples of such approaches include those that encourage a two-way exchange of knowledge and collaboration between individuals of various backgrounds and organizations (e.g., policy, practice, and academia). Acknowledging this, we at IRISS have sought to utilize our Web 2.0 capabilities in an effort to make *Confidence through Evidence* a more interactive and social tool kit.

At present, tool kit users have the ability to receive updates through RSS feeds on events designed to facilitate the sharing of ideas around evidence and practice among staff across the sector. Through such events, it is hoped that individuals will have the opportunity to adapt and test findings from evidence within local contexts in ways that will support positive practice change. Tool kit users are also able to register to become part of an online network that we hope will help foster communities of practice and allow for best practices to be shared across organizational boundaries.

In the future, we aim to expand the functions of the tool kit in ways that will enable users to comment on the resources provided and to rank and recommend resources and evidence-based practices to other users. In this way, our ultimate aim is for the tool kit to become shaped by its users and for its guidance to be driven by their evidence and practice needs.

The *Confidence through Evidence* tool kit has been developed from the perspective that any tool designed to facilitate evidence use must be based on a dual understanding of how ideas spread through systems and of what capacities, both individual and organizational, are required to effectively act on evidence. While other tools have been developed to promote research use in the UK (e.g., Think Research, Firm Foundations), the strength of *Confidence through Evidence* arguably lies in its ability to go beyond facilitating access to evidence to providing guidance around the much more fraught process of implementing and evaluating evidence-based practices. An important part of that guidance has been to harness Web 2.0 technologies to facilitate collaboration between social services practitioners, academics, and service users in determining the value of research evidence and the uses to which it can be put.

IMPACT ASSESSMENT

The developments outlined above add to a range of resources developed within the evidence utilization sector over the last decade. Common to all these initiatives is a requirement to practice what is preached; that is, to examine their effectiveness. Impact assessment is currently much discussed but rather more rarely implemented. Notable exceptions include Hagell and Spencer (2004) and White, Booth, Cooke, & Addison (2005). The former examined the effectiveness of audio tape in engaging social services staff, exploring the response to a tape produced by Research in Practice (Barratt & Hodson, 2006) on young people leaving care. Those sampled confirmed that individuals tended to pursue research findings only when they had a specific demand generated by their own practice; moreover the preference for the presentation of learning materials was "interpersonal, informal, conversational," yet pitched at a level commensurate with their professional status. The authors conclude that "some accommodation needs to be reached that can bring together the preferences of practitioners on one hand and the evidence of effectiveness of different dissemination methods on the other" (p. 195). The evaluation by White et al. (2005) of information skills training for social care practitioners and librarians again underlines the need not to be overly ambitious, to adjust delivery to the needs of the individual if attitudes and practice are to change.

IRISS will seek to ensure careful evaluation of the different initiatives outlined above and in particular the extent to which they contribute to ensuring a workforce better equipped to deliver improved outcomes for Scotland's children. This is one element within a wider exploration of the nature of impact within research utilization. This is perhaps best conceived as a continuum, allowing for different interpretations of impact at stages of the continuum. An initial exploration, for example, may seek to ensure that individuals have accessed and made use of a resource. A second stage may wish to ascertain changes in individual practice as a result of engagement with the resource. Further along the continuum is a concern with the wider changes within the service system. Ultimately, the litmus test for impact is whether the initiative has made a difference in terms of the outcomes for the individuals who use services. This brings with it all the difficulties of attribution: to what extent can particular outcomes be considered a direct result of the particular intervention or initiative? Perhaps change might have occurred anyway.

Social welfare is a complex and messy process; often there is no direct linear association between input and outcome and judgment has to be on the basis of probability. Increasingly, however, we will focus on seeking to demonstrate, in as robust a fashion as possible, the value of the range of activities, some of them explored here, which collectively contribute to the art and the science of research utilization.

ENDNOTES

1. For a fuller description see: www.en.wikipedia.org/wiki/Web_2.0.
2. Dublin Core: www.dublincore.org, and Learning Object Metadata: www.en.wikipedia.org/wiki/Learning_object_metadata.
3. IMS is a non-profit standards organization concerned with establishing interoperability for learning systems and learning content: www.imsglobal.org.
4. A widely used access and identity management system: www.athensams.net.
5. Creative Commons is a worldwide licensing system that allows copyright holders to specify the purposes for which their work may be used or copied without seeking permission. Use of this system greatly simplifies the sharing and reuse of information: www.creativecommons.org.
6. Go to iTunes and search for "social work."
7. Who Cares? Scotland is a voluntary organization working with and for children and young people in care: www.whocaresscotland.org.
8. The dramatization is available at www.iriss.org.uk/resources/nrcci-future-who-cares-scotland.
9. Different models are seen to have different utility for different groups in the sector.
10. These evidence summaries are called "Progress Maps" and cover a broad range of topics from the well-being of disabled children to child poverty strategies.

REFERENCES

Barratt, M.O., & Hodson, R. (2006). *Firm Foundations: A practical guide to organisational support for the use of research evidence.* Dartington, England: Research in Practice.

Booth, S., Booth, A. & Falzon, L. (2003). The need for information and research skills training to support evidence-based social care: A literature review and survey. *Learning in Health and Social Care, 2,* 191–201.

Cadman, M., & Cameron, K. (2009). *Case study: Children, families, and child protection.* Retrieved October 21, 2010, from http://content.iriss.org.uk/childprotection/

Cooke, J., Bacigalupo, R., Halladay, L., & Norwood, H. (2008). Research use and support needs, and research activity in social care: A cross-sectional survey in two councils with social services responsibilities in the UK. *Health and Social Care in the Community, 16,* 538–547.

Daly, E., & Ballantyne, N. (2009). Retelling the past using new technologies: A case study into the digitization of social work heritage material and the creation of a virtual exhibition. *Journal of Technology in Human Services, 27,* 44–56.

Fixsen, D.L., Naoom, S.F., Blase, K.A., Friedman, R.M., & Wallace, F. (2005). *Implementation research: A synthesis of the literature.* Tampa, FL: University of South Florida, Louse de la Parte Florida Mental Health Institute, National Implementation Research Network.

Guldbrandsson, K. (2008). *From news to everyday use: The difficult art of implementation.* Stockholm, Sweden: Swedish National Institute of Public Health.

Hagell, A., & Spencer, L. (2004). An evaluation of an innovative audiotape method for keeping social care staff up to date with the latest research findings. *Child and Family Social Work, 9,* 187–196.

Horder, W. (2007). "Reading" in professional practice: How social work practice assessors access knowledge and information. *British Journal of Social Work, 37,* 1079–1094.

Information Literacy. (2009). *The information literacy website.* Retrieved October 21, 2010, from www.informationliteracy.org.uk/Information_literacy_definitions/

Intrallect. (2009). *Intralibrary digital repository.* Retrieved October 21, 2010, from www.intrallect.com/index.php/intrallect/products

Institute for Research and Innovation in Social Services. (2007). *The assessment triangle–Introduction.* Retrieved October 21, 2010, from http://content.iriss.org.uk/assessment/

Institute for Research and Innovation in Social Services. (2008). *The golden bridge: Child migration from Scotland to Canada.* Retrieved October 21, 2010, from www.iriss.ac.uk/goldenbridge

Institute for Research and Innovation in Social Services. (2010a). *The learning exchange.* Retrieved October 21, 2010, from www.iriss.org.uk/openlx

Institute for Research and Innovation in Social Services. (2010b). *Podcast.* Retrieved October 21, 2010, from www.iriss.org.uk/category/resource-categories/podcast

Institute for Research and Innovation in Social Services. (2010c). *Information literacy interactive tutorial.* Retrieved October 21, 2010, from www.iriss.org.uk/informationliteracy

Institute for Research and Innovation in Social Services. (2010d). *Confidence through evidence toolkit.* Retrieved October 21, 2010, from http://toolkit.iriss.org.uk/

Marsh, J. (2002). Using knowledge about knowledge utilisation. *Social Work, 47,* 101–104.

Moseley, A., & Tierney, S. (2005). Evidence-based practice in the real world. *Evidence and Policy, 1,* 113–119.

Multi-Agency Resource Service. (2010). *Multi-Agency Resource Service.* Retrieved October 21, 2010, from www.mars.stir.ac.uk

Ning. (2010). *Ning: Create your own social network.* Retrieved October 21, 2010, from www.ning.com/

Nutley, S., Walter, I., & Davies, H. (2003). From knowing to doing: A framework for understanding the evidence-into-practice agenda. *Evaluation, 9,* 125–148.

Nutley, S., Walter, I., & Davies, H. (2007). *Using evidence: How research can inform public services.* Bristol, England: The Policy Press.

Pfeffer, J., & Sutton, R.I. (2006). Hard facts, dangerous half-truths and total nonsense: Profiting from evidence-based management. Boston, MA: Harvard Business School Press.

Scottish Executive. (2000). *For Scotland's children.* Edinburgh, Scotland: Author.

Scottish Executive. (2006). *Changing lives: Report of the 21st century social work review.* Edinburgh, Scotland: Author.

Scottish Government. (2008). *A guide to getting it right for every child.* Retrieved October 21, 2010, from www.scotland.gov.uk/Publications/2008/09/22091734/0

Sheldon, B., & Chilvers, R. (2000). *Evidence-based social care: A study of prospects and problems.* Lyme Regis, England: Russell House Publishing.

Sheldon, B., & Macdonald, G. (1999). *Research and practice in social care: Mind the gap.* Exeter, England: University of Exeter, Centre for Evidence Based Social Services.

Social Services Knowledge Scotland. (n.d.). *Social Services Knowledge Scotland: Sharing knowledge, improving practice, changing lives.* Retrieved October 21, 2010, from www.ssks.org.uk/Default.aspx

Society of Information Technology Management. (2010). *Social media: Why ICT management should lead their organisations to embrace it.* Retrieved October 21, 2010, from www.socitm.net/downloads/download/255/social_media-why_ict_management_should_lead_their_organisations_to_embrace_it%22

Stevens, M., Liabo, K., Roberts, H., & Witherspoon, S. (2009). What do practitioners want from research, what do funders fund and what needs to be done to know more about what works in the new world of children's services? *Evidence and Policy, 5,* 281–294.

Vimeo. (2008). *Forgotten citizens conference.* Retrieved October 21, 2010, from http://vimeo.com/album/24133

Vimeo. (2010). *IRISS on Vimeo.* Retrieved October 21, 2010, from http://vimeo.com/iriss

Walter, I., Nutley, S., Percy Smith, J., McNeigh, D., & Frost, S. (2004). *Improving the use of research in social care practice* (Knowledge Review 7). London: Social Care Institute for Excellence.

White, C., Booth, A., Cooke, J., & Addison, F. (2005). SCISTER Act: Delivering training in information skills for social-care professionals. *Health Information and Libraries Journal, 22,* 54-62.

Systemic-Level Efforts to Improve the Use of Evidence-Informed Practice

CHAPTER 8

INFORMING POLICY WITH EVIDENCE:
SUCCESSES, FAILURES, AND SURPRISES

CATHY HUMPHREYS, GABY MARCUS, ANN SANSON, KELLY RAE, SARAH WISE, MARILYN WEBSTER, *and* SARAH WATERS

ABSTRACT

In this paper we discuss the issues involved in informing policy with evidence, framed around Banks's quote below; thus we consider what constitutes the right evidence, the right people, and the right time.

INTRODUCTION

> [The evidence to inform policy] needs to be the right evidence, it needs to occur at the right time and be seen by the right people. (Banks, 2009, p. 8)

Policy and practice are inexorably interwoven, but the strategies through which evidence is brokered or translated to inform either policy or practice are different. Exploration of the ways in which evidence is used to support social policy change invites an analysis of successes, failures, and surprises in what, at first glance, appears to be an unpredictable arena. In this chapter we discuss the issues involved in informing policy with evidence, framed around the opening quote by Banks (2009), who draws from Kingdon's seminal work on 'opening the policy window' (Kingdon, 1984).

We have used case study extracts drawn from the work of the authors to illustrate how the right evidence, the right people, and the right time has contributed to a range of policy initiatives in Australia. Particular aspects of the case studies have been used to illustrate specific points. However, the complex relationship between all the key ingredients outlined by Banks (2009) as being fundamental to bringing about evidence-based policy change are evident in each case study.

A basic assumption underlying efforts to inform policy with evidence is similar to the arguments for evidence-based practice: that this will lead to better policy. The recent emphasis on evidence-based policy is strongly tied to the increased government focus on efficiency and effectiveness (Head, 2008), and is intended to ensure that "what is being done is worthwhile and is being done in the best possible way" (Davies, Nutley, & Smith, 2000, p. 2). Reliable evidence should allow better long-term planning (British Academy, 2008) and reduce the risk of unintended outcomes (Petersen, 2006). More cynically, there are also "PR" reasons for being seen to be implementing an evidence-based approach (Banks, 2009), and sometimes evidence is selectively cited by policy-makers simply to justify existing or planned agendas rather than to guide their development (Shonkoff, 2000).

Using the learning from our own case examples, we discuss the deployment of the right evidence, by the right people, at the right time.

THE RIGHT PEOPLE

Banks (2009) refers to the "right people" as an essential element in evidence-informed policy-making. He speaks of the need for policy workers and senior bureaucrats with research skills and research backgrounds who are interested and able to sift and synthesise evidence to inform policy. He argues that they are a dying breed in the Australian public service where so much of this intensive work is now resourced to consultants.

However, the following quote from the senior policy worker involved in the Victorian Family Services Reform (Humphreys et al., in press) refers to "the right people" in a slightly different context.

> From my end, the research wasn't as important at getting the reform up as the people themselves were. The research was important for showing Treasury, Premier's and Cabinet that there is a business case here. The important stuff was getting the Department to work within the sector— the people stuff was most important. You still need the policy, and the research to inform the policy—you couldn't do without them. (senior policy worker commenting on the Victorian Family Services Reform, personal communication)

From this perspective, people committed to policy reform were pivotal and research but an element in this process. The policy workers needed more than an understanding of research as suggested by Banks (2009). The case studies that form the background to this chapter suggest an alignment with the Victorian senior policy worker's perspective. The "actioning" of the evidence in a policy context was the result of influential people from community sector organizations and researchers backing, supporting, creating the alliances, and making the evidence available at strategic moments to policy-makers and politicians. Such a lens adds some weight to the following truism:

> It takes people to bring about change. Every public policy has its champions and advocates. (Silverstein, 2003, p. 1)

It is a truism that hides as much as it reveals. In the context of using research evidence to support policy shifts, it could beg the question of whether "the right people" are the researchers, the policy workers, or the community advocates. Each will have a role to play and the role will differ.

For researchers, there arises a clear question about the stance they take in relation to influencing public policy. In particular, whether the stance is derived from

1. a consensual approach (a situation of broad agreement between policy-makers and researchers to focus on improving the efficacy of decision making and the outcomes of service activities);
2. a contentious approach (researchers are on the margins of public policy and hold a critical stance to the government, society, and its institutions);
3. a paradigm-challenging approach (researchers use their work to problematize established frameworks and ways of thinking). (Nutley, Walter, & Davies, 2009, p. 6)

At times researchers may position themselves differently depending upon the policy context.

From a policy perspective, much of the literature in the area refers to "policy change agents" and "change champions" (Ulrich et al., 2003): people with highly developed skills in working with others, reading the strategic context, and building the alliances necessary to implement a change process. High-quality leadership marked by the ability to build a team of other people also committed to the change process is given constant reference (Caldwell, 2001). Without a "policy champion" or champions it would seem unlikely that research evidence will find its way to inform policy change.

Credibility is seen as a key ingredient of "the message." Evidence uptake is greater if the source is known, reliable, and responsive to policy-makers and politicians. Hence, relationships between the holders and recipients of the evidence are key, but building long-term interpersonal relationships can be challenging because of the fast movement in public service positions. In this sense, making "organizational" relationships may be the only and often less "potent" solution.

It is nevertheless the relationship between researchers and policy-makers that may provide one of the keys to opening the policy window. It is a complex process in which building relationships between the sectors and the people within them is pivotal, though not always straightforward (Pyra, 2003).

Box 8.1

Case Study 1: No Interest Loans Scheme

Good Shepherd Child Youth and Family Service is a Melbourne-based community service with a specific mission to support the welfare of women and their children. Within the organization is a small but experienced group of policy workers and researchers. They have been a stable group who, over many years, have networked with government, practice organizations, and business to advocate for policy to support the most vulnerable.

In 1981, a worker with Good Shepherd Youth and Family Service developed an idea for supporting young women with the provision of a no-interest loan for the purchase of basic household goods as they moved into independent accommodation following hostel care. The funding was provided by the Good Shepherd sisters. Since then, the No Interest Loans Scheme (NILS) has grown to provide loans through 280 programs based in community service organizations with millions of dollars of support from state and federal government and the banking sector. The goals of the program are not only to increase individual and family assets at a very basic level but to enhance social well-being, participation, and social capital. NILS is targeted very specifically to social security recipients and consistently this has been shown to be women, especially women with children.

Research about the impacts of NILS has been an influence on the development of both government and commercial sector support for its expansion. The research reports showed that the NILS loans offer real solutions to essential needs when other options are not available. NILS assisted people experiencing hardship, improved people's daily lives, strengthened money management skills, and helped people feel more positive about the future.

The evaluations were strategic. Each evaluation report identified the question of sustainability and scalability of NILS because of the difficulty in securing ongoing capital injections in the face of the slow erosion of capital. Each evaluation report identified the need for significant ongoing government support.

An essential element in the NILS strategy lay with ensuring that senior members of the organization held the evaluation reports at their fingertips as they networked and negotiated across both government and the corporate banking sector. These "policy champions" within the organization actively sought out responsive and influential people within the government bureaucracy as well as ministers who might want to be seen to be associated with such a successful program. A similar process occurred within the banking sector as "champions" for change were sought out to carry and broker the corporate partnership.

Following the release of a research report (Ayres-Wearne & Palafox, 2005) launched by the Deputy Premier of Victoria and the Minister for Community Services, the first government funding for NILS in Victoria was announced. More importantly, however, the National Bank used the report and its findings to facilitate discussions between the Victorian Government and Good Shepherd Youth and Family Service, resulting in a $10 million capitalization of NILS by the National Bank in 2006 and a matching $5.4 million operational support strategy by the Victorian Government in 2007. This activity was subsequently echoed by commitments from other state governments in Queensland and New South Wales and followed prior commitments by the Western Australian and Tasmanian governments to operational support for NILS.

In October 2009, the Prime Minister of Australia announced further funding of $18.5 million over three years to enhance the number and capacity of NILS programs around Australia. The funding was granted as part of the response to the global financial crisis but rests within the social inclusion strategy developed by the government as part of their election platform in 2007.

This case study shows how the interest and involvement of the right people was achieved as a result of their access to, and engagement with, research. The policy workers at Good Shepherd Child Youth and Family Service were a motivational force behind the project. However, it was their ability to engage key partners in the state governments, the corporate banking sector, and the federal government that resulted in NILS becoming the largest micro finance program in Australia.

THE RIGHT EVIDENCE

The Evidence Hierarchy Pyramid shows the traditional scientific view of what constitutes evidence.

This view of evidence has been expounded and developed by the Cochrane Collaboration that champions random controlled trials as the evidence "gold standard" or the "right evidence." However, this understanding of evidence does not fit comfortably within a social science paradigm where ethical considerations often do not allow for double-blind control trials to be conducted to assess the effectiveness of interventions. Other forms of evidence have also been utilized and valued by social scientists to inform policy-makers. Strong arguments are made about "what counts as evidence" and whose voice is allowed to be heard and have influence in the "knowledge debate" (Humphreys, Berridge, Butler, & Ruddick, 2003).

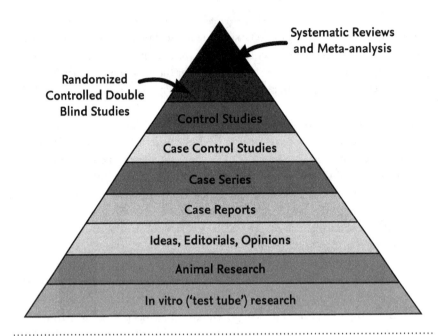

Figure 8.1 The Evidence Pyramid

Petr and Walter (2001) are social scientists who have been instrumental in counteracting and formulating alternative frameworks that broaden the knowledge base to include a "multidimensional evidence base." This involves: identifying the precise question to be answered; articulating and summarizing consumer-based perspectives; identifying and summarizing professional perspectives; identifying both qualitative and quantitative research studies; and culminating with a value-based critique of current best practice. Petr states:

> The broadened notion of evidence based practice recognizes the importance of the professional and the consumer in determining the relevance of the evidence to the situation at hand. (Petr, 2009, p. 20)

The perspective has much in common with the framework of "the knowledge diamond" developed by social work researchers at the University of Melbourne, which works with an action research model to bring together consumers, policy workers, practitioners, and empirical evidence to inform the development of both policy and practice through valuing and interrogating knowledge from each sector (Humphreys, 2009).

This view of multiple dimensions of evidence gathering is aligned to the

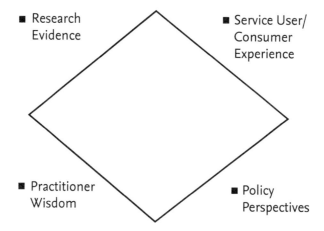

Figure 8.2   The Knowledge Diamond

assertion by Banks (2009) that gaining the right evidence through canvassing a broad spectrum of knowledge sources ensures that the evidence-gathering process is comprehensive and inclusive. He stresses that getting the right evidence depends on using the right methodology, and we would argue that this is also dependent upon ethical and value considerations. Banks argues that the methodology must be appropriate for the particular task, produce good data, and be transparent. He defines transparency as "opening the books" in terms of data, assumptions, and methodologies, such that the analysis could be replicated. He advocates strongly for broad consultation not only with the relevant experts but also with those people who will be affected by the policy. Again, it is a process reflected in the development of "the knowledge diamond."

These multi-dimensional models argue for a much broader view of evidence than that which fits within the evidence hierarchy. When a consensual approach to policy-making is in place, the right evidence is determined and gathered on a case-by-case basis by going through a systematic process that includes formulating an answerable question, tracking down and critically appraising the evidence, integrating the research with consumer expertise, understanding the characteristics of the client or the situation, and then evaluating the effectiveness of the intervention (Patteson, Miller, Carnes, & Wilson, 2004). Organizations can therefore play a valuable role in assisting policy-makers and practitioners by synthesizing knowledge into a form that makes the right evidence accessible to key people at the right time.

Box 8.2

Case Study 2: High-Frequency Contact for Infants in Out-of-Home Care

Case vignette: Tom was born substance-affected. He spent the first three weeks in hospital and was then moved to a foster care placement. The Children's Court of Victoria ordered supervised access five days per week involving 50-minute journeys each way. Child protection workers contested this order, but failed in their attempt to gain a less intensive parental contact arrangement. The foster care agency reported that, in a week, usually five different people supervised contact visits. Sometimes family visits went well, but at other times Tom's mother slept through the visit. In general, her attendance was inconsistent. Tom is reported to be having difficulty establishing a sleep routine and is suffering from frequent colds.

This case vignette provides an example of an issue that creates significant disagreement and conflict between the Court and child protection workers, family support workers, and foster carers. A research study was undertaken to explore questions about the best interests of babies where high-frequency contact was being ordered by the Court in circumstances in which babies were constantly being transported by multiple workers to supervised contact venues. The study was undertaken with a view to influencing the policy agenda in this contentious area.

The researchers developed a project brief in conjunction with a number of stakeholders to guide the research. The research methodology involved a case file audit of the contact arrangements and outcomes of all infants in care at August 2007, and 12 focus groups involving 118 people that included: lawyers for the parents; lawyers representing child protection workers; foster carers; high-risk infant specialist workers; counsellors from the Children's Court Clinic; and foster care managers from community sector organizations. The latter method not only provided qualitative data but also ensured the involvement of a wide range of stakeholders in the project.

The findings from the research raised a number of issues:

- Serious concerns about the welfare of infants involved in high-frequency family contact arrangements (four to seven times per week) were consistently raised in focus groups with key stakeholders
- A division surfaced with the legal advocates for parents and some Children's Court Clinic staff who felt strongly that parents had a right to very frequent contact with their infant in order to provide the best chance for family reunification.

> - No difference was found in the rate of reunification between infants with high-frequency contact and those with lower levels of family contact
> - The only point of consensus across all focus group participants was that the environment for contact between parents and infants needed substantial improvement to support better quality family contact
>
> A significant number and range of other strategies to support the dissemination and utilization of research findings were undertaken. These included establishing a high-level reference group of key stakeholders, reporting back of interim findings, a written report in accessible formats (full report, executive summary, key findings) available in both printed form and online, presentations at more than 20 conferences, seminars and workshops, two seminars for magistrates, and the researcher presenting to a high-level task force established to explore less adversarial legal processes for matters before the Children's Court.
>
> Even though the evidence was regarded as strong by many of those with an interest in the outcomes of this study, its impact on policy has not been clearly evident. To date the anecdotal evidence is that the research has had limited impact on the numbers of infants with orders for high-frequency contact (a further case file audit would be required to confirm this), the magistrates are unconvinced by the findings that high-frequency contact is not leading to higher levels of reunification, and that serious concerns are arising about the impact of travel and multiple handling on infants. However, there have been strong ramifications at the policy level as reform of the Children's Court is now under discussion.

This case study indicates that in this particular circumstance where the courts hold sway, the evidence uncovered by this study was not the right evidence to bring about a policy change on a highly controversial issue. It may not be evidence about the impact on babies that will be convincing for magistrates and lead to a policy shift, but evidence of a different kind. As Shonkoff (2000) notes and as this case study clearly shows, science is not the only (or even the preferred) source of policy guidance; other factors, in this case judicial independence, impinge on the process and affect the outcome.

THE RIGHT "TIME"

Another important ingredient for policy-making is timing; that is, synchrony in the availability of the right evidence when needed by policy decision-makers (Banks, 2009).

One of the barriers to research use identified in the literature is the different time scales that operate within the research and policy communities (Lewig,

Arney, & Scott, 2006). Co-production of knowledge, where researchers and policy-makers work closely together, can promote better understanding of time frames for results, and help to align research and policy decision-making. However, this approach relies on good, systematic policy-making and planning, whereas the policy process is typically reactive, messy, unpredictable, and requiring immediate action, resulting in little time to wait for high-quality research.

In this environment existing evidence that policy-makers can access "off the shelf" is crucial. Ongoing data collections that are designed to suit a broad range of policy purposes and can be tapped quickly can be particularly useful in responding to the immediacy of policy-making. However, in order for research findings to be "timely," research sometimes needs to be developed ahead of policy agendas, so researchers must anticipate the requirements of policy-makers. Getting the timing right is not a precise science. It requires astute political antennae to understand emerging policy issues and the future political landscape.

Research may be deliberately undertaken on important issues that are completely off the policy radar screen, because they are out of political favour, go against public opinion, or are not seen as a priority. Sometimes there is no "right" time for this research, irrespective of how well articulated it is. However, it may contribute to a larger evidence base and/or contribute to community education that eventually sways political opinion. Hence there can be a "sleeper effect" in the outcome of research, where it is initially ignored or disregarded and then a policy window suddenly opens. Further, certain times are better than others to raise a particular issue in terms of its chance of influencing policy decision-making, relating, for example, to a particular stage in the election cycle, shifts in public opinion, and other external pressures.

Alignment of research and policy-making is enhanced if knowledge is generated in a shared manner. However, the policy process cannot always wait for high-quality research. Large, ongoing research projects are helpful to ensure evidence is within easy reach of policy-makers. The impact of research that is not in step with current political agendas may be enhanced if messages from research are timed according to political events and pressures.

The slow process of research often fits poorly with the political need for speed. This case study illustrates how in this instance the timing was perfect. The research was available just at the time when the government was engaged with the issue of improving child protection services. Being a commissioned piece of work, it was produced in a relatively short time frame, while the issue was still "on the burner." This case study also illustrates some aspects of importance regarding the "right people" and "right evidence." The credibility of ARACY, arising from its strong cross-sectoral membership and use of broad consultative processes,

Box 8.3

Case Study 3: Systems Change in Child Protection

The need for a change in the way that we address child abuse and neglect has been a common concern by governments and many organizations for some time. The bulk of the response and resourcing has traditionally been focused toward treatment, rather than prevention of abuse and neglect. To resolve this imbalance, in early 2008 the Australian Research Alliance for Children and Youth (ARACY) harnessed the diverse views of its membership across policy, practice, and research (over 1,300 organizational and individual members), and came to the conclusion that the issue required a systems solution, using a public health lens. This led to the idea of a research study on the current national and international evidence of best practice organizational change strategies and processes for protecting children, while reducing demand on tertiary child protection services.

ARACY commissioned the Allen Consulting Group to undertake the research, using a systems analysis methodology. The resulting report, *Inverting the Pyramid: Enhancing Systems for Protecting Children* (2008), made the case for rebalancing service provision to provide greater resourcing for universal and secondary targeted services for children and families.

To broker this knowledge into practice and policy, ARACY worked through its membership to devise a long-term and highly consultative solution that aimed to generate a shared vision, supportive organizational culture, and integrated governance arrangements to enable a wide range of practitioners to better respond to early indicators of need, before problems escalate to crises.

Countless meetings, submissions, and briefings culminated in a meeting with the Minister responsible for Child Protection, who agreed to work with ARACY to implement the key research findings of the report. This involved commissioning ARACY to establish the Common Approach to Assessment, Referral, and Support (CAARS) project, which included a task force with the same name. This task force is co-convened by ARACY and a federal government department (FaCHSIA), supported by broad representation from nongovernmental organizations, government departments, and professional organizations engaged in supporting children and young people. The task force aims to develop a common assessment "mechanism" plus related referral and information processes that can be used by agencies within the primary- and secondary-level services to help identify the early signs of children "at risk" or "vulnerable" or having developmental issues.

The CAARS project was adopted within the new National Framework for Protecting Australia's Children 2009–2020 as the first of more than 70 projects that are intended to be funded under this Australian government strategy.

ensured that the "right people" were engaged in developing and disseminating the evidence. The commissioned report, while comprehensive, was also highly accessible and reader-friendly. These factors operating together led to the rapid uptake of the research in policy processes. However, it remains to be seen whether adequate resourcing of the task force's recommendations eventuate.

DISCUSSION AND CONCLUSION

While Banks' (2009) framework outlines three key elements in the process of creating evidence-based policy, it is clear that the process is more complex and unpredictable than the coincidence of these three elements.

The use of evidence in policy-making is a process beset by many challenges. First, decision-making within a government policy setting is governed by multiple priorities and considerations, including party platforms, ministerial concerns, budgetary constraints, vested interests, lobbying, and opinion polls. Banks (2009) himself goes on to note that "[v]alues, interests, personalities, timing, circumstance and happenstance—in short, democracy—determine what actually happens" (p. 4), and policies emerge "from a maelstrom of political energy, vested interests and lobbying" (p. 7).

Second, while it is difficult to measure the impact of research on policy (Davies & Nutley, 2008), it is clear that research evidence (whether qualitative or quantitative) is only one of the types of evidence impinging on the policy-making process. Head (2008) summarizes the multiple sets of evidence that inform and influence policy as "systematic ('scientific') research, program management experience ('practice') and political judgement" (p. 1). Hence, it is not surprising that some policy issues appear "'data-proof' or 'evidence proof', in the sense that their evidence base has been narrowed and buttressed by political commitments" (Head, 2008, p. 5).

Third, there are factors in the research arena that mitigate against the take-up of evidence in policy. In the absence of close relationships between the research and policy worlds, research often fails to answer questions that policy-makers need to answer (Banks, 2009). Researchers' commitment to detail and accuracy often limits their capacity to tell a compelling story with explicit policy implications. Researchers are often unaware of how to disseminate their findings to policy audiences (British Academy, 2008) and there are few rewards in academic life for doing so (Cortis & Head, 2009). Hence, evidence is not often presented in the brief, clear, digestible, and non-technical formats, which are needed by time-pressured, non-expert policy makers (Head & Cortis, 2009).

Our final case study indicates the complexity of the policy-making process.

Box 8.4

....

Case Study 4: The Staying Home, Leaving Violence Program in New South Wales (NSW), Australia

Since the resurgence of feminism in the 1970s that brought with it a concerted effort by feminists to assist women experiencing domestic or family violence, the predominant model used to assist women has been to place women and their children in a refuge or other accommodation, leaving the perpetrator of the violence in the home.

McFerran (2007) notes that in the mid-1990s women in Australia started to question this policy. She believes this was due to concern by feminists that refuge accommodation was a band-aid by the state that was not really addressing issues of women's safety as well as their concern that moving women and children into refuges was contributing to women's homelessness.

WESNET, the peak body for women's homelessness services in NSW, produced a policy paper calling for increased resources to allow women and children experiencing violence to stay in their own homes, but this resulted in no changes in policy by the NSW government.

In 2002, the Violence Against Women Specialist Unit conducted a research project that found almost no exclusion orders (ouster orders, which would facilitate women remaining in their own homes) had been issued by the court. The research was brought to the attention of the NSW Department of Community Services, which manages the funding for the provision of emergency housing.

The Department then provided funding for additional research, which was carried out by the Australian Domestic and Family Violence Clearinghouse (the Clearinghouse). The research identified the removal of the perpetrator and keeping him out over time as key requirements along with the implementation of a range of safety measures and supports for the woman to remain at home.

This research led to the funding by government of two pilot projects that were well received by the community and service users, but experienced difficulties as a result of a lack of consistent response from government agencies, especially the police and the courts. This inconsistency can be clearly linked to the lack of government policy to support this new initiative.

In 2007, to encourage policy change, the Clearinghouse published a paper examining the efficacy of this model, and the infrastructure and policy supports required to allow it to operate successfully. A forum aimed at transferring the knowledge directly to policy-makers and practitioners was conducted and was well attended by decision-makers from most states.

In addition, both pilots projects were evaluated, showing successful outcomes for the service users but deficiencies in government agency engagement. Following the evaluations, the NSW government announced the allocation of funding for 16 additional sites to be established over two years. They also established a series of advisory groups including one on which the Clearinghouse is represented. One of the roles of the advisory groups is to develop policy to support the program. The rollout of these additional sites has begun, although the required polices and protocols to ensure agency engagement and consistent models of service delivery are still being developed.

In 2009, the federal government committed itself to a policy supporting women and children to remain in their own homes. Resources to support this policy have yet to be allocated.

As this case study indicates, the right evidence, the right people, and the right timing are crucial. The early policy paper developed by WESNET did not have strong evidence to support a policy shift. This emerged through the subsequent research. It also came at the wrong time, as the political climate was not conducive to change. It was also conducted by "the wrong people" in the eyes of the policy-makers, as WESNET was regarded by the then federal government and most state governments as a radical group that lacked credibility. The subsequent work by the Clearinghouse, which is regarded as highly credible by government, provided evidence that encouraged policy change at a time when governments across Australia were seeking new ways of addressing a seemingly intractable and ever more costly problem. Nevertheless, the idiosyncrasies of the policy-making process still result in a far-from-perfect process, with services being funded in the absence of a comprehensive policy framework to support the program. The political imperative has clearly overtaken the lengthy process required to make and test good policy.

As Davies et al. (2000) suggest, and as this case study illustrates, it may often be more realistic to aim for evidence-*informed* policy, rather than evidence-*based* policy when the knowledge base is partial. It is also worth returning to "the knowledge diamond" and multi-dimensional framings of the knowledge base to support both policy and practice. In this process, the ethical base of knowledge building is recognized and the significance of both consumer and practitioner experiences is understood alongside that of empirical research. Inevitably their contributions inform the contextual understanding of an issue: a necessity when analyzing the successes, failures, and surprises in the policy-making process.

References

Australian Research Alliance for Children and Youth (ARACY) and The Allen Consulting Group. (2008). *Inverting the pyramid: Enhancing systems for protecting children.* Melbourne, Australia: The Allen Consulting Group.

Ayres-Wearne, V., & Palafox, J. (2005). *NILS small loans-big changes: The impact of no interest loans on households.* Collingwood, Australia: Good Shepherd Youth and Family Service.

Banks, G. (2009, February 4). *Evidence-based policy-making: What is it? How do we get it?* ANU Public Lecture Series, presented by ANZSOG, Productivity Commission, Canberra, Australia. Retrieved May 15, 2010, from http://www.pc.gov.au/speeches/cs20090204

British Academy. (2008). *Punching our weight: The humanities and social sciences in public policy making.* London: The British Academy. Retrieved March 15, 2010, from www.britac.ac.uk/reports/wilson/index.cfm

Caldwell, R. (2001). Champions, adapters, consultants and synergists: The new change agents in HRM. *Human Resource Management Journal, 11,* 39–52.

Cortis, N., & Head, B. (2009). *Tensions and challenges in Australia's early years field: Views from the inside.* Paper presented at the Australian Social Policy Conference, "An Inclusive Society? Practicalities and Possibilities," Sydney, Australia, July 8–10.

Davies, H.T.O, Nutley, S., & Smith, P. (2000). Introducing evidence based policy and practice in public services. In H.T.O. Davies, S.M. Nutley, & P.C. Smith (Eds.), *Evidence-based policy and practice in public services.* University of Bristol, England: The Policy Press.

Davies, H.T.O., & Nutley, S.M. (2008). *Learning more about how research based knowledge gets used: Guidance in the development of empirical research.* New York: William T. Grant Foundation.

Head, B. (2008). Three lenses of evidence-based policy. *The Australian Journal of Public Administration, 63,* 1–11.

Humphreys, C. (2009). *The knowledge diamond.* Retrieved March 15, 2010, from http://research.cwav.asn.au/AFRP/OOHC/WAMI/Reports_Papers/default.aspx

Humphreys, C., Berridge, D., Butler, I., & Ruddick, R. (2003). Making research count: The development of knowledge-based practice. *Research, Policy and Planning, 21,* 41–50.

Humphreys, C., Holzer, P., Scott, D., Bromfield, L., Arney, F., Lewig, K., et al. (in press). The planets aligned: Is child protection policy good luck or good management. *Australian Social Work.*

Kingdon, J.W. (1984). *Agendas, alternatives and public policy.* Boston: Little, Brown and Co.

Lewig, K., Arney, F., & Scott, D. (2006). Closing the research-policy and research-practice gaps: Ideas for child and family services. *Family Matters, 74,* 12–19.

McFerran, L. (2007). *Take back the castle: How Australia is making the home safer for women and children.* Australian Domestic and Family Violence Clearinghouse, Sydney. Retrieved March 15, 2010, from www.austdvclearinghouse.unsw.edu.au/Issues_Paper_14.rtf

Medical Research Library of Brooklyn. SUNY Downstate Medical Center. (2004) Evidence Based Medicine Course. A Guide to Research Methods: The Evidence Pyramid. Retrieved March 1, 2010 from http://library.downstate.edu/EMB2/2100.htm

Nutley, S., Walter, I., & Davies, H. (2009). Past, present and future possibilities for evidence-based policy. In G. Argyrous (Ed.), *Evidence for policy and decision making* (pp. 1–26). Sydney: UNSW Press.

Patterson, J.E., Miller, R.B., Carnes, S., & Wilson, S. (2004) Evidence-based therapies for marriage and family therapists. *Journal of Marital and Family Therapy, 30,* 183–195.

Petersen, A. (2006). Conducting policy-relevant developmental psychopathology research. *International Journal of Behavioural Development, 30,* 39–46.

Petr, C. (2009). Multi-dimensional evidence based practice. In C. Petr (Ed.), *Multi-dimensional evidence based practice: Synthesizing knowledge, research and values.* Oxon, London: Routledge.

Petr, C., & Walter, U.M. (2001). Best practices inquiry: A multidimensional, value-critical framework. *Journal of Social Work Education, 175,* 79–80.

Pyra, K. (2003, October). *Knowledge translation: A review of the literature.* Retrieved March 15, 2010, from www.nshrf.ca/AbsPage.aspx?id=1280&siteid=1&lang=1

Shonkoff, J. (2000). Science, policy, and practice: Three cultures in search of a shared mission. *Child Development, 71,* 181–187.

Silverstein, J. (2003). *A congressional insider guide to influencing disability policy.* Center for the Study and Advancement of Disability Policy. Retrieved March 15, 2010, from www.bcm.edu/ilru/html/publications/bookshelf/change_agents.html

Ulrich, D., Carter, L., Goldsmith, M., Bolt, J., & Smallwood, N. (Eds.). (2003). *The change champions fieldguide: Strategies and tools for leading change in your organisation.* LLC New York: Best Practice Publications.

CHAPTER 9

FACING THE CHILD WELFARE AND MENTAL HEALTH INTERFACE CHALLENGES THROUGH EVIDENCE-INFORMED APPROACHES: AN IRISH CASE STUDY

JOHN CANAVAN, AISLING GILLEN, KATHRYN HIGGINS, and BRENDAN DOODY

ABSTRACT

Using policy, services, and practices on the island of Ireland as a case study, this chapter examines the interface between child welfare and child mental health systems. Our goal is to clarify key interface challenges and explore the potential for evidence-informed frameworks and approaches to meet these challenges, with the ultimate aim of better meeting the needs of the children and young people.

INTRODUCTION

Two significant trends can be identified in children's policy globally. First is the idea of a whole-child approach, reflecting the fact that children's needs are interconnected ,and policy and service responses must be similarly integrated (McTernan & Godfrey, 2006). A second identifiable trend is a commitment to policy and services that are grounded in evidence—whether scientific, practice-based, or an amalgam of both (Canavan, Coen, Dolan, & Whyte, 2009; McDonald, 1999). Policy-makers and service providers are increasingly being challenged to present robust research that supports the new initiatives they wish to develop and implement.

The purpose of this chapter is to explore the intersection of integrated policy and service delivery and the implementation of evidence-informed practice and policy initiatives, and to suggest a framework for knowledge and action development in this key area. In meeting these aims, the chapter focuses on the substantive policy and service area of the interface between the Child Protection and Welfare (CPW) and Child and Adolescent Mental Health (CAMH) sectors, what the needs of children are, and how these are or are not met. Evidence-informed approaches[1] to policy and services development are the lens through which these interface issues are considered, while experiences of the Republic of Ireland and Northern Ireland provide case study material.

It is important to note at the outset that this chapter is the result of collaboration between academics and senior officials in service delivery systems. For this reason, its arguments are derived from an engagement with research literature and a detailed and nuanced understanding of the feasibility of the framework that it proposes. The first section of the chapter outlines some of the key issues identified in the literature in relation to the child welfare and child mental health interface, while the second presents the case study material. In the third section, the framework is presented as the basis from which some of the challenges faced in Ireland north and south, and most likely in other settings, can be addressed.

OVERVIEW OF THE LITERATURE

If one starts with the needs of children in mind, two issues arise in relation to the interface between child welfare and child and adolescent mental health. First are the unmet and often unidentified mental health needs of children within the CPW system, especially those in the care of the state. Second are the safety needs of children whose parents suffer from mental illnesses. This latter area is covered in the overview, as the interface issues are similar to those where child protection and child mental health concerns coexist.

The Unmet Needs of Children

In relation to the first point, the unmet mental health needs of children in child welfare systems is a well-documented international phenomenon. Within the welfare system in the United States, research indicates that while 42 percent of children have mental health problems, 28 percent received specialized mental health services. In a recent UK study, Sempik, Ward, and Darker (2008) found that 77 percent of children between 5 and 15 years of age in the care of six local authorities had some emotional or behavioural problem or disorder. This level of need was higher than the 50 percent rate identified by Melzer et al. (2003). Unlike the Sempik et al. study, the data in the study by Melzer and colleagues was based on psychiatric diagnostic information, while the former was based on psychological assessments subsequent to these being recorded by social workers.

In a sample of children aged 0–17 who had entered care for the first time in an area of Melbourne, Australia, Milburn, Lynch, and Jackson (2008) identified that 62 percent met the criteria for a major psychiatric diagnosis, with 18 percent of these children and young people having a previously recorded mental health history. Egelund and Lauten (2009) found 20 percent of a cohort of Danish children born in 1995, who either at the time of the research or previously had been in state care, had at least one psychiatric diagnosis and that almost half scored in the abnormal range of the Strengths and Difficulties Questionnaire (Goodman, 1997). The needs of such children have also been identified in states with less developed social policy provision. For example, in Turkey, Erol, Simsek, and Munir (2010) found higher levels of psychiatric-related needs among children in care than the general population.

The needs of children in the CPW system, whose parents suffer from mental illness, is also a significant challenge. Often cited in this area is Falkov's (1996) research, which identified parental psychiatric illness in one-third of reviews of 100 child abuse tragedies. In spite of this, however, Gilbert et al. (2009), in a comprehensive international review on recognizing and responding to child maltreatment, did not find any study "that investigated recognition of child maltreatment as part of the care of adults using mental-health services" (p. 175).

Whether it arises from their own mental health problems or those of their parents, the requirement to respond immediately to the suffering of a child or adolescent is obvious. The need to intervene to prevent longer-term consequences for the individual and costs to society are also apparent. Southerland, Casaneuva, and Ringeisen (2009) highlight the range of negative longer-term outcomes for transition-age youth with mental health difficulties apparent in the literature (relating to education, work, housing, and criminal behaviour). Interestingly, in their own research using longitudinal data on a cohort of transition-age children involved with CPW services in the United States, having mental health problems only caused additional risk of negative outcomes in the criminal justice area, specifically, being arrested.

In reflecting on these current and longer-term consequences for children, an obvious policy response would appear to be the encouragement of greater links between the CPW and child and adolescent mental health systems, and agencies and practitioners within them. It is therefore something of a surprise that previous research from the United States is equivocal. Thus, while Hurlburt et al. (2004) demonstrated that greater co-ordination is associated with increased use of mental health services, Glisson (1994) found that service gaps were more likely where coordination teams existed. And research by Bickman and colleagues indicated that while coordination may have increased service use, it was not associated with improved outcomes (Bickman, 1996; Bickman, Lambert, Andrade, & Penaloza, 2000).

More recent research is more positive. Bai, Wells, and Hillemeier (2009), using longitudinal data on a nationally representative sample of children who have had contact with the CPW system, found "greater intensity of IORs (interorganizational relationships) was associated with higher likelihood of both service use and mental health improvement, controlling for a variety of predisposing, enabling and need factors" (p. 378). Notably, Bai et al. conceptualized intensity of IORs as incorporating various ties, including joint budgeting or resource allocation and cross-training of staff, among a range of other indicators, and not just collaboration at case level. At a more general level, Wells (2006) suggests a number of reasons for the ambivalent findings on the value of such links. These included failure to measure some benefits, the fact that benefits of collaboration may take time to emerge, the nature of individual relationships, unresolved governance and accountability issues, and competing paradigms. As with most services, adequate resourcing is a basic challenge for collaboration. For example, if an agency is resource-poor, collaboration can be seen as a luxury. At a basic level, time spent on collaboration can be at the cost of meeting core service responsibilities.

Specific Collaboration Challenges and Emerging Good Practices

Barbour, Stanley, Penhale, and Holden (2002) report on a small-scale qualitative study exploring inter-agency work between CPW and mental health staff where parental mental health and child protection concerns coexisted. They identified different perceptions of risk as a core issue, both in the child care assessment and in relation to severity and impact of parental mental health on parenting capacity. The fluctuating nature of mental illness was also identified as a significant practice-level issue, according to Darlington, Feeney, and Rixon's (2005) findings from similar research in Australia. Gilbert et al. (2009) suggest that the key issue in the interface between CAMH and CPW services is the readiness of clinicians to consider that maltreatment is part of the reason for a child's presentation to their service; and that perceptions that involvement with CPW services will impede clinical work could relate to under-reporting of welfare concerns.

Based on survey research between adult mental health services and CPW services in Queensland, Australia, Darlington and Feeney (2008) suggest that improving processes and outcomes at the interface requires "effective communication strategies at both the organizational and service-delivery (case) levels; enhancement of professionals' knowledge and skills; and appropriate resource allocation" (p. 195). Included under communication strategies are a range of formal and informal processes and protocols; for example, documents specifying areas of potential conflict between agencies or the provision of opportunities for workers to share information on cases. Knowledge and skill enhancement refers to mutual understanding of systems and service issues, with joint training advocated as an important "structural" support for collaboration (p. 196). While resources alone are insufficient for the achievement of good collaboration, adequate resourcing was identified as fundamental. Interestingly, Darlington and Feeney note that resources can be seen as the focus of joint proposals instead of the focus for inter-agency turf wars. As part of qualitative research connected to their survey research, Darlington et al. (2005) arrived at an additional dimension to support collaboration, that of role clarity. Thus, when workers from the different agencies had separate and agreed-upon roles, collaboration was enhanced.

A number of more specific examples of practices in this area are to be found in the research. Callaghan, Young, Pace, and Vostanis (2004) report on the development of a specialist CAMH team in the UK that focused on meeting the needs of vulnerable children, including children in care. A key role of the team was to develop the mental health skills of front-line residential staff and foster carers and to improve their capacity to identify young people at risk for mental illness. Critically, primary mental health workers, of different disciplinary hues, provide time-limited interventions for children with identified needs and support for carers. Where needs required it, more intensive support is provided by mental health specialists on an outpatient or residential basis.

Kelly, Allan, Roscoe, and Herrick (2003) report on a pilot intensive assessment and intervention team approach to meeting the needs of children in care in another UK local authority area. The service is multi-agency, with shared ownership among health, education, and social service. It prioritizes children with complex health, social, and educational needs, providing intensive assessment and service planning on an in-patient basis. Also in the UK, Cotterill, Lucy, Porter, and Walker (2000) outline system changes resulting in more effective linking between social services and mental health services in Leeds. Central to the systems changes were structures and processes to prioritize referrals from social work to mental health services, consultation by mental health services on complex cases held by social work, and training for social work on mental health issues. Tye and Precey (1999) similarly call for the creation of practice development groups comprising workers from the two sectors working on an action-learning basis as a means to overcome difficulties.

Milburn et al. (2008) discuss a program developed in Australia, which arose out of the experience of mental health professionals consulting to CPW services. The experience had been that, by the time children were referred to them, their needs were significant and that earlier identification and assessment could have reduced immediate distress and instances of poor planning. Because of the distress and disruption associated with entry to care for both children and families, this was identified as a key point for intervention. Helping the child directly, helping parents and carers understand the child's needs, and assisting the planning processes toward meeting the child's needs were the program aims. Milburn et al. (2008) identify high levels of parental involvement and increasing the focus on the child's needs as strengths of the assessment program. They highlight systemic difficulties in CAMH service provision and the fact that parents in the children protection systems, who face difficult life issues, may not be able to identify children's mental health needs, identify supports that their children need, or access these services.

The Role of Evidence-Informed Practice

One way of approaching the challenge of achieving collaboration between CPW and child mental health systems is to ground it in a commitment to evidence-informed practice. Within the literature, the focus tends to be on programs targeting mental illness with the direction of influence from psychiatry to social work. Thus, Kolko, Herschell, Costello, and Kolko (2009), in a study involving a survey of administrators in CPW systems, found little emphasis on what they call evidence-based treatments (EBTs) among more general calls to expand the scale and scope of mental health services. They cite the absence of reference to programs such as the Incredible Years or Multisystemic Therapy as indicative of a lack of training in the EBTs and the reason opportunities to treat significant mental health problems within CPW systems is missed. Leathers, McMeel, Prabhughate, and Atkins (2009) similarly offer the view that the CPW literature is slow to impart new ideas and programs from child mental health to the practice community. A wider issue arises, however, in that there is no reason for evidence-informed practice to be conceptualized simply as an issue for therapeutic intervention. Practices in collaboration are equally amenable to being informed by evidence, as are practices in how to establish strong baseline data on children's needs and current services responses.

The key is to achieve a balance between quantitative knowledge, based, in particular, on experimental research studies and meta-analyses, and other forms of evidence. Petr and Walter (2005) usefully suggest that best practice is multi-dimensional, requiring quantitative and qualitative sources of knowledge, wisdom of consumers of services and professionals, and processes that analyze findings from these sources and their quality. Most significantly, it demands using this knowledge as part of a value-based critique of existing practices in moving toward their improvement.

CASE STUDY

How then, might the specific needs of children in Ireland who appear at the interface between CPW and CAMHs services be considered? The following section sets out the broad policy context for child protection and mental health, the nature of services provision in these areas, and what is known about children's need at the interface and subsequent key issues.

Demographics and Policy and Service Structure

In the Republic there are just over a million children (0–17 years of age), while Northern Ireland's child population stands at just over 400,000; in both cases, this represents just under one-quarter of the total population. Both jurisdictions have adopted long-term strategies for children, which are informed by whole-child approaches (Department of Health and Children, 2000; Office of the First Minister and Deputy First Minister, 2006; Office of the Minister for Children/ Department of Health, 2007). These high-level documents are outcomes-driven, proposing that all children's services should be orientated toward a set of high-level outcomes in health, mental health, safety, and so on.

Other similarities between the systems are the operation of statutorily based, independent offices focusing on children's rights: the Northern Ireland Commissioner for Children and Young People in Northern Ireland, and the Ombudsman for Children in the Republic of Ireland. Northern Ireland is also interesting in that it operates within an integrated health and social care system. While similar in many respects, what clearly differentiates the child and adolescent populations is the experience of those in Northern Ireland of living in a conflict/post-conflict society. The Chief Medical Officer (CMO) report (Department of Health and Children, 2000) estimated that 20 percent of children in Northern Ireland would be suffering a significant mental health problem by their 18th birthday. The Bamford review report similarly estimates that 10 percent of the population will have moderate to severe mental health problems. It also points out that Northern Ireland has a higher overall prevalence of mental illness compared to England, estimated at 25 percent (Department of Health and Social Services and Public Safety (2007). Although our understanding of the specific long-term effects of such violence is not fully clear, increasingly a range of initiatives operate in Northern Ireland focusing on mental health needs associated with living in a transitional situation.

As outlined in Figure 9.1 below, in the Republic of Ireland and Northern Ireland, CPW and CAMH services operate within the same organizational structure. In theory at least, collaboration on common concerns should be more easily achieved.

Child and Adolescent Mental Health

Mental health services in both in the Republic and Northern Ireland are undergoing a period of significant change. In the case of the Republic, a major process of

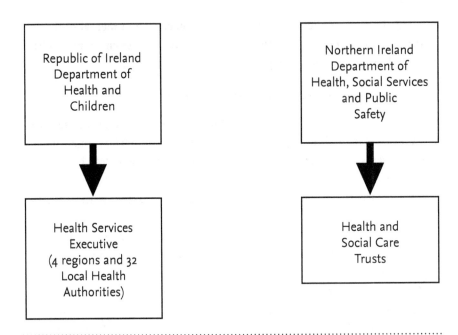

Figure 9.1

development is being guided by *A Vision for Change*, the Department of Health and Children's 2006 policy statement (Government of Ireland, 2006). *A Vision of Change* proposed 99 multidisciplinary CAMH teams (11 services) based on 7 per 300,000 population. The service delivery framework reflects the distinction between primary care, wherein mental health needs are met by a range of professionals, secondary care, delivered through multidisciplinary CAMH teams, and tertiary in-patient and other specialist services. In 2008, the first annual report on CAMH services in the Republic was produced, and data included a month-long survey of service activity (Health Services Executive, 2009). According to the report, in 2008, 54 multidisciplinary teams were in place, comprising 49 community teams, two day-hospital teams, and three pediatric hospital liaison teams. In 2008, 3 percent of referrals to CAMH teams came from social services, 4 percent of children attending CAMH were in state care, while 11 percent had contact with social services.

In Northern Ireland, a similar process of major development is taking place, shaped by the *Bamford Review on Mental Health and Learning Disability*. In 2002, the Department of Health, Social Services and Public Safety (DHSSPS) initiated a major, wide-ranging and independent review of the law, policy, and provision affecting people with mental health needs or a learning disability in Northern Ireland. The review, which took five years to report (DHSSPS 2007), highlighted the inadequacy of CAMH in existence in Northern Ireland and outlined a program of unprecedented change that is currently being implemented.

CAMH Northern Ireland services are structured according to a four-tiered model and replicate those operational throughout the UK. The first tier involves non-specialist staff taking some responsibility for identification, prevention, and promotion of mental health issues, and the second involves mental health professionals working as part of wider networks that provide a range of services including training and consultation and assessment. Tier three is similar to the secondary-care structure, and tier four is akin to the tertiary level in the Republic of Ireland system, respectively. In 2008–2009, there were 6,555 referrals made to CAMH teams across Northern Ireland; that number increased to 7,038 for 2009–2010. Around 70 percent of referrals were accepted in both years. Of those, 20 percent were for crisis assessment.

No publicly reported statistical data were currently available on referrals from CPW services to CAMH services, or on proportions of children attending CAMH who are in state care or have had contact with CPW services. Indeed, data on mental health needs of children and young people had been collected in different formats by different trusts on a number of separate systems.[2] Currently, there are major changes underway to streamline the collection of data on the mental health needs of children and young people. Additionally, a CAMH network has been tasked with establishing uniform assessment and monitoring protocols for any child referred.

Some data is available from research studies in Northern Ireland highlighting the CPW and CAMH interface. A study by Teggart and Menary (2005) suggests that 60 percent of children 4–10 years old in the 'in care' population may have a diagnosable psychiatric disorder. Fulton and Cassidy (2007) undertook a retrospective investigation of one regional in-patient unit for children in Northern Ireland (tier 4 level CAMH). Among the findings were that during a three-year period there were 115 admissions to in-patient care. Forty-five young people fulfilled diagnostic criteria for more than one ICD(International Classification of Diseases)-10 diagnosis while 37 had experienced permanent parental separation. Ten young people were exposed to violence within the parental relationship. Five young people were on the Child Protection Register and 13 were children in care. Eighteen mothers had a history of depression.

CHILD PROTECTION AND WELFARE

In the Republic of Ireland the Health Services Executive (HSE) provides this comprehensive CPW service through 32 Local Health Offices, which are managed by Local Health Managers under four distinct Integrated Service Areas in the country. The overriding legislation is the Child Care Act, 1991. Every HSE Local Health Office has a designated child care manager/equivalent officer with responsibility for coordinating CPW services. It is normally the role of the social workers in the HSE CPW services to carry out enquiries into reported concerns, but other disciplines may be allocated this task in certain cases. If a child protection concern has been notified to An Garda Siochána (the police force), it may conduct a parallel investigation in coordination with the HSE CPW Services. The HSE has recently developed proposals for the restructuring of CPW services in the Republic of Ireland to ensure a standardized approach across the country.

In 2008, there were almost 25,000 reports to social work departments in the Republic of Ireland. Currently, nationally collected data on children who are offered a service by CPW services includes three categories generally related to mental health: children's own emotional and behavioural issues, their own mental health/intellectual disability needs (categorized together), and the mental health needs of other family members. A small-scale analysis of the use of these categorization schemes undertaken for this chapter indicated limitations of the categorization scheme and the scope for inconsistency in recording in relation to them. Focused on a small number of cases in one services catchment area, the analysis found generally good relationships between CPW services and CAMH.

In Northern Ireland, CPW services are delivered through the five Health and Social Care Trusts, under their Family and Childcare Programs. The main underpinning legislation for CPW services is the Children (Northern Ireland) Order (1995). Two recent policy statements set out arrangements for inter-agency working on child protection in particular. A new strategic body called the Safeguarding Board Northern Ireland will coordinate a range of activity on safeguarding children and will unify the previous four area child protection committees into one.

Another significant development in Northern Ireland has been the development, piloting, and implementation of a single assessment framework, including risk assessment and a mental health needs component, for children in need across Northern Ireland. A common assessment form, called Understanding the Needs of Children in Northern Ireland (UNOCINI), was developed and introduced. Appropriate training and guidance was provided for its use by a wide range of people working with children and families, including key workers such as health visitors, social workers, the community nursing sector, and also the voluntary and community sector. This has just become fully operational, and data from the assessments relating to mental health needs is not yet available.

Shared Issues and Responses

Both jurisdictions share an experience of general neglect of child and adolescent mental health, with recent significant policy and service development strategies in place. In reviewing data from CPW and CAMH in both jurisdictions, it is apparent that information systems need significant strengthening. This applies both to the separate CPW and CAMH information systems and in relation to possible interface data.[3] Particularly important for both jurisdictions is the development of good epidemiological data on mental health needs. Certainly, while at the policy level, the issue of the interface between systems is acknowledged in both Northern Ireland and the Republic of Ireland, and there are good inter-agency practices in operation locally, there is less evidence of any convincing concerted system-wide program of action to address it in either context. Indeed, the nature of the data gathered for the purpose of this chapter is strongly suggestive of systems operating generally in isolation. On a positive note, there is evidence of change. The development of a common assessment framework in the North offers the promise of better data on children's needs, and in addition, an epidemiological study on child and adolescent mental health needs is being planned at the time of writing.

A FUTURE FRAMEWORK

The earlier overview of the literature was focused on three concerns—epidemiology, interagency cooperation, and the promise of evidence-informed practice as the basis for an integrated approach in meeting children's needs. In both north and south, the absence of solid epidemiological and service provision data is a major cause of concern. Without understanding the needs of children, and listening to their own and their parents' voices in order to do so, the development of policy and services will be continually hamstrung. The minority of children in focus in this paper will remain invisible in the absence of appropriate data systems.

In preparing this chapter, the authors actively sought formal research on the experience of working at the interface between CPW and CAMH systems, with little success. Although the minor review undertaken for this chapter indicated positive relationships between services, it is likely that the same challenges faced by professionals internationally exist in Ireland. As suggested above, evidence-informed practice should be conceptualized equally as a concern for agency-level and inter-agency structures and processes as for what works in intervention for children and their families. In that context, empirical research is required. This could be exploratory in nature, in line with Bai et al. (2009) or Darlington,

Feeney, and Rixon (2004; 2005), or focused on an action research approach as per Cotterill et al. (2000) or Milburn et al. (2008).

One of the most promising possibilities for the CPW/CAMH interface is that offered by evidence-based preventive and early-intervention-focused models. While Leathers et al. (2009) express concerns about the limited adoption of good practice from the child and adolescent literature in CPW practices, recent developments in Ireland suggest otherwise. In part reflecting the efforts of motivated individuals and collaborative groupings, and also reflecting the value of philanthropic funding, a range of evidence-based programs are currently being tested in Ireland including the Incredible Years, Triple P Parenting, Big Brothers Big Sisters Mentoring, and Treatment Foster Care. Their common prevention concerns suggest that these programs should appeal to both CPW and CAMH systems—indeed professionals from both are involved across these innovative practices.

Taken together, these elements (epidemiology, services data, good practice in collaboration, and the use of evidence-based models) can be thought of as a preliminary framework around which CPW and CAMH systems can become more integrated as in the framework presented in Figure 9.2.

Each of the components can be seen as representing an area of possible research to be undertaken as part of the development of an evidence-informed approach to meeting the needs of children at the interface of CPW and CAMH systems, north and south.

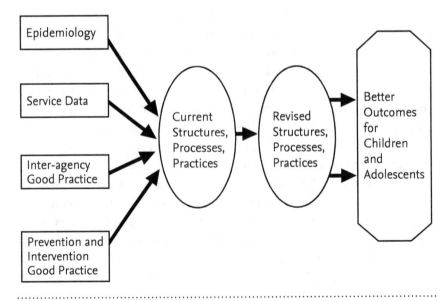

Figure 9.2

CONCLUSION

In summary, this chapter has been developed on that basis that an evidence-informed practice orientation should be adopted as a strategic approach to addressing a real practice and policy issue in Ireland—that of the needs of children who appear at the interface of CPW and CAMH systems. In this specific context, there is a major evidence gap in relation to epidemiological data and the level and nature of services provision. Material contained in the earlier literature is indicative of some of the available evidence on inter-agency work generally, and joint working by CPW and CAMHs systems specifically. As stated, some of the good practice models associated with the achievement of outcomes relevant to both disciplinary areas are already operational in both jurisdictions, and skills and capacity are developing in the implementation of such models in culturally appropriate ways. In terms of the operational basis for the development of evidence-informed practice, the Change Project model developed by Research in Practice and outlined by Bowyer and Moore in this volume (Chapter 5), represents a solid foundation from which a project could develop. The fact that a high-level state-appointed cross-border group currently exists in the CPW field offers a very positive specific context for such a project to proceed.

The Irish and Northern Irish experience reflects the major challenge facing policy and service delivery systems globally in achieving integrated responses to the needs of children and young people. The experiences presented of the interface issues between CPW and CAMH systems illustrate the cost to children, families, and society of not facing these challenges. While by no means offering a quick fix, through the model it proposes, this chapter demonstrates that a commitment to the generation and thoughtful application of evidence is central to solutions.

ENDNOTES

1. This chapter is written from the perspective of evidence-informed practice. It is guided by Gambrill's (2008) distinction between evidence-informed practice, which involves decision making reflecting "ethical, evidentiary and application concerns" (pp. 446–447), and evidence-based practice, which reflects a more narrow concern with the use of particular approaches in practice.

2. While Trusts are required to report annually to the Health and Social Care Board on children in need (including the local advisory committee (LAC)), on those waiting for an assessment or receiving treatment with Child and Adolescent Mental Health services, attempts to gain these statistics for this chapter proved problematic as data was inconsistent or not available across the different Trusts.

3. For example, children known to Child Protection services who have mental health issues or whose parents have mental health issues; children in statutory care who have mental health issues and, from the perspective of CAMH, children using mental health services who have contact with Child Protection services or who are in statutory care.

REFERENCES

Bai, Y., Wells, R., & Hillemeier, M.H. (2009). Coordination between child welfare agencies and mental health service providers, children's service use, and outcomes. *Child Abuse and Neglect, 33*, 372–381.

Barbour, R.S., Stanley, N., Penhale, B., & Holden, S. (2002). Assessing risk: Professional perspectives on work involving mental health and child care services. *Journal of Interprofessional Care, 16*, 323–334.

Bickman, L. (1996). Implications of a children's mental health managed care demonstration evaluation. *Journal of Mental Health Administration, 23*, 107–117.

Bickman, L., Lambert, E.W., Andrade, A.R., & Penaloza, R.V. (2000). The Fort Bragg continuum of care for children and adolescents: Mental health outcomes over 5 years. *Journal of Consulting and Clinical Psychiatry, 68*, 710–716.

Callaghan, J., Young, B., Pace, F., & Vostanis, P. (2004). Evaluation of a new mental health service for looked after children. *Clinical Child Psychology and Psychiatry, 9*, 130–148.

Canavan, J., Coen, L., Dolan, P., & Whyte, L. (2009). Privileging practice: Facing the challenge of integrated working for outcomes for children. *Children and Society, 23*, 377–388.

Cotterill, D., Lucy, D., Porter, I., & Walker, D. (2000). Joint working between child and adolescent mental health services and the Department of Social Services: The Leeds Model. *Clinical Child Psychology and Psychiatry, 5*, 481–489.

Darlington, Y., & Feeney, J.A. (2008). Collaboration between mental health and child protection services: Professionals' perceptions of best practice. *Children and Youth Services Review, 30*, 187–198.

Darlington, Y., Feeney, J.A., & Rixon, K. (2004). Complexity, conflict and uncertainty: Issues in collaboration between child protection and mental health services. *Children and Youth Services Review, 26*, 1177–1192.

Darlington, Y., Feeney, J.A., & Rixon, K. (2005). Practice challenges at the intersection of child protection and mental health. *Child and Family Social Work, 10*, 239–247.

Department of Health and Children. (2000). *Report of the Chief Medical Officer of the Department of Health and Children.* Retrieved November 2, 2010, from www.dohc.ie/press/releases/2000/20000316.html

Department of Health and Social Services and Public Safety (DHSSPS). (2007). *The Bamford review of mental health and learning disability (Northern Ireland): A comprehensive legislative framework.* Belfast, Ireland: Author.

Egelund, T., & Lauten, M. (2009). Prevalence of mental health problems among children placed in out-of-home care in Denmark. *Child and Family Social Work, 14*, 156–165.

Erol, N., Simsek, Z., & Munir, K. (2010). Mental health of adolescents reared in institutional care in Turkey: Challenges and hope in the twenty-first century. *European Child and Adolescent Psychiatry, 19*, 113–124.

Falkov, A. (1996). Study of working together 'part 8' reports. Fatal child abuse and psychiatric disorder: An analysis of 100 area child protection committee case reviews. London: Department of Health.

Fulton, K., & Cassidy, L. (2007). Northern Ireland Tier 4 Child and Adolescent Mental Health Services: A survey of admissions to the Child and Family Centre. *Child Care in Practice, 13*, 237–250.

Gambrill, E. (2008). Evidence-based (informed) macro-practice: Process and philosophy. *Journal of Evidence-Based Social Work, 5*, 423–452.

Gilbert, R., Kemp, A., Thoburn, J., Sidebotham, P., Radford, L., Glaser, D., et al. (2009). Child Maltreatment 2: Recognising and responding to child maltreatment. *The Lancet, 373*, 167–180.

Glisson, C. (1994). The effect of services coordination teams on outcomes for children in state custody. *Administration in Social Work, 18*, 1–23.

Goodman, R. (1997). The strengths and difficulties questionnaire: A research note. *Journal of Child Psychology and Psychiatry, 38*, 581–586.

Government of Ireland. (2006). *A vision for change: Report of the expert group on mental health policy.* Dublin, Ireland: Stationery Office.

Health Services Executive. (2009). *Child and adolescent mental health services: First annual report.* Dublin, Ireland: Author.

Hurlburt, M.S, Leslie, L.K., Landsverk, J., Barth, R.P., Burns, B.J., Gibbons, R.D., et al. (2004). Contextual predictors of mental health service use among children open to child welfare. *Archives of General Psychiatry, 61,* 1217–1224.

Kelly, C., Allan, S., Roscoe, P., & Herrick, E. (2003). The mental health needs of looked after children: An integrated multi-agency model of care. *Clinical Child Psychology and Psychiatry, 8,* 323–335.

Kolko, D.J., Herschell, A.D., Costello, A.H., & Kolko, R.P. (2009). Child welfare recommendations to improve mental health services for children who have experienced abuse and neglect: A national perspective. *Administration and Policy in Mental Health, 36,* 50–62.

Leathers, S.J., McMeel, L.S., Prabhughate, A., & Atkins, M.S. (2009). Trends in child welfare's focus on children's mental health and services from 1980–2004. *Children and Youth Services Review, 31,* 445–450.

McDonald, G. (1999). Evidence-based social care: Wheels off the runway? *Public Money and Public Management, 19,* 25–32.

McTernan, E., & Godfrey, A. (2006). Children's services planning in Northern Ireland: Developing a planning model to address rights and needs. *Child Care in Practice, 12,* 219–240.

Melzer, H., Corbin, T., Gatward, R., Goodman, R., & Ford, T. (2003). *The mental health of young people looked after by local authorities in England.* London: The Stationery Office.

Milburn, N.L., Lynch, M., & Jackson, J. (2008). Early identification of mental health needs for children in care: A therapeutic assessment programme for statutory clients of child protection. *Clinical Child Psychology and Psychiatry, 13,* 31–47.

Office of the First Minister and Deputy First Minister. (2006). *Our children and young people: Our pledge.* Belfast, Ireland: Author.

Office of the Minister for Children/Department of Health. (2007). *The agenda for children's services.* Dublin, Ireland: Stationery Office.

Petr, C.G., & Walter, U.M. (2005). Best practices inquiry: A multidimensional, value-critical framework. *Journal of Social Work Education, 41,* 251–267.

Sempik, J., Ward, H., & Darker, I. (2008). Emotional and behavioural difficulties of children and young people at entry into care. *Clinical Child Psychology and Psychiatry, 13,* 221–233.

Southerland, D., Casaneuva, C.E., & Ringeisen, H. (2009). Young adult outcomes and mental health problems among transition age youth investigated for maltreatment during adolescence. *Children and Youth Services Review, 31,* 947–956.

Teggart, T., & Menary, J. (2005). An investigation of the mental health needs of children looked after by Craigvon and Banbridge health and social services trust. *Child Care in Practice, 11,* 39–49.

Tye, C., & Precey, G. (1999). Building bridges: The interface between adult mental health and child protection. *Child Abuse Review, 8,* 164–171.

Wells, R. (2006). Managing child welfare agencies: What do we know about what works? *Children and Youth Services Review, 28,* 1181–1194.

CHAPTER 10

ACHIEVING AN OUTCOMES-DRIVEN SYSTEM:
CRITICAL DECISION POINTS FOR LEADERS

SYBIL K. GOLDMAN, M.S.W., *Assistant Professor and Senior Advisor, National Technical Assistance Center for Children's Mental Health, Georgetown University Center for Child and Human Development*

KAY HODGES, PH.D., *Professor, Department of Psychology, Eastern Michigan University*

PATRICK KANARY, M.ED., *Director, Center for Innovative Practices, Institute for the Study and Prevention of Violence, Kent State University*

JAMES R. WOTRING, M.S.W., *Director, National Technical Assistance Center for Children's Mental Health and Assistant Professor, Georgetown University Center for Child and Human Development*

ABSTRACT

Numerous reports and commissions have called for the broad implementation of evidence-based or evidence-informed practices (EIP), yet few states, territories, tribal nations, provinces, and communities have implemented these on a large-scale basis.[1] This chapter proposes a systemic framework that outlines the key decision points leaders need to consider in building a sustainable infrastructure for an outcomes-driven system for children and youth with mental health challenges and their families.

INTRODUCTION

Numerous studies over the past decade have concluded that children with mental health challenges and their families can benefit from a more science/research-based array of treatments and supports, including the use of evidence-informed practice (EIP), coupled with outcome data that inform improvements in service quality. The American Psychological Association Task Force on Evidence-Based Practice for

Children and Adolescents (2008) concluded, "There is a rich evidence base of sound assessment and intervention strategies tailored to particular conditions, contexts, and needs demonstrating structured, empirically tested treatment programs can have beneficial effects with children and their parents" (p. 13). The President's New Freedom Commission on Mental Health (2003) concluded that people with mental health problems fail to receive effective community-based services and called for the expansion of evidence-based practice. As a result, policy-makers and other funding entities are increasingly demanding that the services they fund are grounded in empirical research and evidence of effectiveness (McCall, 2009). Cooper et al. (2008), however, concluded in the monograph entitled *Unclaimed Children Revisited*, "states have limited capacity for using outcomes-based decision making, planning, and quality improvement and determining program and policy effectiveness" (p. 8).

EIP are provided all across the United States and Canada, as well as in other countries. According to the National Center for Children in Poverty (Cooper et al., 2008), 50 states promote, require, or support the use of evidence-based practice; however, less than 20 percent reported they support these statewide. Promising practices are also being used all across the states. But no state provides a comprehensive set of evidence-based or promising practices across youth-serving systems, within one system, or even on a statewide basis. Cooper et al. (2008) found that there are only eight states that have advanced statewide performance measurement systems (PMS) capable of producing and using client-level outcome data for planning, continuous quality improvement, and determining systems' outcomes. There are many reasons for this, including funding, need for supportive organizational environments, lack of infrastructure and training capacity, complexity of implementation across systems, and numerous other barriers. While studies cited focus on the US, these issues are also relevant to Canada and other countries as well. Implementation of a statewide or provincial "science to service" system, driven by outcomes and accountability, requires an integrated approach that addresses policy, systems, infrastructure, and practice. This chapter offers a framework for state, regional, territorial, provincial, or tribal decision-makers to consider in developing an outcomes-driven system for children and their families.

FRAMEWORK

The framework proposed in this chapter, as shown in Figure 10.1, recognizes that to achieve an outcomes-driven system in real-world environments is highly complex. There are multiple domains that need alignment and integration. Each of these domains requires a set of decisions from state and provincial leaders and involves different options, challenges, planning processes, and strategies with the ultimate goal being the achievement of positive outcomes for children, youth, and families. Decisions need to be supported by data. These domains include: (1) determining the population of focus and outcomes to be achieved; (2) determining the systems to be engaged and aligned at a state and local level, as well as strategies for fostering supportive organizational environments; (3) establishing a performance measurement system; (4) selecting and implementing EIP; (5) investing in the workforce and changing practice; and (6) building in continuous quality improvement. The focus of this chapter's discussion is on the first four domains.

Context

In the US, the largest federal effort to reform children's mental health has been the Comprehensive Community Mental Health Services for Children and Their

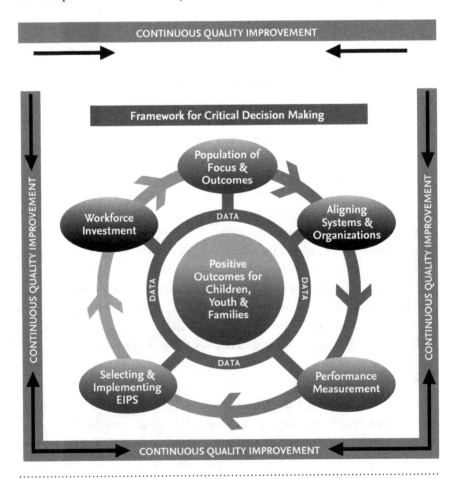

Figure 10.1

Families Program, mandated by Congress in 1992 and administered by the Substance Abuse and Mental Health Services Administration to support the development of systems of care across the country. Over 98,750 children in 164 communities have been served to date, with appropriations of over $1.3 billion. An ongoing national evaluation of this initiative has demonstrated positive outcomes for children and their families. The 20-year experience in the US of building systems of care for children and youth with mental health challenges provides both data and lessons learned in developing comprehensive cross-agency service delivery systems grounded by a strong set of values (Stroul & Blau, 2008a). Core values include partnering with families and youth at all levels of decision making; addressing cultural and linguistic competence and issues of disparities; and building community-based services and supports across child-serving systems. Increasingly, systems of care are embracing the value of data for making decisions, incorporating EIPs within their service array, and building an infrastructure for performance measurement. In fact, the federal request for application for systems of care now includes the requirement that the selected grantee implement an EIP as part of its service delivery approach. The value base and organizational structure of systems of care provide an important context for developing a quality-driven system, a frame for determining a common set of outcomes to be achieved, and a vision that enables critical stakeholders to come together to align service systems.

KEY DECISION POINTS

The next section highlights the key domains for decisions by leaders to ultimately achieve an outcomes-driven service system. Critical challenges and options for each will be discussed.

1. Population of Focus and Outcomes

Determining the population of children to target and the outcomes to be achieved represents the first and most critical set of decisions to be made. Issues for consideration include how broadly or narrowly to define the population and whether to phase in certain population groups. These decisions have implications for funding, stakeholder involvement, and implementation. Some states may want to select a broad population, such as children with mental health challenges or those at risk. Other states may want to focus on a population similar to that defined in the systems of care legislation, which targets children with significant mental health disorders in all the child-serving agencies. Still other states may want to focus on a population in a particular system, such as those children with significant mental health challenges in the juvenile justice system. Alternatively, some states may want to address youth in one system and progressively add other systems. What is significant is that decision-makers consider the pros and cons of these approaches and implications of their decision. It is critical that decisions are informed by data—demographic data on the population of children and youth including cultural diversity and disproportionality, socio-economics, prevalence and incidence, costs, service use, unmet need, and risk factors.

Once the population of focus is determined, the next task is identifying the outcomes to be achieved for that population. Increasingly, states and communities are adopting the outcomes articulated by systems of care, which include both clinical and functional outcomes for children with mental health challenges. These correspond with National Outcome Measures proposed by the US Government's Substance Abuse and Mental Health Services Administration (SAMHSA). Common outcomes include reduction of clinical symptomatology, living at home or in the community, stable living environments, attendance and performance in school, staying out of trouble with the law or diversion from the juvenile justice system, and child welfare outcomes of permanence and safety.

Families and young people should be involved in the determination of outcomes meaningful to them. Selection of outcomes also has important implications for achieving buy-in across systems, for measurement, for selection of appropriate EIPs, and for client level and system accountability.

2. Alignment of Systems and Development of Supportive Organizational Environments

In the US, delivery of mental health services is fragmented across multiple systems including mental health, education, child welfare, juvenile justice, substance abuse, and general health (American Psychological Association Task Force on Evidence-Based Practice for Children and Adolescents, 2008). Such cross-sectoral fragmentation also seems to be a challenge for other countries as well. Each of these systems and organizations has a variety of quality improvement processes; however, there are neither consistent standards for quality of care nor consistent measurement systems used across sectors. An outcomes-driven system that is to be adopted statewide needs to address these issues of fragmentation and consistency. As mentioned above, systems of care provide a context for developing this collaboration across agencies and systems and partnering with families and youth. The vision and mission of the outcomes-driven system to be achieved needs to be compatible with the vision and mission of participating state and provincial agencies.

In addition, it is important to get the buy-in of these key systems to engage them in planning, to achieve common outcomes for cross-cutting populations, and to develop statewide standards. The more systems align their investment in performance measurement systems, technology, EIPs, and training, the more cost efficiencies and effective allocation of limited state resources are achieved. Coordination of all systems at the outset may be challenging and decision-makers may want to bring key systems in on an incremental basis. However, it is important to try to involve all relevant systems in the planning stages from the beginning.

State and provincial systems are also in a position to promote vertical integration with state, county, and community agencies and organizations to develop supportive environments for the implementation of outcomes-driven service systems. Policies, regulations, contracts, and standards are all tools that states and provinces have to influence local agencies and organizations. Moving the implementation to the community level is necessary for the systems to ultimately impact children and families because that is where families live and services are delivered. Work also needs to occur at the local level in order to create an environment conducive to collectively engaging stakeholders in implementation of EIPs. This environment has to support managers and supervisors as well as their staff in the day-to-day operation and delivery of EIPs and in performance measurement functions (Barratt & Hodson, 2006).

3. Performance Measurement System

The third key domain in the framework for an outcomes-driven delivery system is a performance measurement system (PMS). For the purpose of this paper, a PMS is defined as a means of collecting client-level data on outcomes, which can be used for

- case decision making;
- accountability and continuous quality improvement (CQI);
- informing higher level decisions, via aggregated data.

The end-point objective is attaining meaningful clinical and functional outcomes for the youth, which in turn should positively impact the quality of life for the family. Data aggregated across populations of children also provide valuable information to communities and states about the effectiveness of their investment in service delivery. Implementation of a PMS promotes greater accountability, more transparency among stakeholders, and increased use of data to inform policies and practices. In addition, it can greatly facilitate the implementation of EIPs. This section will: (1) elaborate on the characteristics and advantages of a

PMS, (2) provide guidelines for selecting measurement tool(s), (3) describe how a PMS can facilitate EIP implementation and collaboration across systems, and (4) discuss implementation issues.

Essential Characteristics of a PMS

To be truly accountable for the outcomes of the youth served, data must be collected at the level of the individual client and used for improving the youth's functioning. Furthermore, client data should be immediately available, meaning that data need to be delivered in "real time." This is essential so that the practitioner can optimally utilize the information to benefit, and share with, the client and family at the time of receiving services. The PMS must inform practitioners (and their supervisors) as they make decisions about the case as well as track client progress during services. In order to be useful for continuous quality improvement (CQI) efforts, client information from the PMS should be available at all levels, including family members, front-line practitioners, supervisors, and agency leadership. Data should also be aggregated in order to be shared with a wide range of stakeholders and used to help shape treatment practices, program development, policies, and workforce development initiatives. Use of the data by local, county, or regional directors and state/provincial administrators can facilitate collaborative problem solving.

Advantages of a PMS

A PMS can greatly facilitate the implementation of EIPs in contrast to "treatment-as-usual" and the improvement of outcomes, if appropriate EIPs are implemented. Using aggregated outcome data to determine the types of clients most in need of more effective services results in selecting EIPs that are likely to have the greatest impact on outcomes for the population of youth served. For example, this data-informed approach to selecting EIPs used in Michigan generated sustained support for statewide implementation and led to the widespread adoption of EIPs that matched the needs of the youth served by the state (Hodges & Wotring, 2004; Wotring, Hodges, Xue, & Forgatch, 2005). Data collected as part of the PMS can be used to objectively identify the target population (e.g., youth's profile of specific problem(s) and associated level of impairment), to select EIPs most likely to achieve positive results, and ensure more appropriate referral and enrolment.

Assessing the EIP

In addition, the PMS can be used to assess the effectiveness of the EIP. This is important because the results observed from the original research studies may not be applicable, or generalizable, to the local culture or the characteristics of the youth. Also, it is assumed that strict adherence to implementing the treatment as taught by the progenitors, typically referred to as "fidelity," is required to obtain outcome results similar to those observed in the original research studies. Continuing to monitor outcomes for EIPs is recommended (Fixsen et al., 2005) because fidelity may be reduced by adaptations introduced or delivery of the EIP by subsequent cohorts of trainees not trained by the progenitors. The state of Hawaii, for example, used data from their PMS to study the relationship between implementation of EIPs and outcomes. The state found that use of EIPs was associated with the youths' functioning improving at a faster rate, which was summarized as "getting better at getting them better" (Daleiden et al., 2006).

Collaboration across Systems

A PMS can facilitate collaboration with other child-serving systems to improve access to appropriate care. It helps remove barriers to delivering appropriate services to any youth with serious mental health issues, regardless of the agency to which the youth was referred. A measure that helps determine the extent of the youth's mental health needs can be an objective means of identifying youth in the juvenile justice or child welfare systems who should receive mental health services. The result should be increased access to mental health services, more transparent and objective criteria for receiving specialized mental health services, and reduction in disparities in treatment availability. The mental health agencies can also assess the outcomes of the services they offer and share these results with their system partners. Collaborating around objective criteria and data-based outcomes fosters more widespread collaboration around other needed reforms.

Measurement Tools

In order for a PMS to accomplish these goals, a measurement tool(s) is needed, which has demonstrated evidence that it can both assess the needs of youth at entry into care and can assess outcomes in children and adolescents with mental health needs. Guidelines for selecting a measure are available in the literature (Newman, Ciarlo, & Carpenter, 1999) and include the following criteria. The tool must be: (1) relevant to the target group and independent of the treatment provided (i.e., relevant to determining and differentiating mental health issues and functioning); (2) useful in assessing the outcomes that are considered the most critical (i.e., functioning in home, school, and the community); (3) able to regularly assess progress in treatment so that the course of treatment can be changed if needed while the youth is still receiving services; (4) capable of using objective, well-defined referents, such as behavioural descriptors; (5) psychometrically strong, including evidence of concurrent and predictive validity and sensitivity to change, for the target population (e.g., youth with mental health needs); (6) useful in clinical services (e.g., helps to describe client service needs, identify goals for treatment planning, and, if the client is not improving, identify specific areas of functioning that are non-responsive to treatment); and (7) able to generate results that can be shared with the family and easily understood. A measure that is considered clinically relevant by practitioners (i.e., helpful in case decision making and tracking progress) will more likely be implemented more successfully. A variety of tools are available (Maruish, 2004) and can be evaluated using these criteria.

Beginning the Implementation Process

Establishing a PMS involves deciding on the target population (i.e., which youth, from which systems), a measure(s) that can both assess a youth's needs and track their outcomes, and a means of electronically collecting client-level data so that data can be used for the benefit of the child and family, the agency, community, and state. Making these decisions requires bringing into the process individuals who will be responsible for using the PMS. Including the administrative and clinical stakeholders in the process increases the likelihood they will make full use of the data to improve performance. Leaders need to convene groups of stakeholders who will assist in the design and gathering of the data. Throughout the implementation process, families and youth need to be involved. These groups need to identify ways the data can be used and embedded at various levels in organizations and systems. Getting buy-in to own and understand the data is the key objective. Using the client-level data to improve practice is the ultimate goal, which seeks to align the system(s), organizations, programs, and clinicians around client-level data and helps focus the attention on the child and family accomplishing their goals for improvement. This is at the heart of the CQI process. The end goal is to fully use the data at all levels. If the data are infused at all levels, it is more likely that the data will be used to improve performance of the clinicians, organizations, and systems (Barratt & Hodson, 2006).

Electronic Tracking System

Adequate funding is necessary to put into place an effective PMS. Funding must support the electronic means for information collection, the instruments, training, and hardware. Web-hosted systems, which are now common, do not require installation or maintenance of software and permit access to groups of users, who are not on the same computer system or server. An electronic system that generates information in "real time" is needed in order to embed the use of the information throughout the organization and at all levels. Involving information technology staff from the beginning is critical. They can be helpful in getting the system up and operational, troubleshooting problems, and integrating the PMS with the organization's other information management systems. Once linked to a management information system, additional aggregated reports can be generated that may be useful to the various stakeholders. An investment in an effective electronic tracking system, as a needed component of infrastructure, can save money in the long term for systems.

Achieving Supportive Agency Environments

Within an organization, it is critical to build the necessary infrastructure and support to sustain and improve PMS. This involves allowing time for administrators, supervisors, and clinicians to use and study the data and then plan for improvements in the systems and organizations. The environment needs to be supportive for the staff to be willing to critically review how they are performing in relation to others and help them understand how they are performing with different types of clients. Some staff will perform better with children who have behavioural disorders while other staff are better suited at working with children who have anxiety or depression. Using end point data enables staff to identify their strengths as well as areas of improvement. Taking a critical look at staff performance requires supportive supervision and a supportive environment for the supervisors. Administrators need to recognize that time will also be required for staff to develop new skills to improve their performance. The successful implementation of a PMS aligns systems, organizations, and individuals to improve the quality of the services that children and families receive.

4. Evidence-Informed Practices

Despite the emerging priority of EIPs within the behavioural health system, there is limited guidance specific to the challenges of selection and implementation—the process of identifying EIPs and determining the "fit" of the EIP (systemically, organizationally, and clinically)—within the context of an outcomes-driven system. For the purposes of this chapter, selection is defined as "the set of activities involved in identifying an EIP for implementation within an organization and/or community setting." Implementation is defined as "a specific set of activities designed to put into practice an activity or program" (Fixsen et al., 2005, p. 5).

Each of these undertakings has a set of challenges that must be addressed in order to maximize the success of the adoption. State and provincial leaders, as well as local decision-makers (e.g., providers), must evaluate a wide range of clinical, fiscal, and systemic factors when considering investing in EIPs. Although this section primarily focuses on EIP interventions, it is important to note that there are certain inter-system and organizational activities, such as Wraparound, integrated case planning, and inter-system case reviews that can be considered best practices. These practices, while not direct treatment interventions, can help support quality and effectiveness by assuring accurate identification of youth, appropriate dosage, family and youth satisfaction, and the management of service coordination and delivery.

Selection

Perhaps second only to implementation, an informed selection of an EIP is the most critical factor for optimizing successful adoption. More attention and guidance are needed in the areas of selection and implementation. The conditions that lead to selection of an EIP are often diverse and likely include one or more of the following:

- Response to an identified need/target population
- A grant or other opportunity that requires the implementation of an EIP
- Federal, state, and/or local mandates that require implementation of an EIP
- Availability of funding that requires implementation of EIPs
- Influential advocacy promoting EIPs
- Consumer choice
- Administrative/policy/legislative directive (often the result of a negative situation and/or lawsuit settlement)

These influences begin to set the stage for implementation, but all need to be embedded within a planning process (Stroul & Blau, 2008b). Taken out of a planning context, they can have unintended consequences and may result in short-cutting critical steps needed for successful adoption, implementation, and sustainability. The selection process should be developed by and with the key stakeholders, including systems (funders) and organizations (implementers, practitioners, and customers). The fundamental elements that are core to the process typically include

- identifying an impact area and/or a specific population of youth and families with a specific set of behaviours, challenges, or conditions to be addressed;
- utilizing available selection tools, resources, and research;
- assessing feasibility that the EIP can actually be adopted, implemented, and sustained with fidelity (this area includes both financing and workforce issues).

Target Population/Impact Area

Ultimately, the success of implementation rests on clearly identifying either the specific target population of youth/families (e.g., adolescents with serious behaviour disorders that are not completing school) and/or the specific need areas (e.g., high rate of youth violence in a particular neighbourhood) that the proposed intervention is designed to impact. The identification of need can be generated from any number of places, but to assure meaningful implementation, the following factors should be carefully assessed for both target population and impact/need area:

- Sufficient and credible data to confirm and support the need (anecdotal is not sufficient)
- Determination of the level of evidence standard that is sufficient to meet the defined needs
- Analysis of what programs/interventions have already been tried
- Assessment of the factors driving the need
- Precisely defined characteristics of the target population
- Description of intended outcomes of the intervention or how the conditions will be improved

As awareness of use of EIPs has increased, so have the number of resources or tools that can assist in selection and implementation. Most of these take the form of a list or some type of matrix. In the US, a variety of organizations have developed these lists, including the federal government, universities, and professional associations. These resources often are targeted for a specific system, for example, The Office of Juvenile Justice and Delinquency Prevention (OJJDP) Model Programs Guide focuses on the juvenile justice population's needs. Some of the common elements that the lists share are: identification of a named practice/intervention; description of the practice; and description of the target population/area for which the practice is intended. More sophisticated tools may also include: level/description of research associated with the practice; a rating of the practice via some independent process; and cost-benefit analysis (e.g., the Washington Institute for Public Policy).

Informed use of selection tools and resources can add to the likelihood of a quality decision. Planners and decision-makers should become familiar with the range of tools and assess the strengths and limitations of each, and match those against the specific task at hand. The purpose of using a selection resource is to refine the range of options for decision-makers. It is important, then, to determine the acceptable levels or thresholds for the various items on a particular list. For example, is it important that decision-makers only consider interventions that have undergone randomized clinical trials? Is it essential that the intervention apply to a specific gender, cultural, or ethnic group? How is the states' or provinces' target population or high need area reflected in the choices being made? Websites for some of these resources are listed in the endnotes.[2] Other approaches (Daleiden et al., 2006) examine the active ingredients that appear to be the reason that certain EIPs are effective and provide training modules and consultation on the ingredients to change practice and improve outcomes.

Feasibility, Fidelity, and Implementation

These areas are perhaps the most relevant to "on the ground" organizations and practitioners who are seeking guidance on EIPs. The underlying feasibility question is: What is the likelihood that an identified EIP can be successfully implemented for this particular population/need, within this particular environment, at this particular time? Assessing for feasibility is critical at multiple levels: organizational, clinical, workforce, and fiscal. Each of these areas must be analyzed and prioritized within an implementation planning framework. Only until each area is analyzed and given weight or priority can a decision on selection be reached. The underlying fidelity questions are: (1) Can the identified organization (within the context of its local system of care) meet the fidelity standards that are required in order to achieve the desired outcomes? and (2) Can agency, state, and provincial fiscal and administrative policies support the selected intervention? (Stroul & Blau, 2008b).

There are a myriad of reasons that certain practices may seem feasible, but upon closer examination, the edges may not line up so neatly. For example, some interventions have undergone rigorous scientific study and have been replicated in real-world settings with consistently high levels of outcomes. At a glance, it might seem like choosing such an intervention would be obvious, but as the conditions of feasibility are applied, the likelihood of successful adoption may diminish. Such factors as the need for a highly skilled workforce; ability to bill for services at a case rate; low caseloads; targeted geographic area; flexible hours; ongoing consultation fees, and so forth, all serve to impact the final analysis of feasibility. So, feasibility must include a close review of at least:

- adoptability of the program with fidelity (the way it is intended to be implemented);
- room for adaptability based on local circumstances;
- compatibility of the potential provider with the unique characteristics/ requirements of the model;
- adequate funding amounts and sources to support the program model;
- cultural relevance and consumer salience;
- the fit of the program within the local systems of care structure.

The EIPs typically have explicit directions regarding the conditions needed for successful adoption and ultimately achieving fidelity. Decision-makers need to be keenly aware of what these (often rigorous) requirements are and map those against the ability of the provider and system to achieve those conditions. Highly successful interventions can fall significantly short of their expectations without scrupulous attention to feasibility and what it takes to achieve fidelity.

As decision-makers utilize more thoughtful selection processes and more carefully assess the feasibility factors, the likelihood of successful adoption increases. In the end, it is the success and process of implementation that will ultimately impact sustainability and build a strong platform for future efforts to improve the service system. The implementation phase is all about management, oversight, maintenance, and ongoing assessment.

To address some of the particular concerns about EIP's appropriateness for serving different cultural groups, the US has also taken a service-to-science approach related to indigenous practices. This approach is often referred to as "practice-based evidence," a concept that takes into account that there are local practices and interventions that have not necessarily been studied (and may not contribute to data collection or PMS approaches) but may be deemed important and effective by a particular population or community. States and communities are finding that "practice-based evidence" and "evidence-based practice" approaches can be compatible.

5. Considerations about Workforce

Throughout this chapter there have been references to workforce related issues, such as skills-level training and support, and a need for investment in workforce capacity. While these cannot be underestimated as factors related to building an outcomes-driven service system and represent a critical domain in the framework proposed, we can only outline some of the key issues within this chapter that decision-makers need to consider. The issues include:

- Incentives to improve the capacity and capability of practitioners to successfully implement selected EIPs and track outcomes
- Support for ongoing training and consultation
- Identification of professional characteristics that are compatible with the fidelity requirements of an EIP
- Collaboration with universities to develop curricula (and field opportunities) that bridges pre-service preparation and community provider expectation/ need
- Examination of the role of a non-traditional workforce (parents as peers, youth as mentors)

This chapter proposes that implementing the strategies in the first four domains of the framework lays the groundwork for establishing a supportive workforce for an outcomes-driven system.

CONCLUSIONS: KEY DECISIONS THAT IMPROVE QUALITY AND PROMOTE DISSEMINATION OF EIPs

In a science-to-service model, implementation requires careful consideration of "real-world issues" while striving to improve the quality of care. Based on the framework outlined in this paper, there are several critical factors that decision-makers need to consider:

1. Determine the values and principles that will serve as a foundation and provide common ground for key stakeholders.
2. Decide on the population of focus and the overarching goals for achieving progress on quality improvement and practice dissemination.
3. Address the issues of scope and scale; discuss the longer-term vision and stages toward full implementation; and develop a plan to guide the implementation process.
4. Determine the time, tools, and resources needed to develop and/or refine a performance measurement system, which includes client-level outcome data and yields meaningful information that can be effectively used at the clinical, administrative, and system(s) levels.
5. Include data and outcomes in the development of policy and programs.
6. Map out both incremental and going-to-scale strategies and assess each for strengths and challenges.
6. Make a commitment to implementation of practices that are research/science-based or informed.
7. Address issues of cultural diversity and disparities.
8. Maximize opportunities that can bring some degree of alignment (e.g., data collection, program evaluation, critical outcomes) among multiple systems that are engaged with the same target populations.
9. Employ multiple resources and tools (e.g., research, registries, credible lists) to guide the process of selection of EIPs.
10. Articulate the real world limitations and opportunities related to feasibility of implementation of EIPs.

A meaningful performance measurement system, coupled with effective EIP selection and implementation processes, can improve system and service quality, increase access to effective practices, increase the likelihood of positive outcomes, and improve the quality of life for youth and their families.

ENDNOTES

1. For purposes of this paper the term "evidence-informed practices" will be used to include other similar terminology such as evidence-based practices or evidence-based treatment. This chapter incorporates the views presented in Barratt and Hodson (2006), that states "research evidence is one of the factors that needs to influence practitioner's decisions and judgments.... [T]he practitioner goes through a thoughtful process where a range of factors (including research) influence judgment.... [I]t is this thoughtful process we call evidence-informed practice (EIP). The evidence-informed practitioner carefully considers what research evidence tells them in the context of a particular child, family, or service, and then weighs this alongside knowledge drawn from professional experience and the views of service users to inform decisions about the way forward" (p. 14).
2. National Registry for Effective and Promising Practices: www.nrepp.samhsa.gov
   OJJDP Model Programs Guide: www.ojjdp.ncjrs.gov/programs/mpg.html
   Promising Practices Network: www.promisingpractices.net
   Washington State Institute for Public Policy: www.wsipp.wa.gov
   Blueprints for Violence Preventions: www.colorado.edu/cspv/blueprints

REFERENCES

American Psychological Association Task Force on Evidence-Based Practice for Children and Adolescents. (2008). *Disseminating evidence-based practice for children and adolescents: A systems approach to enhancing care*. Washington, DC: American Psychological Association.

Barratt, M.O., & Hodson, R. (2006). *Firm foundations: A practical guide to organisational support for the use of research evidence*. Dartington, England: Research in Practice.

Cooper, J.L., Aratani, Y., Knitzer, J., Douglas-Hall, A., Masi, R., Banghart, P., et al. (2008). *Unclaimed children revisited: The status of children's mental health policy in the United States*. New York: National Center for Children in Poverty, Columbia University.

Daleiden, E.L., Chorpita, B.F., Donkervoet, C., Arensdorf, A.M., & Brogan, M. (2006). Getting better at getting them better: Health outcomes and evidence-based practice within a system of care. *Journal of the American Academy of Child & Adolescent Psychiatry, 45*, 749–756.

Fixsen, D.L., Naoom, S.F., Blasé, K.A., Friedman, R.M., & Wallace, F. (2005). *Implementation research: A synthesis of the literature*. Tampa, FL: University of South Florida, Louis de la Parte Florida Mental Health Institute, The National Implementation Research Network.

Hodges, K., & Wotring, J. (2004). Role of monitoring outcomes in initiating implementation of evidence–based treatments at the state level. *Psychiatric Services, 55*, 396–400.

Maruish, M.E. (Ed.). (2004). *The use of psychological testing for treatment planning and outcome assessment* (3rd ed.). Mahwah, NJ: Lawrence Erlbaum Associates.

McCall, R.B. (2009). Evidence-based programming in the context of practice and policy. *Social Policy Report, 23*, 3–19.

Newman, F.L., Ciarlo, J.A., & Carpenter, D. (1999). Guidelines for selecting psychological instruments for treatment outcome assessment. In M.E. Maruish (Ed.), *The use of psychological testing for treatment planning and outcome assessment* (pp. 153–170). Hillsdale, NJ: Lawrence Erlbaum Associates.

President's New Freedom Commission on Mental Health. (2003). *Achieving the promise: Transforming mental health care in America*. Rockville, MD: National Mental Health Information Center.

Stroul, B.A., & Blau G.M. (Eds.). (2008a). Systems of care: A strategy to transform children's mental health care. *The system of care handbook: Transforming mental health services for children, youth, and families* (pp. 3–23). Baltimore, MD: Brookes Publishing.

Stroul, B.A., & Blau G.M. (Eds.). (2008b). Implementing evidence-based practices within systems of care. *The system of care handbook: Transforming mental health services for children, youth, and families* (pp. 155–179). Baltimore, MD: Brookes Publishing.

Wotring, J.R., Hodges V.M., Xue, Y. & Forgatch, M. (2005). Critical ingredients for improving mental health services: Use of outcome data, stakeholder involvement, and evidence-based practices. *The Behavior Therapist, 28*, 150–157.

CHAPTER 11

LET'S COME TOGETHER:
A MACRO-ORIENTED MODEL FOR ORGANIZING THE SUPPORT OF EBP

KARIN ALEXANDERSON, ELISABETH BEIJER, ULF HYVÖNEN, PER-ÅKE KARLSSON, and KRISTIN MARKLUND

ABSTRACT

In this chapter, a preliminary model for organizing the support for an evidence-based practice (EPB) in the Swedish social welfare services is outlined. The model is based on a theoretical framework where EPB is understood in a broad sense, and it assumes the co-operation between different national and regional actors to be an important prerequisite for supporting and performing EBP in the social services. The chapter contends that (1) these actors, given their complementary positions, can promote EBP by producing knowledge for practice, by governing knowledge into practice, by contributing to collaborative knowledge development, and by supporting knowledge use in practice; and (2) the possibilities of establishing such an infrastructure in the Swedish welfare system, in spite of several obstacles and difficulties, are fairly good.

INTRODUCTION

The discussion on evidence-based practice (EBP) is worldwide and ongoing. Nationally, regionally, and locally based organizations make strong efforts to promote EBP and, as a result of the workshops on evidence-informed practice held in England in 2008 and in Canada in 2010, an international network in this field is being established. In this chapter, four key actors in the Swedish arena are identified: The National Board of Health and Welfare, The Swedish Association of Local Authorities and Regions (SALAR), the universities, and the Research and Development (R & D) milieus. Their actual and potential roles in providing support for EBP is discussed in relation to a theoretical framework built on an understanding of evidence-based practice in an organizational context, combined with a wide interpretation of knowledge, knowledge use, knowledge production, and learning. The aim of the chapter is to outline a model for how these actors, given their different assignments and roles, can promote knowledge production and utilization in practice. The main interest is the interplay between research and practice, and one of the crucial issues is how to maximize the capacity to implement evidence-based knowledge in the social service agencies.

Our view is very similar to those actors in the "promoting EBP field" who prefer to use the term evidence-*informed* practice (EIP) or multidimensional evidence-based practice. For example, we embrace their broader interpretation of knowledge, that there are "different ways of knowing" (Dill & Shera, 2010, p. 5). Still, we have chosen to use the concept EBP—interpreted in this broader sense—since it is established and used in our Swedish context.

EVIDENCE-BASED PRACTICE

EBP is rooted in evidence-based medicine (EBM) (Trinder & Reynolds, 2001). David L. Sackett defines EBM in a way that is often quoted: "the conscientious, explicit, and judicious use of current best evidence in making decisions about the care of individual patients" (Sackett, Scott-Richardson, Rosenberg, & Haynes, 1997, p. 2). In another quotation, the role of the professional is emphasized:

> Without clinical expertise, practice risks becoming tyrannized by external evidence, for even excellent external evidence may be inapplicable to or inappropriate for an individual patient. (Sackett et al., 1997, p. 2)

Sackett also points out the importance of the service users' (i.e., patients, clients) perspectives: "and the integration of best research evidence with clinical expertise and patient values" (Sackett, 2000, p. 1). Consequently, Sackett identifies three essential sources for EBM: the views and expectations of service users, the best research evidence available, and the experience-based knowledge of the practitioners. The latter means that it is important in EBP that the professionals also incorporate earlier experiences and think critically in relation to the sources being mentioned while analyzing and deciding how to provide the best help. In this chapter, "evidence" means that there is scientific/empirical support that a method or a way of working leads to desired effects, or at least does not cause individuals unnecessary harm.

The model in Figure 11.1 illustrates that EBP is embedded in an organizational and environmental context, which includes historical and cultural influences

Figure 11.1

(Alexanderson, 2006; Powell & DiMaggio, 1991). These are circumstances that must be taken into account while investigating the possibilities to support research utilization in social work practice.

The discussion on "evidence-based" has been rather extensive in different parts of the Swedish social sector (Bergmark & Lundström, 2006; Eliasson-Lappalainen et al., 2010; Oscarsson, 2006; Ronnby, 2006; Sundell, Soydan, Tengvald, & Anttila, 2010). Our impression, however, is that there is a growing consensus about the importance of focusing on outcomes and having an evidence-based approach in relation to individual clients or groups of clients.

THE SWEDISH EBP MOVEMENT

During the last decades, at least three waves have shaped the development of Swedish social welfare services. The first wave concerned cost limitation (i.e., cost containment), the second concerned work quality (i.e., quality assurance), and the third was called knowledge-based or evidence-based practice (i.e., "what works"). The common foundation for these measures was to bring about as much value as possible in the form of good results for the resources invested in the business (i.e., to get one's money's worth). This aspect has a high priority in current Swedish social welfare services and is closely related to the fact that, during the past 40 years, costs have increased in a way that is considered to be unsustainable in the long run. This trend is related to the growth of the New Public Management and a market-oriented delivery of welfare services.

This is one of the reasons the National Board was commissioned by the Swedish government in the early 2000s to investigate ways to support knowledge development in the social services. Some years later, a report was published by the Swedish government: *Evidence-Based Practice in the Social Services: For the Benefit of the Client* (SOU, 2008).[1] It shows that the basis for the efforts, work procedures, and methods in social work practice is fairly weak. It also emphasizes that, in this field, the national support for knowledge development to a large extent is based on short-term projects without adequate coordination between research, practice, learning, and implementation. The report points out a lack of research and evaluation of client effects, results, and outcomes (i.e., evidence) internationally, as well as in a Swedish context. One of the suggestions put forward in the report is to strengthen EBP in the social sector by producing systematic reviews from research, and national guidelines with recommendations and measurable quality indicators for practice, and it is stressed that this form of knowledge should be spread, implemented, and used in practice. However, definitions of terms and quality standards for social work need to be clarified to form a better foundation for follow-up systems. It also pointed out that national quality indicators and systems for comparisons available for both citizens and professionals are other parts of the required infrastructure. The need for measuring, describing, and disseminating best practice and developing platforms for collaboration between research and practice is highlighted. The report also points out that, in some cases, politicians instead of social workers are obliged to make decisions about individual clients, which is not the case for the politicians in the health sector. This is a condition that complicates the ambition of developing EBP in social work. Last but not least, the report accentuates the perspective of service users as an urgent area for development in relation to EBP.

In 2009, SALAR initiated joint work with government representatives to build a platform for coordinated long-term efforts for supporting evidence-based practice in the social services. The point of departure for this process was the report mentioned above (SOU, 2008). The project team was to prepare future agreements between national actors on how to strengthen possibilities and capacities to produce and make use of knowledge in the social services. The project team is expected to present model(s) for providing long-term requirements of structures that support knowledge development, implementation, evaluation, and so forth.

KNOWLEDGE AND KNOWLEDGE UTILIZATION

Evidence-based practice is supposed to draw on a solid knowledge foundation. However, the knowledge concept can be understood in different ways. In a stricter fashion, originating from EBM, there is a hierarchical approach to knowledge where difference in quality is determined by the strength of scientific evidence. The strongest evidence is provided by meta-analyses or well-performed, large-scale Randomized Controlled Trial (RCT) studies. The international Campbell Collaboration research network has taken on the task of summarizing the best available research in the field of social welfare and made it accessible by publishing so-called systematic reviews. A systematic review must have clear inclusion/exclusion criteria, an explicit search strategy, systematic coding, analysis of included studies and, where possible, meta-analysis.[2]

In contrast to a hierarchical view, there are inclusive, non-hierarchical approaches that map out the knowledge basis for social care and social work (Gould, 2006). Including theoretical knowledge is one such approach that exceeds the notion of EBM. An exponent of this view is Trevithik (2008), who claims that the knowledge basis for social work includes three interweaving features: theoretical knowledge, factual knowledge (including research), and practical/personal knowledge. In social work, she argues, knowledge must incorporate both theoretical and practical knowledge—"knowing about" and "knowing how" (Trevithik, 2008, p. 1214). This framework acknowledges that practitioners, other professionals, as well as the involved clients bring something valuable into the encounter with one another. A knowledge review, conducted by The Social Care Institute for Excellence (SCIE) in England, expresses a view where there is no hierarchy between different types of knowledge (Pawson et al., 2003). Instead, the different types are assumed to play vital roles in building up the evidence basis for social care and social work, allowing different types of knowledge to underpin good practice.

This wider definition of knowledge, in accordance with SCIE and Trevithik, fits well with our view on EBP and on how the interplay between research and practice should be organized to maximize the capacity to implement evidence-based knowledge in social service agencies. This leads to the complexity of translating what we know from research into practice, and, of course, from practice into research. In an article on social service organizations in the era of evidence-based practice, Maynard (2009) claims that the EBP paradigm requires a different sort of social service organization: one that "can learn on a continuous basis and adapt quickly and responsively to knowledge, research and the changes in the field that are occurring at a rapid pace" (Maynard, 2009, p. 3). She proposes the "learning organization" as a theoretical framework for bridging the gap between science and service. We will return to this later in the chapter.

We can conclude that there are different types of knowledge that support EBP and that there are different actors in the field who can promote the knowledge production and utilization needed, which is highly dependent on their separate commissions. This can be illustrated by adding four main activities, or positions, to our model (see Figure 11.2): governing knowledge into practice, knowledge use in practice, knowledge development in collaboration with practice, and producing knowledge for practice.

Figure 11.2

The activities or positions in the figure represent four main perspectives in knowledge use and production. The key actors that can be supportive within these perspectives, beside or in collaboration with practice itself, will be addressed in the next section of this chapter.

According to Nutley, Walter, and Davies (2007), there are three models or archetypes of how research can be put into practice: the research-based practitioner model, the embedded research model, and the organizational excellence model. A previously published article (Alexanderson et al., 2009) argued that the third model, the organizational excellence model, has great potential as a starting point for building a theoretical basis to underpin the development of EBP. This model is focused on collaboration between managers and social workers as parts of a learning organization with participating researchers from universities and other organizations. Research findings are regarded as something more than the effects of interventions, and welfare organizations are not seen merely as recipients or users of research findings but as milieus for local initiatives, evaluations, and practice development based on research. In fact, the welfare organizations might play more of an active role in producing knowledge, for example, by hosting clinical researchers, formulating new research questions, and making use of their own systematic documentation by using it as a source of reflection and as a base for building experience-based knowledge (Alexanderson et al., 2009).

FOUR ACTORS SUPPORTING EBP

In this section, four different types of locally-, regionally-, and/or nationally-based organizations are introduced as key actors in promoting EBP in Swedish social welfare agencies. In addition to a brief description of their work, reflections on their potentials in relation to EBP are presented with reference to the theoretical framework outlined in Figure 11.2.

The National Board of Health and Welfare

The National Board is a government agency under the Ministry of Health and Social Affairs with a wide range of responsibilities for social services. One of its commissions is to compile, disseminate, and compare information about social work interventions and practice evaluation. Another is to develop a common terminology in systematic documentations. Other responsibilities are to produce guidelines and perform inspections of the social services. It can be seen as governing knowledge into practice but also producing knowledge for practice (Figure 11.2).

The National Board produces knowledge in EBP and is commissioned to work with knowledge translation to support local authorities. This work includes the following:

1. Providing systematic knowledge reviews to professionals who work in the social services in terms of what works
2. Supporting the development of standardized methods for assessing the needs of clients/ users and supporting the use of such methods
3. Supporting and implementing the results from studies on social initiatives and structured action programs
4. Disseminating the results of reviews and studies in order to support evidence-based social work practice

The National Board has produced a method guide (Clearinghouse) on the Web where common interventions and evaluation methods (standardized assessment instruments) are described. This is to make it easier for practitioners to find information about current research on methods and their effects on social work practice.

Working with disseminating and supporting the implementation of EBP has become an increasingly important issue for the National Board. This assignment requires smooth communication and collaboration between national and local authorities, with new communication strategies to be tested and evaluated in the future.

The Swedish Association of Local Authorities and Regions

The Swedish Association of Local Authorities and Regions (SALAR) represents the governmental, professional, and employer-related interests of Sweden's 290 municipalities and 21 county councils. SALAR strives to promote and strengthen local self-government and the development of regional and local democracy.

As an actor on the national level, SALAR is obliged to represent the interest of its owners. Whereas the National Board has a formal responsibility in supervising and controlling social work practice and health care, SALAR has an active role in relation to developmental issues. One important task for SALAR is knowledge dissemination. A current example of this is the ongoing project regarding the implementation of the national guidelines for treatment of alcohol and drug abuse. In this work, SALAR also takes on the role of governing knowledge into practice. Another assignment for SALAR, which is regarded as more urgent by representatives for the organization itself, is to support the knowledge development that takes place in or near practice (see Tydén, 2009).

The Universities

Important supporting actors for EBP are the universities, who provide basic and advanced training for social workers or research on social work. In relation to Figure 11.2, universities may play different roles: they may produce knowledge for practice, which can be seen as the "classic" position, or participate in joint work between universities and social work practice (e.g., in a research project or a master program that contributes to knowledge development in collaboration with practice). For example, in collaboration with R & D units, they can support knowledge use in practice; or researchers from universities can provide knowledge reviews on behalf of the government with the purpose of producing national guidelines, which is governing knowledge into practice.

A national evaluation of the basic education programs for social workers was recently conducted by the Swedish National Agency for Higher Education (Högskoleverket, 2009), but it paid scant attention to EBP. It merely mentioned that EBP and its prerequisites are briefly presented in the programs. The use of quantitative methods is rare in evaluations in social work and doctoral dissertations (Dellgran & Höijer, 2000; Socialstyrelsen, 2010) for which both education and research have been criticized (Tengvald, 1995).

Our assessment is that universities need to focus and put effort into contributing to a more elaborate view on EBP in social work. Working in closer cooperation with the other actors would promote such a necessary development.

Research and Development Milieus

In Sweden, the social services are the responsibility of the local municipalities, which have a high degree of autonomy in relation to the government and other national actors. During the 1990s a large number of R & D units emerged, owned by one or several municipalities/counties. Sometimes they are established in partnership with the health care services. Collaboration with a local university is also quite common. Target groups include children and families, the elderly, persons with disabilities, persons with income support, and/or persons with alcohol or drug abuse problems. Today, almost all municipalities in Sweden have access to such R & D milieus.

The activities of an R & D unit vary, and there is no consensus or established theoretical basis for what the units should do. Still, there are some common features that have been observed in different evaluations (Ekermo, 2002; Engström, 2007, 2008; Socialstyrelsen, 2002). They are mostly small-scale with limited resources and are closely tied to practice. They are locally based with an interactive and development-oriented research approach. The subjects for their R & D activities correspond to local knowledge and developmental needs (i.e., a bottom-up approach). Their decisions as to what needs to be done are mostly achieved by dialogue and negotiation. Their core activities are studies in fields important for the region and are often conducted in a multidisciplinary way.

R & D milieus can be supportive in conducting evaluations and follow-up activities in practice in a systematic way. This is a constituent of EBP and performance development. One example is their training and coaching to support the implementation of the Addiction Severity Index (ASI) in the social services. The role of the units can be described as supporting the governing of knowledge into practice through the implementation of the assessment tool, but it also creates possibilities for the development of knowledge through the learning processes that R & D units can facilitate through dialogues on how to use the results (in this example, ASI), individually and organizationally.

R & D units provide arenas for practitioners to express, document, and communicate their experiences but also to seek, find, interpret, and use evidence (i.e., knowledge use in practice). Continuously, various activities are arranged, such as research circles or seminars where researchers and practitioners meet on core tasks for developing the practical work in the region. Quite recently, different units have started to find ways for giving this support in a network, where research circles are offered to different regions at the same time. In this sense, the role of knowledge development in collaboration but also knowledge facilitation is put into practice.

The National Board of Health and Welfare and the universities are the main actors for outcome studies that demand huge compilations of materials (e.g., evaluations with experimental designs). The R & D units can contribute in collecting such material, form multi-sites, and become speaking partners for designing studies and discussing results. In this way, the R & D units can be described as partners of knowledge production for practice. The "gravity centres" for R & D units, however, can be described as supporting knowledge use in practice as well as knowledge development in collaboration with practice.

Summary

Four important actors and their possibilities—actual and potential—to support EBP have been introduced. As shown, they play different roles in relation to promoting EBP; sometimes complementary, sometimes overlapping. So, what would be the main assignment for our four key actors in relation to our EBP model? The National Board primarily promotes governing knowledge into practice by providing knowledge reviews, guidelines, handbooks, and so forth. The main role of SALAR is somewhat more difficult to identify, but we would argue that it is to support knowledge use in practice. To fulfill this mission, SALAR must co-operate with other actors as well facilitate the co-operation between other actors, both at the national and local level. The main role for the universities is to produce knowledge for practice, whereas R & D units have a main role as active parts in knowledge development in collaboration with practice.

The support and performance of an evidence-based practice in the Swedish social services is highly dependent on the co-operation between these key actors.

ANALYSIS AND DISCUSSION

In this chapter, we have suggested a preliminary model for supporting EBP in the social services. This model is built on the complementary contributions from the four supporting key actors facilitating EBP. We will end by discussing the professional social worker who adheres to EBP in his or her everyday work with clients and service users in an organization that supports EBP. Finally, some possibilities and obstacles for realizing EBP in the social services in Sweden will be highlighted.

Two points mentioned earlier are crucial for our discussion. The first is the claim that different sorts of knowledge are needed to underpin EBP. Well-performed RCT-studies can provide useful knowledge, but useable knowledge can and must be produced by using various (research) methods and be performed in different settings (i.e., universities, R & D units, and social service organizations). The second point is our conviction that the organizational excellence model can help in understanding knowledge utilization in the social services. This model emphasizes that knowledge use is an issue for the whole organization and not only for professional social workers. Our argument for the necessity of strengthening the knowledge base and creating a genuine learning organization is strongly related to the character of Swedish social work, where professional autonomy is restricted and politicians sometimes make decisions in complicated individual social work cases.

EBP from a Practitioner's Point of View

A professional social worker in the EBP-supporting organization in social work is, for purposes of our example, a woman with a master's degree in social work. By education and experience, she is trained to integrate research evidence with the needs of the individual client in the decision-making process. She has integrated the latest demands of the legislation as well as local circumstances and policies. Her work takes place in a learning organization where politicians and managers support an evidence-based decision-making process, with an open mind toward the wants and needs of the clients and their relatives. In performing the job, she is supported by user-friendly access to updated knowledge reviews, scientific journals, national guidelines, and manuals for relevant methods. She makes her decisions by referring to different sources of knowledge in dialogue with her client.

In carrying out her everyday work, this professional social worker is familiar with different sources of knowledge and the different roles of the actors. She knows what the National Board does to produce knowledge to govern social work, including where and how to find such knowledge. She has regular contact with the universities to keep up to date with relevant ongoing research. She is also familiar with the ongoing discourse about the limits of "evidence" in connection to social welfare. Furthermore, she has experiences with collaborative knowledge development projects from working together with researchers at the local R & D unit. From such experiences, she knows how to conduct the necessary local monitoring and evaluation of social work interventions. Finally, this professional social worker knows what the regional organization of SALAR does to promote knowledge use in practice by their conducting of seminars, courses, workshops, and so on, often arranged in co-operation with the other actors.

Her local organization has a documented policy where different sorts of knowledge are expected to support and promote professional expertise. In order to integrate this, she is guaranteed a minimum of 10 percent of her working time to develop herself as a "professional tool" by taking part in supervision, seminars, reflections, reading textbooks, journals, and so on.

Obstacles and Possibilities

This is an image of a professional social worker who works actively in accordance with the EBP ideal in a learning organization. Of course, there is a long way to go to achieve such a situation, but there are strong forces that promote this development. First, we need to acknowledge some of the obstacles to and difficulties of such an achievement:

- Many municipalities are small and have limited economic and personal resources, and sometimes it is difficult to recruit educated social workers.
- Political and economic restrictions govern the work more than knowledge; focus is usually on "output" rather than "outcome" for the clients.
- EBP is not integrated as a natural part in social work education.
- Effectiveness studies are not common.
- Social workers have limited knowledge about and practically no tradition of working in accordance with EBP.
- The potential supporting actors often work in an uncoordinated fashion; sometimes it appears that the organization's needs supersede the common good.

Second, we can identify some important possibilities:

- There are strong forces in Swedish society that push the social services to show results; at different levels, politicians and citizens want evidence for their money's worth, not just output.
- The professions want a more solid knowledge base from which to act.
- Nowadays, clients/service users are more active and demand better services; also, the service must be relevant to the individual.
- There is a general growth of formal knowledge among society's citizens.

In addition to the factors supporting the possibility of working with EBP mentioned above, we believe that there is a growing tendency in Sweden to see evidence-based practice in an organizational context and its development as strongly dependent on organizational support at all levels. Furthermore, we think that the long tradition of open dialogue and negotiations upon which the welfare system in Sweden is built can provide a firm ground for a constructive co-operation between our key actors. We would like to see these parties in serious discussion with social workers on how to co-operate to develop the content and the use of the three main knowledge sources for an evidence-based social work practice. Hopefully, our model can make a contribution to such discussions—both in Sweden and internationally.

ENDNOTES

1. This report is only available in Swedish.
2. Further information is available at www.campbellcollaboration.org.

REFERENCES

Alexanderson, K. (2006). *Vilja, kunna, förstå—om implementering av systematisk dokumentation för verksamhetsutveckling i socialtjänsten.* Akademisk anhandling (Diss.) Örebro universitet. Universitetsbiblioteket. (Willingness, comprehension, capability—About implementation of systematic documentation for developing social work in the public social-work services).

Alexanderson, K., Beijer, E., Bengtsson, S., Hyvönen, U., Karlsson, P.-Å., & Nyman, M. (2009). Producing and consuming knowledge in social work practice: Research and development activities in a Swedish context. *Evidence & Policy, 5,* 127–139.

Bergmark, A., & Lundström, T. (2006). Mot en evidensbaserad praktik. Om färdriktningen i socialt arbete. *Socialvetenskaplig tidskrift, 2,* 99–113.

Dellgran, P., & Höjer, S. (2000). *Kunskapsbildning, akademisering och professionalisering i socialt arbete.* Akademisk avhandling (Diss.) Göteborgs universitet, Göteborg.

Dill, K., & Shera, W. (2010). *Pushing the envelope: Future directions for evidence informed practice.* Paper presented at the Conference "Connecting the Dots: Making the Evidence Informed Practice a Reality," Toronto, ON, April 8–10.

Ekermo, M. (2002). *Den mångtydiga FoU-idén: lokala FoU-enheters mening och betydelse.* Akademisk avhandling (Diss.) Örebro universitet.

Eliasson-Lappalainen R., Edebalk, P.G., Meeuwisse, A., Sunesson S., Svensson, K., & Swärd, H. (2010). Socialstyrelsen vill dirigera forskning. *Universitetsläraren,* 10–11.

Engström, B. (2007). *FoU-enheter med inriktning äldreomsorg.* Stockholm: Socialstyrelsen.

Engström, B. (2008). *FoU-enheter med inriktning mot individ-och familjeomsorgen—en uppföljning.* Stockholm: Socialstyrelsen.

Gould, N. (2006). An inclusive approach to knowledge for mental health social work practice and policy. *British Journal of Social Work, 36,* 109–125.

Högskoleverket. (2009). *Utvärdering av socionomutbildningen vid svenska universitet och högskolor.* Stockholm: Swedish National Agency for Higher Education.

Maynard, B.R. (2009). Social service organizations in the era of evidence-based-practice. *Journal of Social Work, 9,* 1–16.

Nutley, S.M., Walter, I., & Davies, H.T.O. (2007). *Using evidence: How research can inform public services.* Bristol, England: The Policy Press.

Oscarsson, L. (2006). Evidenskravet och socialt arbete. *Socionomen, 4,* 31–34.

Pawson, R., Boaz, A., Grayson, L., Long, A., & Barnes, C. (2003). *Types and quality of knowledge in social care.* London: Social Care Institute for Excellence.

Powell, W.W., & DiMaggio, P.J. (1991). *The new institutionalism in organizational analyses.* Chicago: University of Chicago Press.

Ronnby, A. (2006). Det sociala arbetets konst. *Socionomen, 6,* 29–32.

Sackett, D.L. (Ed.). (2000). *Evidence-based medicine* (2nd ed.). Edinburgh, Scotland: Churchill Livingstone.

Sackett, D.L., Scott-Richardson, W., Rosenberg, W., & Haynes R.B. (1997). *Evidence-based medicine: How to practice and teach EBM* (5th ed.). New York: Churchill-Livingstone.

SOU. (2008). *Evidence-based practice in social services: For the benefit of the client.* Stockholm: Ministry of Health and Social Affairs.

Socialstyrelsen. (2002). *Utvärdering av FoU.* En studie av FoU-enheter inriktade på individ och familjeomsorgen. Stockholm.

Socialstyrelsen. (2010). *Effektutvärderingar i doktorsavhandlingar.* Stockholm.

Sundell, K., Soydan, H., Tengvald, K., & Anttila, S. (2010). From opinion-based to evidence-based social work: The Swedish case. *Research on Social Work Practice, 20,* 714–722.

Tengvald, K. (1995). A need for result-oriented knowledge development in social work. Swedish Government Official Reports (SOU). 58. Stockholm, Sweden.

Trevithik, P. (2008). Revisiting the knowledge base of social work: A framework for practice. *British Journal of Social Work, 38,* 1212–1237.

Trinder, L., & Reynolds, S. (Eds.). (2001). *Evidence-based practice: A critical appraisal.* Oxford, England: Blackwell Science.

Tydén, T. (Ed.). (2009). *Gott och blandat.* Om FoU-miljöer i kommuner, landsting och regioner. DFR report.

Multi-level Initiatives in the Implementation of Evidence-Informed Practice

CHAPTER 12

FACILITATING EVIDENCE-INFORMED PRACTICE:
PARTICIPATORY KNOWLEDGE TRANSLATION AND EXCHANGE

DR. ROBYN MILDON, *Parenting Research Centre, Melbourne, Victoria, Australia*

Associate Professor LEAH BROMFIELD, *Australian Centre for Child Protection, University of South Australia, Adelaide, Australia*

Associate Professor FIONA ARNEY, *Menzies School of Health Research, Darwin, Northern Territory, Australia*

KERRY LEWIG, ANNETTE MICHAUX, *and* GREG ANTCLIFF, *Benevolent Society, Sydney, New South Wales, Australia*

ABSTRACT

Increasingly, participatory knowledge translation and exchange strategies are being used to enhance evidence-informed practice in child and family services. The use of these strategies is based upon the understanding that organizational change to promote best practice is a dynamic process that requires sustained interactions between researchers, knowledge brokers, management, and practitioners, as well as an understanding of the contexts in which child and family service agencies are operating. This chapter describes knowledge translation and exchange strategies that utilize participatory approaches to enhance evidence-informed practice in two practice contexts.

INTRODUCTION

Research is highly valued for its potential to improve policy and practice decisions in the child and family welfare sector. For example, in a survey of 495 child and family welfare professionals in Australia, the majority of participants reported that research was important for informing their work (Holzer, Lewig, Bromfield, & Arney, 2008). While the value of research is highly recognized, achieving the goal of evidence-informed practice has proven difficult. It is now recognized that there is frequently a significant time lag between the development of a rigorous evidence-base and its implementation in policy and practice. For example, Lewig, Arney, & Scott (2006) in their review of the literature reported that, where there was a high-quality evidence base to inform practice, the incorporation of this evidence in practice was frequently unpredictable, slow, incidental, or haphazard. The limitations of traditional research to practice activities (e.g., training) have also been highlighted (Saks, 2002). This has prompted new fields of inquiry that have sought to investigate and identify the barriers that have prevented the use of research in policy and practice (for example, Cultures in Context Model, Holzer et al., 2008). In addition, a diversity of approaches have emerged to enhance the use of evidence in practice.

The fields of knowledge translation and exchange (KTE) have become prominent in guiding strategies designed to increase the use of research in policy and practice. KTE refers to an interactive interchange of knowledge and activities between research users and research producers (Manion et al., 2009) and includes research production, dissemination, and utilization. The prominence of KTE is based on evidence that the successful uptake of knowledge requires more than one-way communication; instead, it requires genuine interaction among researchers, decision-makers, and other stakeholders (Lavis, Ross, McLeod, & Gildiner, 2003; Lomas, 2000). The degree to which researchers and research users interact will vary from no interaction through to an active and equal partnership between researchers and research users who together "co-produce" knowledge and apply that knowledge to the policy or practice environment.

This chapter will explore how higher levels of utilization might be achieved with different KTE strategies and varied levels of participation by practitioners in child and family services. The first section of the chapter will set the scene by exploring the literature for participatory KTE. This is followed by a discussion of two KTE projects that utilize different participatory approaches to enhance the use of evidence in specific practice contexts.

EVIDENCE-INFORMED PRACTICE

To explore KTE strategies aimed at improving utilization of evidence, it is helpful to clarify what is meant by evidence-informed practice. The terms "evidence-informed practice" and "evidence-based practice" are often used interchangeably in the literature (Kessler, Gira, & Poertner, 2005). However, there is a distinction between the two terms. Evidence-based practice is the "conscientious, explicit and judicious use of current best evidence in making decisions about individual patients" (Sackett et al., 1996, p. 71). Evidence-informed practice is the use of current best evidence combined with the knowledge and experience of practitioners and the views and experiences of service users in the current operating environment (Chaffin & Friedrich, 2004; Petch, 2009). The term "evidence-informed practice" will be used in this chapter as it fits well with the broad definition of evidence and participatory approaches applied in KTE.

In facilitating evidence-informed practice, it is worth noting that research can be used in different ways: (1) to change levels of knowledge, understanding, and attitudes (conceptual use); (2) to change policy, practice, and behaviour (instrumental use); and (3) to justify a position or action that has already been taken or to justify inaction in a particular area (symbolic use) (Amara, Ouimet, & Landry, 2004). The purpose of KTE is primarily to enhance the conceptual and instrumental use of evidence in practice.

DETERMINING THE CONTENT OF KTE STRATEGIES— THE NATURE OF THE EVIDENCE

Having defined "evidence-informed practice," it is also necessary to define "evidence." An implication of the interactive two-way knowledge exchange approach of KTE strategies is that the term "evidence" refers to the many forms of knowledge relevant to practice. This includes research evidence (e.g., evaluations on what interventions and practices improve program outcomes, research on reasons for failures in treatment adherence), as well as evidence from routine service monitoring data and other statistical data, expert knowledge, stakeholder consultations, and program and service cost-effectiveness. Petr's (2009) systematic approach (multidimensional evidence-based practice; MEBP) for combining sources of evidence to determine best practice evidence-informed approaches in child and family services involves identifying and synthesising evidence from consumer, practitioner, and research perspectives and critiquing this evidence against research standards and the values of the organization. In this way, evidence about the effectiveness of interventions and practices identified in impact and outcome evaluations (Chaffin & Friedrich, 2004) as well as about key processes (e.g., client engagement, preferred service delivery modes) can be utilized in a critical analysis.

PARTICIPATORY APPROACHES TO FACILITATING EVIDENCE-INFORMED PRACTICE

The MEBP process aims to increase the relevance and breadth of approaches to working with children, young people, and their families. It highlights the importance of service providers having power and agency in determining the relevance of research to their context. However, it provides little information on dissemination and implementation (KTE) strategies to enhance evidence-informed practice.

Walter, Nutley, and Davies (2003a) assessed the relative effectiveness of different KTE mechanisms, reviewing studies of research use interventions in the health care, education, social care, and criminal justice fields. The authors concluded that the evidence we have about "what works" to improve research use is limited and emphasized caution when considering the review's findings. Notwithstanding this caution, the review concluded that interactive approaches showed the most promise in improving the use of research. These strategies ranged from facilitating greater discussion of findings between researchers and practitioners, local collaborations between researchers and research users to test out the findings from research, to formal, ongoing, large-scale partnerships to support better connections between research and practice over the longer term.

Primarily interactive KTE strategies have used different ways of bringing researchers and service providers together, but still largely situate service providers as recipients of research findings (albeit active recipients). KTE strategies that give service providers agency and control over research dissemination and implementation, and that have a broad conceptualization of evidence that includes practice knowledge are emerging, but do not have a robust evidence base to guide their use. However, the well-developed area of participatory research provides some direction for participatory approaches to KTE.

Participatory research has been defined by the Royal Society of Canada as the "systematic enquiry with those affected by the issue under study to effect action or social change. Participatory research involves researchers and end users as a team for decision making throughout the process from developing the research question; developing tools; collecting, analyzing and interpreting the data; developing conclusions and a dissemination strategy; and disseminating results" (Green et al., 1995).

Participatory research comprises three goals: (1) to undertake high-quality research; (2) to benefit the research users who are working with the researchers to undertake the project; and (3) to develop knowledge that is generalizable/applicable to other settings (Green et al., 1995). Studies of research use have shown that opportunities for service providers to be involved in participatory research activities are associated with a greater likelihood that the findings of such research will be implemented (e.g., Holzer et al., 2008). This is likely because the findings are of high relevance to the organization, and there has been significant investment by the organization in producing the knowledge.

Another area that provides some direction for participatory KTE is the also emerging concept of "co-production." "The term 'co-production' is increasingly being applied to new types of public service delivery in the U.K., including new approaches to adult social care. It refers to active input by the people who use services, as well as—or instead of—those who have traditionally provided them. So it contrasts with approaches that treat people as passive recipients of services designed and delivered by someone else" (Needham & Carr, 2009, p. 1). Applying the concepts of participatory research and co-production to participatory KTE, we propose a distinction between interactive and participatory KTE. Interactive KTE brings researchers/research disseminators and research users together while participatory KTE is characterized by an equal and active partnership between researchers/research disseminators and research users. Participatory KTE can be further categorized according to who engages in the participatory approach to pro-duce and implement the KTE strategy: "the organization" (specified member(s) of the organization given the task of producing and implementing the KTE strategy); front-line practitioners; service users; or a combination of these groups.

In this chapter we specifically focus on participatory KTE strategies designed to enhance evidence-informed practice and are composed of an equal and active partnership between service delivery organizations and front-line practitioners and those who have traditionally developed evidence-based programs, practice tools, and practice guidance.

Organizing Frameworks: Systemizing KTE

There are a number of different KTE strategies that have been applied to try to improve the use of evidence in practice. Examples of strategies include: web-based information and electronic communications; using "actionable" messages tailored to the audience; publishing practice implications of research findings; education and training; face-to-face exchange through regular meetings, joint workshops, networks and communities of practice; the inclusion of practition-ers in the research process as part of interdisciplinary research teams; the use of intermediaries that understand both roles, known as "knowledge brokers"; and co-production of programs and materials to enhance their fit with services and organizations (Mitton et al., 2007).

Many argue that it is useful to establish a categorization of these activities to help systematize thinking and understanding about how to improve the use of evidence (Davies, Nutley, & Smith, 2000; Nutley, Walter, & Davies, 2007). However, just as there are multiple KTE strategies, there are also multiple organizing frameworks for understanding KTE. They range from simple dichotomies to multi-dimensional frameworks. We describe three different types of organizing frameworks for KTE: classifying the degree of engagement; classifying according to the form and type of KTE strategy being used; and classification according to the mechanisms that underpin the KTE strategy.

Strategies can be distinguished based on the degree of engagement with the potential audience (Tetroe et al. 2008). In this conceptualization, activities are considered to be "push," concentrating on diffusion and efforts to disseminate to a broad audience; "pull," focused on the needs of users, thereby creating an appetite for research results (Lavis et al., 2003); or "linkage and exchange," building and maintaining relationships in order to exchange knowledge and ideas (Lomas, 2000).

Another way to categorize KTE strategies is to group them by the form and type of intervention being used (Walter, Nutley, & Davies, 2003b). For example, categories might include written materials (including journal articles, research reports, and evidence briefings), professional interventions (such as education and training, audits, reminders, and feedback), or boundary spanners, such as knowledge brokers or practitioner-researchers (see the taxonomy of interventions to achieve practice change developed by the Effective Practice and Organisation of Care [EPOC] group within the Cochrane Collaboration as a good example of this type of classification).

Walter et al. (2003b) took an innovative approach and developed a taxonomy that focuses on the underlying mechanisms that underpin the strategies rather than their form or content. The authors argue that a focus on underlying mechanisms forces us to be clear about why it is that we believe any KTE approach will be successful in any given circumstances. The five main mechanisms that they proposed were at play in research use strategies included:

1. Dissemination: circulating or presenting research findings to potential users, in formats that may be more or less tailored to their target audience. This mechanism typically assumes a one-way flow of information from research to practice, and views research users as relatively passive consumers of evidence.

2. Interaction: developing stronger links and collaborations between the research and policy or practice communities. This mechanism assumes that two-way flows of information are required so that researchers are better able to orient their work to users' needs and research users are enabled to adapt and negotiate research findings in the context of the use.

3. Social influence: relying on influential others, such as experts and peers, to inform individuals about research and to persuade them of its value. This mechanism emphasizes the importance of the attitudes and behaviour of "significant others" in prompting practice change.

4. Facilitation: enabling the use of research, through technical, financial, organizational, and emotional support. This mechanism stresses the importance of giving practical assistance for individuals and groups to change.

5. Incentives and reinforcement: using rewards and other forms of control to reinforce appropriate behaviour. This mechanism assumes that behaviour can be influenced by controlling external stimuli.

The Research Unit for Research Utilisation (Walter et al., 2003b as cited in Nutley et al., 2007) has proposed a method for bringing together these different approaches to promoting the use of research. They propose a two-dimensional taxonomy that categorises KTE strategies according to

1. "Intervention Type—grouping interventions that are similar in form and content" (p. 129), for example, the taxonomy of interventions to achieve practice change developed by the Cochrane Collaboration;
2. "Underlying Mechanism—grouping interventions according to their underlying mechanism(s)" (p. 130) (dissemination, interaction, social influence, facilitator, and incentives and reinforcement).

In this chapter we draw upon these organizing frameworks for understanding KTE to critically analyze two KTE projects that used different degrees of participatory KTE. It is worth noting that taxonomies describe "typical" categories. In reality, a KTE strategy may draw on several different categories simultaneously. In the following two examples, we have recognized that multiple interventions or underlying mechanisms may be operating.

DEVELOPING PRACTICE GUIDES: CO-PRODUCING KNOWLEDGE

This KTE strategy was a project undertaken by The Benevolent Society (the practice context) in partnership with the Australian Institute of Family Studies, an organization whose primary activities are research and research dissemination. The project was designed by The Benevolent Society and the Institute to co-produce practice guides to sit under The Benevolent Society's overarching practice framework and provide additional guidance to practitioners in cases where specific complex problems exist (e.g., cumulative harm, specific vulnerable subgroups such as infants).

The Context and Collaborators

The Benevolent Society is a not-for-profit agency operating in New South Wales and South Eastern Queensland. Between 2003 and 2010, the organization experienced rapid expansion and increased its range of child, family, and community programs. These programs now include: community development, education and care, children's hubs, parenting programs, family support, child protection services, and out-of-home care. The rapid expansion required new staff with a diversity of qualifications and experience. The organization needed an overarching practice framework that would provide a unifying approach to service delivery in its child, family, and community programs. It also realized that practitioners would benefit from additional guidance for responding to complex problems or vulnerable subgroups. Specific evidence-based programs were not deemed appropriate given the diversity of programs, locations, and variation in staff qualifications and experience.

The Australian Institute of Family Studies, National Child Protection Clearinghouse is a highly regarded research and research dissemination organization that was already developing practice guides in the child, family, and community area in partnership with another service delivery agency. The Benevolent Society commissioned the Institute to undertake the practice guides KTE project (i.e., this was a "pull" strategy).

Purpose

Practice guides are primarily designed to enhance practitioners' conceptual knowledge, but also include some instrumental knowledge—particularly within the "tool" section of the guide. It is expected that as practitioners are involved in developing the practice guides, the development process itself will contribute to both conceptual and instrumental knowledge.

What Is Being "Produced"

The KTE project is the development of practice guides, which are brief and evidence-informed. Practice guides are different from a traditional literature review as they are embedded within the organizational context (i.e., this is a tailored KTE strategy). The guides are composed of two parts. The first provides a brief overview of the issue under investigation (e.g., what is cumulative harm, and how it impacts upon children) and any organizational policy or state legislation that has direct relevance to the issue. The second, and more substantial portion of the guide, is a combination of research evidence and practice knowledge, and takes practitioners through each of the stages of casework (assessment, planning, intervention, reviewing outcomes) to provide concrete prompts, tips, and guidance on what practitioners might do. The process for developing the guides is summarized briefly in Box 12.1.

KTE Strategy

For the practice guides to be truly embedded within the practice context an interactive co-production approach was adopted. The practice guides are co-produced by

○ 12.1.

Developing Practice Guides: Co-producing Knowledge:

- *Nominate co-authors* must include a researcher and a practice specialist who is part of the practice organization and each must have expertise in the subject area.
- *Initial planning* by co-authors regarding guide content
- *Review of the literature* conducted by the research specialist
- *Workshops* with practitioners in the organization comprising presentation of key research and theory (conceptual content) and interactive activities to develop and refine the "practice tool" component of the guide (instrumental content), followed by facilitated discussion to elicit practitioners' views on (a) how the guide should be structured, and (b) what nature and type of content should be prioritized
- *Compile feedback and refine plan for guide co-authors* to draft and re-draft the guide until they are satisfied the final product is of a high quality, and incorporates both contemporary research and practice knowledge
- *Expert reviewers* within and outside the organizational context to review the guide to ensure it (a) is consistent with the policy and practice framework, (b) incorporates contemporary practice knowledge for working with this client group, and (c) is accurate and informed by the evidence base
- *Revise the guide* based on reviews and finalize the draft
- *Executive endorsement* is required as practice guides are designed to suit the needs of practice organizations. The practice co-author will be delegated to produce the guide in collaboration with the research author. However, the finalized draft will require the endorsement of the organization executive before it is formally recognized. At this point the product is "handed over" to the practice organization and the researcher's role is concluded.
- *Publishing* follows executive endorsement, and the guide can be edited, typeset and published. Consistent with research into the barriers and facilitators of the use of research in policy and practice, careful attention is given to the guide layout and design to ensure the format is appealing and user-friendly.
- *Dissemination and implementation* can be enacted. It is a well-established fact in the research-to-practice literature that production of a product is not sufficient to embed the knowledge into practice. Attention needs to be given to the dissemination and implementation process. The research team work with the practice organization to develop an implementation and dissemination strategy, which is enacted by the practice organization.

the research and practice authors as an equal and active partnership, from initial brainstorming to final content and structure, and includes face-to-face meetings, regular phone and email contact, co-writing time, and co-facilitating workshops.

The primary KTE strategy for involving practitioners and their managers who will ultimately be using the guides is a half-day workshop. The workshop is repeated across work groups (for example, 92 practitioners participated in workshops to provide input into the development of the *Cumulative Harm: Specialist Practice Guide*). The workshop is a learning opportunity in the content area. In addition, workshop participants refine the guide, providing: input into the content and structure of the guide; advice on the service context; feedback on what content is and is not relevant to the service context; validating the scientific evidence; and contributing practice evidence. However, the development of practice guides are full participatory KTE strategy at the organizational level only, as front-line practitioners for whom the guides are intended provide input, but are not equal partners with a decision-making role in the production of the guides (this is the role of the co-authors).

KTE Mechanisms

The underlying mechanisms (Walter et al., 2003b) for the development of the practice guides was "interaction" between researchers and practitioners in the development and the use of "social influence," as the guides are co-authored by a respected research institute in partnership with the organization's senior practitioner who is a highly influential and respected practitioner.

Strengths and Limitations of the KTE Strategy

The primary strength of this KTE strategy is that evidence-informed practice guides are tailored to the practice context through a participatory co-production approach designed to maximize relevance to practitioners. As the project resulted in a written resource, it was not feasible within the project timelines and budget for the project to adopt a full participatory approach with practitioners that gave all practitioners a decision-making role. The research practice partnership approach to the development of an evidence-informed resource that excludes implementation is both a strength and a limitation. The end product provides an exit strategy for the research organization. The co-production approach to authorship means that the practice organization is left with a resource that they own, are content experts for, and have heavily invested in. The resource has an internal social influencer, and this increases the organization's commitment to supporting the implementation of the resource. However, the research organization's exit before implementation means that they may advise, but have no decision-making role in planning and undertaking a participatory KTE strategy for the implementation of the completed resource. Nor do they have any authority to evaluate the effectiveness of the KTE strategy for increasing conceptual and instrumental knowledge. Other challenges included the extended timelines involved in co-producing versus producing a resource, and negotiating the different standards of evidence. Overall, the project has theoretical promise, but evaluation of the impact of the development and subsequent implementation of the practice guides on practitioner's conceptual and instrumental knowledge is required.

CO-PRODUCING A PRACTICE FRAMEWORK: PARTICIPATORY KTE

This KTE strategy was a project undertaken by Wanslea Family Services (the practice context) in partnership with the Parenting Research Centre (an Australian not-for-profit non-government research and development organization that focuses on ways to improve outcomes for children by supporting parents, caregivers, and professionals). The aim of the KTE project was for Wanslea and the Parenting Research Centre (PRC) to co-produce a practice framework that would guide and support the work of family support practitioners who are working with vulnerable families.

The Context and Collaborators

Wanslea Family Services is a not-for-profit agency in Western Australia, which provides a range of services to children and families. Services include community development services, child education and care, play groups, parenting programs, home-based family support and family reunification services, and targeted child abuse and neglect services. The agency had identified that, while they had a mission statement, core objectives, and a set of guiding principles (such as being family-focused and strengths-based), they lacked a specific and detailed framework that could guide practice with families beyond policy and rules and promote evidence-informed approaches and consistent performance among staff at the front line.

The PRC specializes in bridging the research-to-practice gap and community-capacity building through the development, translation, and exchange of evidence-based programs and practice. The PRC uses a collaborative, phased approach to working with agencies to support the development and use of evidence-informed interventions (see Box 12.2). The approach allows for a full consideration and inclusion of the evidence and knowledge from research and practice, a contextual and flexible approach to intervention selection or development and implementation, and a two-way transfer of knowledge between researchers, program developers, managers, and practitioners. Wanslea Family Services engaged the PRC to help with the development of an evidence-informed practice framework for use across their family-focused service and supports (i.e., this was also a "pull" strategy).

Box 12.2

....

Co-producing a Practice Framework: Participatory KTE

A project team is formed. Membership was drawn from the Parenting Research Centre (PRC) and the practice context, Wanslea Family Services. Team members from Wanslea needed to be influential and respected within the organization.

Phase 1: Clarify aims and outcomes of the service. This phase helps to identify or clarify the aims and outcomes of the service. This phase is useful when working across services systems, achieving agreement among executive staff and service managers, and developing the evaluation plan. During this phase, the PRC collaboratively works with nominated Wanslea staff to review and clarify the outcomes and indicators their services are aiming to achieve. This is done in face-to-face working meetings.

Phase 2: Collect and summarize the evidence base focusing on programs and practices that show the best evidence for achieving the current programs' aims and outcomes. Different levels of evidence and a wide array of knowledge sources are explored as well as the interaction between the practice programs and context. At the same time, the Wanslea team work with experienced workers at Wanslea and documented current practice and views about optimal service delivery to the families involved in this service. These two sources of knowledge are analyzed to identify the key characteristics of best practice support for vulnerable families and develop draft recommendations for consultation with Wanslea.

Phase 3: Convene working meetings. These meetings include all levels involved in decision making around the final program or service. They must include practitioners who will implement the framework. Here, findings from Phase 2 are presented. This includes key support strategies associated with the outcomes outlined in Phases 1–2, guidelines for engaging parents and supporting change, and evidence-based approaches to skill building. The working meetings provide a setting for discussion around suitability and accessibility of established programs (if the evidence recommends these), the adaptation of an existing program, or the development of an evidence-informed practice framework.

Phase 4: Design or adaptation of a tailored program or practice framework based on what is agreed in Phase 3. During this phase, the PRC works collaboratively with the Wanslea team to develop the framework that is informed by Phases 2 and 3. This includes the development of the evaluation methodology and tools.

Phase 5: Implementation support. PRC provides face-to-face training workshops in the use of the framework as well as ongoing coaching and support during implementation.

Purpose

The primary purpose of the KTE strategies used in this project was to enhance the instrumental use of evidence in practice. That is, the main aim was to change practice and behaviour. The secondary aim was to enhance the practitioner's knowledge and understanding of the evidence (i.e., conceptual use of the evidence).

What Is Being "Produced"

The KTE project is the development and implementation of a practice framework. Wanslea and the PRC identified that the aim of the practice framework was to outline the values and principles that underlie Wanslea's approach to working with children and families. In addition to this, the framework would describe specific approaches and techniques considered fundamental to achieving outcomes. These approaches would include both research-based approaches and promising practices and approaches that Wanslea practitioners have experienced as effective (i.e., this is a tailored KTE strategy). See Box 12.2 for a description of the process for developing the practice framework.

KTE Strategies

Determining the purpose of the KTE strategies helped determine the type of KTE strategies used in this project. The focus on achieving change in practice and behaviour meant a strong emphasis on using interactive KTE strategies. These included the participation of managers, practitioners, knowledge brokers, and researchers in the project team, face-to-face meetings, regular phone and email contact, and collaboration and co-production of all framework materials to enhance their fit at Wanslea. The development of the framework was a participatory KTE strategy, with practitioners as equal and active partners. To enhance interaction and genuine co-production, a strong focus was placed on positioning the practitioner as one of the experts and identifying the assets they contribute to the collaborative relationship and the final framework itself (see Phases 2 and 3 in Box 12.2). To promote and support implementation, this project included face-to-face training for all practitioners and ongoing monthly coaching provided by the PRC team.

KTE Mechanisms

The main underlying mechanism (Walter et al., 2003b) for this project was "facilitation." That is, the KTE strategies used here all emphasized providing practical hands-on assistance and support directly to the practitioners. As with the practice guides project, this project also utilized the underlying mechanisms of "interaction" between researchers and practitioners and "social influence."

Strengths and Limitations of the KTE Strategy

The primary strength of this KTE strategy is the creation and implementation of a common and tailored practice framework across the agency. Similar to the practice guides, the co-production approach to the development of the practice framework means that the practice organization is left with a resource that they own, are content experts for, and have heavily invested in. As a full participatory approach was used with practitioners, it is hypothesized that practitioners would feel a greater sense of ownership and investment toward the practice framework than those involved in the development of the practice guides. Adopting a full participatory approach in this project allowed the project team to maximize input from and relevance to the "consumers" of the practice framework, that is, the front-line practitioners. Including training and ongoing support may result in an increase in the agency's ability and commitment to implementing the framework in practice.

A number of challenges exist with taking this approach. These challenges, which are similar to those experienced with the practice guides, include extended timelines involved in collaboration and co-production, negotiating the conflicting standards of evidence, and lack of a formal evaluation of the impact of the KTE strategies employed. Adopting a participatory approach with practitioners is more time and resource intensive than the participatory approach with the organization used for the practice guides. It involves new responsibilities that could be imposed on practitioners, leading to a concern that co-production can be used as a way to manipulate or exploit practitioners who implement services or more successfully exploit their labour. In addition to this, some practitioners may be given the opportunity to participate, but do not have the skills or experience to enable them to meaningfully contribute. The PRC's role in assisting the implementation of the practice framework also meant that the end point for the project was not as clear as it was for the practice guides project, which was limited to the development phase.

CONCLUSION

There is not a "one size fits all" model for KTE. The type and number of KTE strategies implemented will vary according to the scale of the project, the aims and outcomes of the intervention or service, the kinds of evidence that the KTE project aims to have implemented, and the context in which it will be implemented (Nutley et al., 2007). Tailored participatory approaches to KTE offer some promise as they theoretically will lead to greater ownership and relevance in the practice context, and ultimately greater research uptake. However, participatory KTE is time and resource intensive. Researchers will not always have the opportunity to undertake participatory KTE as it requires staff to be released to participate in the KTE strategy. This is more likely to occur where the KTE strategy is "pull" rather than "push," and/or where the practice context is heavily invested in increasing practitioners' conceptual or instrumental use of research in the specified content area. For researchers and practitioners, participatory KTE is subject to many of the same challenges as participatory research, such as learning how to work as a member of a team and respect other viewpoints, sharing power and authority, understanding different agendas and time frames, needing to be flexible, and building trust (Green et al., 1995).

Participatory KTE will not always be the most appropriate method for disseminating evidence to practice. Time must be invested early in identifying the context in which the evidence will be used. The Cultures in Context Model (Holzer et al., 2008) provides a framework for assessing the context and setting of service delivery and identifying the barriers and facilitators to research use in that specific environment. The purpose of the KTE strategy (conceptual or instrumental research use) and its strategic importance to the practice context must be clearly articulated. This information will be vital in planning for optimal KTE strategies.

Although KTE is not a new concept, it seems to be of growing importance. Nonetheless, KTE as a field of research is still in its infancy. It is easy to find opinion pieces and anecdotal reports about how to use KTE, but the limited reporting of KTE implementation and limited formal evaluation of KTE approaches leave those wanting to develop their own KTE approach struggling to find evidence-based strategies. It is still unclear whether or not increased inclusion in the development process does in fact achieve high utilization. Research is needed to better understand not only the effectiveness of KTE strategies but which KTE strategies and/or combination of strategies are effective, where, and under what conditions. Some researchers have raised concerns with conducting this research using Randomized Controlled Trial methodology alone, as the results would be difficult to interpret due to the problems with eliminating differences, particularly organizational differences, between organizations or services (Dobbins et al., 2009). Using mixed-method designs shows some promise in allowing us to evaluate effectiveness in a comprehensive way. Designs likely to be useful include intensive case studies and within-subject single case studies. It is through rigorous evaluation of KTE strategies that KTE itself can become evidence-informed and the true promise (including cost-benefit analysis) of participatory KTE compared with less interactive KTE will be identified.

REFERENCES

Amara, N., Ouimet, M., & Landry, R. (2004). New evidence on instrumental, conceptual, and symbolic utilization of university research in government agencies. *Science Communication, 26*, 75–106.

Chaffin, M., & Friedrich, B. (2004). Evidence-based treatments in child abuse and neglect. *Children and Youth Services Review, 26*, 1097–1113.

Davies, H., Nutley, S., & Smith, P. (2000). Introducing evidence-based policy and practice in public services. In H. Davies, S. Nutley, & P. Smith (Eds.), *Evidence-based policy and practice in public services.* University of Bristol, England: The Policy Press.

Dobbins, M., Hanna, S.E., Ciliska, D., Manske, S., Cameron, R., Mercer, S.L., et al. (2009). A randomized controlled trial evaluating the impact of knowledge translation and exchange strategies. *Implementation Science, 4*, 61. doi: 10.1186/1748-5908-4-61

Green, L.W., George, A., Daniel, M., Frankish, C.J., Herbert, C.P., Bowie, W.R., et al. (1995). *Study of participatory research in health promotion: Review and recommendations for the development of participatory research in health promotion in Canada.* Ottawa, ON: Royal Society of Canada.

Holzer, P., Lewig, K., Bromfield, L.M., & Arney, F. (2008). *Research use in the Australian child and family welfare sector.* Melbourne, Australia: Australian Institute of Family Studies.

Kessler, M.L., Gira, E., & Poertner, J. (2005). Moving best practice to evidence-based practice in child welfare. *Families in Society, 86*, 244–250.

Lewig, K., Arney, F., & Scott, D. (2006). Closing the research-policy and research-practice gaps: Ideas for child and family services. *Family Matters, 74*, 12–19.

Lavis, J., Ross, S., McLeod, C., & Gildiner, A. (2003). Measuring the impact of health research. *Journal of Health Services Research and Policy, 8*, 165–170.

Lomas, J. (2000). Connecting research and policy. *Canadian Journal of Policy Research, 1*, 140–144.

Manion, I., Buchanan, D., Cheng, M., Johnston, J., & Short, K. (2009). Embedding evidence-based practice in child and youth mental health in Ontario. *Evidence & Policy, 5*, 141–153.

Mitton, C., Adair, C.E., McKenzie, E., Patten, S.B., & Perry, B.W. (2007). Knowledge transfer and exchange: Review and synthesis of the literature. *The Milbank Quarterly, 85*, 729–768.

Needham, C., & Carr, S. (2009). Co-production: An emerging evidence base for adult social care transformation. *Social Care Institute for Excellence Research Briefing, 31*, 1–23.

Nutley, S., Walter, I., & Davies, H. (2007). *Using evidence: How research can inform public services.* Bristol, England: The Policy Press.

Petch, A. (2009). Guest editorial. *Evidence & Policy, 5*, 117–126.

Petr, C.G. (Ed.). (2009). *Multidimensional evidence-based practice: Synthesizing knowledge, research and values.* New York: Routledge.

Sackett, D.L., Rosenberg, W.M.C., Gray, J.A.M., Haynes, R.B., & Richardson, W.S. (1996). Evidence based medicine: What it is and what it isn't. *British Medical Journal, 312*, 71–72.

Saks, A.M. (2002). So what is a good transfer of training estimate? A reply to Fitzpatrick. *Society for Industrial and Organizational Psychology.* Retrieved April 14, 2011, from www.siop.org/tip/backissues/tipjan02/06saks.aspx

Tetroe, J.M., Graham, I.D., Foy, R., Robinson, N., Eccles, M.P., Wensing, M., et al. (2008). Health research funding agencies' support and promotion of knowledge translation: An international study. *The Milbank Quarterly, 86,* 125–155.

Walter, I., Nutley, S., & Davies, H. (2003a). *Research impact: A cross-sector review.* University of St. Andrews, Research Unit for Research Utilisation: St. Andrews.

Walter, I., Nutley, S., & Davies, H. (2003b). *Developing a taxonomy of interventions used to increase the impact of research* (Discussion Paper 3). University of St. Andrews, Research Unit for Research Utilisation: St. Andrews.

Chapter 13

Engaging the Voice of the Child:
Strengthens Practice-Based Research and Guides Multi-Professional Co-operation

Stina Högnabba, Senior Researcher, City of Helsinki, Social Services Department, The Voice of the Child Development Program

Hanna Heinonen, Development Manager, National Institute for Health and Welfare

Tiina Muukkonen, University Teacher, University of Helsinki

Alpo Heikkinen, Researcher, City of Helsinki, Social Services Department, The Voice of the Child Development Program

Abstract

Our focus is to present a development program (voice of children) in Finland. Developing multi-professional work and using evaluation methods helps us to gather practice knowledge, develop best practices, and involve stakeholders. Because of the increased needs of evidence-informed practice in child welfare, we have several researchers and evaluators working inside the program.

Introduction

In this chapter, we will briefly describe the child welfare situation in Finland. As an example of practice research and development of multi-professional co-operation, we will describe some issues of The Voice of the Child Development Program and two of the seventeen sub-projects.

There are 1.1 million children in Finland. The well-being of children has increased on the whole but, at the same time, malaise has increased for some of the children, young people, and families. Many kinds of problems have accumulated for a small minority. The number of child welfare clients has doubled between 1997 and 2007.

In Finland, municipal decision making has a strong and independent role in the organization of services. Municipalities, thus, are independently in charge of organizing basic services. Services are mainly financed with tax revenue. Municipalities may produce the services by themselves, together with other municipalities, or buy the services from private service producers. The services for children and families, especially foster care services, are bought from private service producers.

The Child Welfare Act was revised in 2008. As a result, the number of child protection notifications increased by 30–40 percent. The Child Welfare Act obligates all of the municipal "actors" to draw up a well-being plan for children and young people. The plan is approved in the municipal council, and it must be taken into account when preparing the municipal budget and estimating the resources needed.

The increased notification and growing outpatient client numbers also impact the increased number of children taken into foster care. The percentage of 16–17-year-old children who have been in foster care has grown in Finland in the 2000s noticeably more than the percentage of other age groups, compared to the corresponding population age group. This trend needs to be stopped by developing new kinds of services for young people that react more quickly to their needs. In order for this to work, these new kinds of services demand co-operation that crosses sectoral boundaries and the implementation of services especially in the growth and development environments of young people (National Institute for Health and Welfare, 2009).

In Finland, at the moment, it is especially difficult to find trained and qualified social workers for municipal child welfare. This is probably one symptom of the unmanageability of the amount of clients and work. The service system cannot indefinitely cope with the fact that a certain sector is constantly growing without significant improvement taking place.

In child welfare, difficult and complex problems that should be solved according to the child's individual needs are often encountered. The challenge is to break the culture within which sectoral co-operation is accomplished, and where people's "eyes are closed" when facing difficult matters.

The strengthening of multi-professional co-operation requires special services work to be more systematic than is currently the case to support basic services. During an economic recession, municipalities see services as expenses, and by no means as investments. Models supporting the resources and activities of the development environments of children and young people should be strengthened with new structures. The idea is that multi-professional work is carried out where children and young people mostly spend their time (Ministry of Social Affairs and Health Finland, 2010).

In Finland, the educational requirement to work in child welfare practice for a social worker is a master's degree. Social workers are independently in charge of advancing the child welfare social work process. Those with a bachelor's degree in social services, who carry out practical work and who graduated from universities of applied sciences, also participate in carrying out child welfare work. Specialization training in social work, in which social workers performing practical work pass a licentiate examination, have strengthened the professional competence of social workers. Social workers, therefore, possess good readiness to implement practice research in their own work.

The structures of client work have not enabled the utilization of research knowledge in the best possible way. For that reason, municipal actions where social workers perform development or research work alongside client work have become common. These developer- and researcher-social workers have especially strengthened the client-oriented development of social work.

The Voice of the Child Development Program

The objective of Finnish child welfare policy programs is to increase participation and reduce social exclusion; increase health and well-being; and improve the quality, effectiveness, and availability of services as well as to narrow regional differences. The national level strives to prevent problems from occurring and intervenes as early as possible by ensuring the knowledge and sufficiency of the field's personnel and by creating intact service entities and good operation models for social and health care.

The Voice of the Child program (Högnabba, 2010) is currently the most extensive program focusing on children and young people in Finland. For 2009–2011, approximately €11 million has been received in government aid. The program covers the Southern Finland region, which has approximately 1.8 million inhabitants (34 percent of the whole country's population), and 22 percent of the target group's population is under 18 years of age. Seventy workers have been hired for the program. The program's main goal is to advance the well-being and participation of children, young people, and families. Its basic premise is that practice methods and working models are strengthened and improved through extensive multi-professional co-operation in the development environments of children and young people. According to many studies and previous development projects, strengthening conditions and services that advance health and social well-being, preventing problems before they occur, and early intervention are influential and cost-effective ways to improve the quality of life of children, young people, and families. Municipal social, health, early childhood education, education and young people's services and institutions of learning, congregations, and organizations participate in the development work. The program produces evaluation and practice research information for the use of the whole region, offers learning environments, and supports municipalities in introducing new practices that have been found to be effective elsewhere.

THREE STRATEGIC GOALS

Early Support

The program has been organized into three strategic operative lines, which consist of 17 sub-projects. The first development line is the early support operative line. The goal is to develop preventive and early support structures, methods, work models, and knowledge in basic services. Concrete development targets are, for example, new forms of family counselling and family training, early support and intervention methods for daycare and schools, parents' peer group activities, and multi-professional teamwork. In many sub-projects, the placement of psychiatric nurses in school environments is piloted, and structures are created for participatory work. School environments are an important hub for preventive mental health work and early intervention in the students' symptoms and concerns. Schools are development environments where intervention of problems with children can occur early on and multi-professionally. In early 2010, those sub-projects where the activities take place in the development environments of children and young people have received good assessments, and the well-being of the children has increased. The target group of many projects are those pupils who are in a so-called transition phase (i.e., pupils starting school and pupils moving from elementary school to middle school). Minimal research information exists in the literature on these transition phases in the educational system.

Intensive Intervention Operative Line

The second development line is the intensive intervention operative line, in which models are created for early recognition of factors threatening the well-being of children and young people. The target group is children and young people who are already child welfare clients. In the sub-projects, situation and risk assessment tools and methods for clarifying and improving the life situations are developed. These multi-professional methods have been proven to work well. Teams composed of different professions meet children and young people in their development environments (i.e., school, home) when concern about the situation of the child or young person has been raised.

Development Networks

The third entity is the development networks. The goal of these is to strengthen regional expertise in child welfare work, and especially dialogical networking skills and multi-professional working methods. The monitoring of the work's cost-effectiveness has begun in the sub-projects.

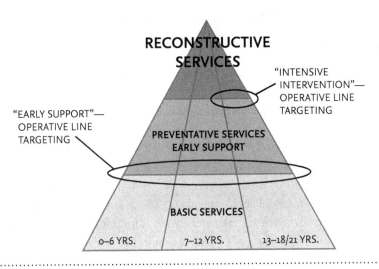

Figure 13.1

The program has put resources into extensive practice research and evaluation. It is common in Finland that the evaluations of large programs are outsourced. The placement of evaluators and researchers as part of the program is a new way of utilizing the expertise of the personnel to highlight practice research information. One researcher is in charge of all evaluations and of supporting and directing the evaluation work of the sub-projects. Researchers in three sub-projects participate in the development of activities and performing the practice research and evaluation. By integrating the evaluation as part of the program, it is assumed that different and new kinds of information on the well-being of children and young people and the influencing work methods will be gained.

The premise of the program work is that, by making clients and workers participate through practice and evaluation research methods, reliable information based on evidence is thereby produced. It is the task of the researchers to increase the evaluation expertise of the workers and add a critical and reflective evaluation aspect to the development work. The premise of information production is realizing that the working procedure or working method is effective and that it requires organizational-administrative information, workers' information, information from the political community, research information, and service-user information (Pawson et al., 2003).

The premise in the utilization of different kinds of information is producing an adequate knowledge base from child welfare work for municipal decision making. This challenge is answered by describing good practices. Describing good practices is process work that is included as part of the development program from the beginning. In Finland, the National Institute for Health and Welfare has developed a model for describing and evaluating good practices.

The premise is an evaluation study based on program theory and logic models, in which evaluation information is produced from development processes as well as client and service structure effects. Common logic models (i.e., descriptions of what kinds of results and outcomes are sought by the interventions) for the above-mentioned operative lines have been established in workshops. With the aid of these evaluation tools, more reliable research information, that is obtained from practice, is gained. One of the program's researchers has led workshops, and practice research and evaluation learning processes have been added to them. The challenge is to bring forth program-theoretical thinking as part of the development work. This—we think—will help us produce practice-based research information about changes in young people's lives (Chen, 2005; Donaldson, 2007; Wyatt-Knowlton & Phillips, 2009).

We are at the starting point in increasing the target group's participation opportunities. What is useful to know is that the participation of children and young people in planning and developing their own ideas has a strong presence (Heath, Brooks, Cleaver, & Ireland, 2009). Conversely, their participation in planning and evaluating the program's actions is rather limited for the time being. After nearly a year of program work, we can state that methods for this can be found, but it is more a question of the attitude of the workers and decision-makers toward the participation of children and young people. We need investment in structures and especially the prevailing work practices so that children and young people will have the opportunity to participate in developing and evaluating work. The empowerment of children and young people requires having opportunities to influence the work—that the voice of a child or a young person is really heard and for it to have an effect on practices. A young person in a sub-project expressed the matter thus: "The voice of the child is not heard if the adults talk all the time."

In the background of the implemented development work is long-term work, with which the development of professional social work has been strengthened in co-operation with the university, the City of Helsinki. and other regional actors. The Heikki Waris Institute, which operates in co-operation with the University of Helsinki and the City of Helsinki, has since the year 2000 strengthened the functioning and permanent co-operation between research, teaching, and practical work. The quickly changing service needs of children, young people, and families has turned toward practice-oriented research and development activities in which the central matter is the information formation arising from basic work and especially information formation crossing boundaries in many respects. This approach has a central role in the program. We think that practice-based research and evaluation are the first steps toward an evidence-informed practice. We will be able to describe effective practices before our program ends in October 2010 (Petr, 2009).

CHILD WELFARE'S PRAKSIS PROJECT

The goal of Praksis is to create new kinds of networks and structures for shared child welfare development work between child welfare practice in the municipalities of the Helsinki region and academic settings that include the University of Helsinki Social Work unit and universities of applied sciences. The Praksis activities taking place at the surface of client work may be described as practice research–oriented. It is characteristic for practice research that social workers from the field focus for a moment on examining a problematic work practice that previously arose in client work in co-operation with the other participants. Through practice research, good practices that can be disseminated are created.

The core actors of Praksis are municipal child welfare teams or networks. The co-operation between the university and the field of social work culminates in teams and networks in the co-operation between developer social workers who have had practical teacher training, leading social instructors of social workers, and university teachers. Municipal actors convene monthly to work on practical training and combine training with the development and research happening in the field (Hinkka et al., 2009; Satka, Karvinen-Niinikoski, & Nylund, 2005).

The goal of the first year (2008–2009) has been to start child welfare's social work teaching in co-operation with the municipalities. The idea is to use social workers as teachers and also to use case work as a learning method to connect it with theoretical thinking. Questions arising from practice have been modified in Praksis into a research-oriented form. Here, the students learn research practices and evaluation. All of the participants in the research support group have the opportunity to produce information. The goal is to increase the working life orientation of the studies, bring theory and practice closer together, and offer support for conducting research work. Here, specifically, we are getting close to the idea of the whole Praksis about the shared information production by students, workers, researchers, and teachers. The goal of all this is to obtain workers for child welfare who are more knowledgeable, and produce better social work and service outcomes for the children and parents who are clients of child welfare.

At the University of Helsinki, social work is taught at the bachelor and master's degree levels, and both feature teaching by Child Welfare's Praksis. Praksis has operated for one and a half years and has provided education to 90 students. A total of 45 practice teachers or lecturer-social workers have participated in the teaching of students. The activities are coordinated by one university teacher with many partners. Child Welfare Praksis education is given in three different practice modules and, in addition to that, to all social work students in the compulsory lecture series *Basics of Child Welfare.*

Through the Praksis activities, the knowledge of both the workers in the field and of the students is strengthened. Students graduating with a master's degree have a better grasp of core child welfare competencies when moving into working life as a child welfare professional. As the knowledge of child welfare professionals strengthens, the clients of child welfare benefit. The contents of the practice modules are developed together with the field, at which time the practice workers must be able to assess what is important in the work and what necessary skills are needed.

Qualified social workers may act as practice teachers in the Praksis network, and qualified social instructors may act as practice teachers for students. Social workers who act as teachers receive practice teacher training as continuing education in which they gain readiness to act as a teacher and develop their own expertise and research orientation. Uniformity is sought in practice training through quality criteria, which have been drawn up to direct the activities of the practice teacher, student, and entire work community as well as institutions of learning. The criteria for the practice teacher are, for example: qualified; experienced; committed; reflexive; inquisitive; conscious of own working methods, attitudes, values; disseminating knowledge, and withstanding doubt. Through shared quality criteria, we are able to process the advancement of teaching, development, and research in the larger network.

There are several benefits of this program for the University of Helsinki. The teaching given at the university meets the needs of the field when it is planned with and partially also implemented with practice social workers. Praksis narrows the gap between theory and practice, in turn building connections between the educational institutions and the field (Satka et al., 2005).

Different kinds of surveys about services have been done with clients and feedback has been received, but we are now looking for the participation of clients in the development work phase, and not merely for their opinion on the completed activities. On a small scale, students have encouraged clients participate such that they have had clients read the analysis of the client work done on them, asked for feedback, had a conversation with the client, and possibly modified the text according to the client's comments. Multi-actor participation is maintained in all activities so that we can speak of a principle that guides the activities. From the viewpoint of the university, it is obviously hoped that the quality of teaching improves. However, the expectation is also for a strengthening of research. We encourage those social workers who have completed research training to conduct research.

There is power and volume in a teaching and research network, but networks are also difficult to manage, and the danger is that the "network's cobwebs" will become tangled. Many people are present in a multi-actor network, but how do all of the members of the network feel that the activities are theirs? An adequate number of distribution forums are needed for common information formation, and they are abundantly needed with a large and multi-actor network. Can all actors find their own role and task, and is it clear? We have also had the courage to ask whether it is disadvantageous that social work students focus only on child welfare. What then is the fate of the generalist idea of social work? Are we forced to specialize in order to cope in the sectored field of social work? As we specialize, do we lose something from the general expertise and knowledge of social work? We have answered these questions by closely co-operating with the adult social work of Praksis.

YOUNG PEOPLE'S INTENSIVE METHOD PROJECT

A flexible outpatient service, "Young People's Intensive Program." is developed in this Voice of Child Development project. The programmatic content brings a new type of thinking into the Finnish helping system. An analyzed and goal-oriented temporary program and structure is typical for intensive methods. In the beginning of the program, the meeting frequency and availability of the helpers follows the young people's needs. Intensive methods feature a solid setting of a goal, a restricted number of clients that can be managed, evaluation of the early phase, the professionals' tight commitment to the support process, and careful monitoring.

In the experimental phase, the duration of the program is 6–12 months. The young person and the family receive intensive support from a multi-professional team. Twenty-four families are chosen for the first program, and the target group is 12- to 14-year-olds who are clients of child welfare's outpatient care. Conditions at home must be such that the young person can live at home, the parenting is adequate, and they must be ready to receive help. The young person and his or her family are supported in their own development environment, for example, at home and in school. The program invests in supporting school attendance and finding solutions for problem situations. The goal is to support the flow of every-day life and prevent the need for child welfare actions.

In the teams, a know-how entity of functional social pedagogical methods and case-specific work, therapy work, and family work is developed. The method includes elements of the international Multisystemic Therapy (MST) method and the Young Intensive Program (YIP). In question is our own Finnish application or method related to these practice initiatives. The family has access to the expertise of the social worker, social instructor, youth worker, psychiatric nurse, and occupational therapist. Some are trained as family therapists or psychotherapists. The young person's mental well-being and motor functions is evaluated through the expertise of the psychiatric nurse and the occupational therapist. In addition, the teams have workers that are familiar with functional group methods and leisure time activities. At least one specializes in functional working methods, and the work contribution is also needed in building the content of the group coaching programs of the young people and their parents and in the implementation of group activities. The program contains individual and family-specific work, activities, groups, and camps (Gasser, 2006; Geldard, 2009; Multisystemic Therapy Services, 2010; Ogden & Hagen, 2006).

The project researcher, who is highly engaged in developing and building the model, partially carries out client work and examines and assesses the functionality and effect of the method. Effectiveness is evaluated by applying a theory-based realistic evaluation, practice research, and participatory observation. This evaluation study asks how the intensive method, as an intervention, is analyzed in the experiences of children and the young people and their well-being, and in what ways the mechanisms that influence well-being change and take shape with the young people during the intervention in different contexts as the work is underway. The focus is also to evaluate and find functional multi-professional ways of working (Peake, Epstein, & Medeiros, 2005).

The survey material is compiled from the clients of the teams. The survey includes traditional scales of well-being, but also an application of the US clinical social work "All About You" form, which always asks in the very beginning what the young people do and do not want to talk about (Peake et al., 2005). The survey has been built up using basic Level of Functioning (LOF) Scales (Martin & Kettner, 2010). The collection of the survey material began in December 2009. The survey's starting-level results are to be analyzed and documented in the spring of 2010. The survey is repeated 6 and 12 months after the starting-level evaluation. The researcher will also collect experience information from the client group through interviews. We are still in the early phase of the work and the challenge is, in addition to developing the intensive program, the modelling of good practices and utilizing research information arising from practice.

FUTURE CHALLENGES

Multi-professional working methods and the collection and utilization of practice and evaluation research information are strengthened as part of our program. For this reason, much information arising from practice is obtained. The mere sharing and dissemination of information are not, however, enough to move and root the good operative models that are present in the program and the researched information into client work and decision making. We need more interactive operating models for the transfer of practice research information. By making workers, clients, and decision-makers participate in the information production process and the critical reflection on information, we can advance the diffusion of good practices. In this way we try, for example, trainings based on social reporting, where the participants include clients and decision-makers in addition to the workers. The training seminars are based on client information produced in the program, into which critical reflections by the workers and decision-makers on the functional prerequisites of the developed interventions are added.

We think that the correct direction is found in co-operation: listening to clients, connecting the experts who are carrying out client work to a new kind of information production, offering easily available support for the systematic evaluation of one's own work and development work, and encouraging management to enable an even braver crossing of administrative boundaries and expertise that is built sector-specifically.

In this phase of our work, we have more questions than answers, including the following:

- How can we produce evaluated and researched information based on evidence regarding the improvement of the well-being of children and young people?
- How can we indicate which interventions are the most effective? How do we indicate which intervention should be used in different problematic situations?
- How do we make sure that the work will not become merely a two-year project without a continuum? How do we show the financiers and decision-makers that early intervention and an intensive approach to work in the development environments of children and young people are cost-effective working methods?
- How do we find better participation structures for children and young people to develop activities, and how do we know how and where the children and young adults want to have an impact?

We will have our first evaluation research report ready soon. We are trying to address at least some of these questions there. We also believe that our practice-based and participatory evaluation approach where the young people produce knowledge will create a basis for an evidence-informed outcome evaluation.

REFERENCES

Chen, H.-T. (2005). *Practical program evaluation: Assessing and improve planning, implementation, and effectiveness*. Thousand Oaks, CA: Sage.

Donaldson, S.I. (2007). *Program theory-driven evaluation science: Strategies and applications*. Mahwah, NJ: Erlbaum.

Gasser, M. (2006). Jugend intensive programm. *Sozial und erlebnisorientierte persönlichkeitsenwiclung fur burschen und mädchen. Informationsbroschhure zur Arbeitsgemeinschaft*. Feldkirch, Austria: Insitut fur Sozialdienste Vorarlberg.

Geldard, K. (2009). Practical interventions for young people at risk. London: Sage.

Heath, S., Brooks, R., Cleaver, E., & Ireland, E. (2009). *Researching young people's lives*. London: Sage.

Hinkka T., Juvonen, T., Kangas, S., Mustonen, T., Saurama, E., Tapola-Tuohikumpu, S. et al. (Eds.). (2009). *Praksis, sosiaalityön käytännön opetus ja oppimisen tutkimus. SOCCAn ja Heikki Waris–instituutin julkaisusarja nro 21*. Helsinki, Finland: SOCCA ja Heikki Waris-instituutti.

Högnabba, S. (2010). *Lapsen ääni—etusivu*. Retrieved July 27, 2010, from www.lapsenaani.fi/

Martin, L.L., & Kettner, P.M. (2010). *Measuring the performance of human service programs*. Thousand Oaks, CA: Sage.

Ministry of Social Affairs and Health Finland. (2010). *Ministry of Social Affairs and Health*. Retrieved February 15, 1010, from www.stm.fi/en/frontpage

Multisystemic Therapy Services. (2010). *Multisystemic therapy: What is it?* Retrieved July 27, 2010, from www.mstservices.com

National Institute for Health and Welfare. (2009). *Child welfare statistical report*. Retrieved November 2, 2010, from www.stakes.fi/tilastot/tilastotiedotteet/2009/Tr19_09.pdf

Ogden, T., & Hagen, K.A. (2006) Multisystemic treatment of serious behavior problems in youth: Sustainability of effectiveness two years after intake. *Child and Adolescent Mental Health, 11*, 142–149.

Pawson, R., Boaz, A., Grayson, L., Long, A., & Barnes, C. (2003). *Types and quality of knowledge in social care*. London: Social Care Institute for Excellence.

Peake, K., Epstein, I., & Medeiros, D. (Eds.). (2005). *Clinical and research uses of an adolescent mental health intake questionnaire: What kids need to talk about*. Binghamton, NY: The Haworth Social Work Practice Press, Inc.

Petr, C.G. (2009). *Multidimensional evidence-based practice: Synthesizing knowledge, research, and values*. New York: Routledge.

Satka, M., Karvinen-Niinikoski, S., & Nylund, M. (2005). Mitä sosiaalityön käytäntötutkimus on? In M. Satka, S. Karvinen-Niinikoski, M. Nylund, & S. Hoikkala (Eds.), *Sosiaalityön käytäntötutkimus*. Helsinki, Finland: Palmenia-kustannus.

Wyatt-Knowlton, L., & Phillips, C.C. (2009). *The logic model guidebook: Better strategies for great results*. Thousand Oaks, CA: Sage.

CHAPTER 14

PARTNERS FOR OUR CHILDREN:
A CASE STUDY OF A PUBLIC-PRIVATE UNIVERSITY-BASED RESEARCH AND DEVELOPMENT CENTRE

MARK E. COURTNEY *and* TESSA KEATING, *Partners for Our Children, University of Washington*

ABSTRACT

This chapter presents a case study of a university-based public-private partnership devoted to using research, demonstration, and workforce development to improve outcomes for children and families involved in a US-state child welfare system. The organizational structure and logic model of the partnership and early lessons learned are described.

INTRODUCTION

This chapter describes a unique model for using research to improve child welfare practice and policy that involves both the generation and use of knowledge to improve outcomes. Founded in 2007, Partners for Our Children (hereafter POC) is a public-private collaboration between the Washington State Department of Social and Health Services, the University of Washington School of Social Work, and private community leaders committed to making positive changes within the child welfare system. Housed at the university, the partnership is based on a shared recognition of the public responsibility for the excellence of the public child welfare system—children in state care are all *our* children and should be treated as such. While recognizing the importance of efforts to prevent children from becoming involved with child welfare services, the focus of this work is on children for whom the public child welfare system bears responsibility, and on their families, a population that is, by definition, very dependent on the provision of public sector services for their health and well-being.

In the first section of the chapter, we describe the creation of POC and describe the four integrated change strategies employed by the partnership. Then we explore some of the assumptions that are implicit in the work. After that, we describe the early activities of POC and present a project case study illustrating how we go about our work. Finally, looking back over the past three years, we gather a few reflections on the challenges and lessons learned.

Parallel Discussions Leading to Creation of the Centre

A rare alignment of ideas and values led to the creation of POC. In this case, the recently appointed Dean at the University of Washington's School of Social Work had met with the leader of the state's public social services agency, the Secretary of the Department of Social and Health Services (DSHS), to think about creating a more productive partnership between the university and the state. Their hope was to facilitate the production of relevant and timely research that might inform practice and to train the workforce responsible for delivering those services more effectively, so that workers would be ready to meet the demands of complex decision making and leadership in child welfare. Around the same time, a small group of individuals in the private sector had begun to think about how to shift the marginalized perception of children in foster care and how to improve the lives and the prospects of children in state care. This culminated in a long-term philanthropic commitment to building a better system of care, in the form of a generous gift of funding to establish the centre and ensure core funding for the first three years.

In conversations the philanthropic group had with the university, the DSHS Secretary, and a wide group of practitioners, advocates, and others with a variety of perspectives in the field of child welfare, a common theme emerged: there is a small but growing field of useful research in child welfare. While we still do not know enough about what works, both practice and policy-makers could benefit from the development of an organization embodying a more engaged approach to research. The concept was to create a long-term funding base to support the public agency and the university in developing what Rosenfeld and Chaskin (2008) call a deep "change-oriented partnership" (p. 165) and, over time, to create a true learning organization. Early in 2007, POC was established through a formal agreement between the University of Washington, DSHS, and a private funder. The agreement called for $3 million in endowment funding and $1 million per year from the funder in operating support for seven years (i.e., a total of $10 million in start-up private support) and annual in-kind contributions from the university (e.g., subsidized office space, research administration, computing infrastructure, salary support for centre leadership, etc.) of $500,000 to $800,000 per year, depending on the level of work of the centre in any given year. The Governor of Washington also included in the state's budget $500,000 per year for the first two years of POC's existence. POC is governed by a board of directors composed of the private funder and other private sector leaders, representatives of the University of Washington, and representatives of state government. Following the establishment of the three-way partnership, POC recruited as its founding director a child welfare researcher who had been involved in the discussions leading to the establishment of the organization.

The mission of POC is to create positive change within Washington's child welfare system to improve the well-being of children, youth, and their families. The organization has three long-term goals:

- To reduce the potential for harm to children in the state's care
- To maintain children in safe, nurturing and permanent families
- To enhance the well-being of children in state care, including their physical and mental health, social development, and educational attainment

Key Operating Principles: Working in Partnership, Using the Best Evidence

POC's founders recognized that pressure from outside of "the system" is often necessary to mobilize the political will and leadership required for policy change. Nevertheless the founders of the organization felt POC would be most effective if it could also work with and within the system, believing that those most involved in delivering child welfare services, if given the tools necessary to do so, are capable of significantly improving outcomes for the children and families they serve. Reflecting this understanding, POC sees as key partners the individuals and institutions directly responsible for providing services to children in state care and their families.

The change-from-within strategy does not mean that POC avoids involvement with outside influences on the state's child welfare system. On the contrary, POC develops strategic relationships with outside influences such as other public institutions (e.g., the courts), the legislature, and policy advocates to inform their efforts to improve child welfare services and to ensure that POC's work has maximum impact on child welfare policy and practice.

A founding principle for the partnership is that sound evidence, rather than ideology or institutional self-interest, should be the basis for change in child welfare policy and practice. The fact that the collaborative partnership is housed at the University of Washington recognizes the university's commitment to employing the highest standards of academic rigour in developing timely solutions to the state's most complex problems. POC's research is inherently applied in nature, leading logically to the use of a wide range of quantitative and qualitative research methodologies, depending on the question at hand, including: survey research using a variety of data collection strategies (e.g., in-person, telephone, and web-based); experimental and quasi-experimental evaluation research; analysis of government program administrative data; focus groups; and key informant interviews.

The long-term stable funding base is intended to enable POC to develop strategies over the long term that empower the child welfare workforce with the knowledge, skills, working conditions, and resources necessary to help children and families in the child welfare system.

POC is ideally positioned to serve as the catalyst for creating a child welfare learning community because of the unique role each partner plays:

- The state (DSHS) brings the perspective of the public institution charged with primary responsibility for children in out-of-home care; it knows which questions are most pressing. The state is also in a position to act quickly to implement promising policies, programs, and practices identified through the work of POC on a scale that can have a real impact on the lives of many children.
- The private sector brings a variety of forms of "capital" to the partnership, all of which enhance POC's potential impact. Private sector funding strengthens POC's independence to pursue work that may not be fashionable or politically expedient; it allows POC to ask the tough questions for which the child welfare community needs answers. Private agency providers of child welfare services are a source of many innovative ideas needed to improve outcomes for children and families. The private sector brings important human capital to the centre and to the child welfare services community (e.g., business models used in the private sector with applicability in child welfare agencies). The private sector can also provide POC with the social capital to open important doors and the political capital to maximize the likelihood that successful projects will actually lead to changes in policy and practice.
- The university brings the expertise of applied researchers and educators from all disciplines concerned with children and families as well as a profound commitment to academic freedom and public dissemination of the findings of POC's work. The university also has a commitment to creating the most innovative education and training programs to ensure a workforce ready to meet the challenges of today's child welfare system.

The state stands to gain knowledge from its partners about how better to serve children and families. The private sector can learn from its partners how to better allocate its resources in support of foster children and their families. From its partners, the university can learn about the pressing issues toward which its research should be directed, can gain assistance in ensuring that knowledge generated reaches those most likely to use it, and can obtain new contexts for student learning opportunities.

At the heart of the vision for the partnership are four essential change strategies:

1. Policy analysis, research, and evaluation
2. Development and demonstration of effective policies, programs, and practices
3. Education and training to support workforce excellence
4. Public education and communications

POC's Model of Strategic Learning and Organizational Change

The diagram on the next page illustrates how POC sees its work leading to change in key long-term outcomes for children and families. The underlying theory of change behind POC's work assumes that child and family outcomes are influenced directly by two change levers: The presence of effective policies, programs, and practices within the child welfare system as well as the presence of a workforce capable of implementing those policies, programs, and practices. Factors outside the purview of the child welfare system also powerfully influence the lives of children and families involved with the system, but POC's primary focus is on the child welfare system and the social institutions most directly involved with that system.

POC's four change strategies inform and are inextricably tied to one another, as illustrated by the two-way arrows between the four strategies in Figure 14.1. For example, the knowledge generated by our research and evaluation work informs our choice of demonstration projects, our workforce development projects, and the content of our communications to members of the child welfare community. Similarly, our engagement with the child welfare workforce helps us to identify pressing issues that require research, and new program and practice ideas worthy of testing through our demonstration work. All of this helps us to improve our communications directed at educating child welfare stakeholders about the needs of the child welfare workforce.

We believe that POC will influence child and family outcomes because its four change strategies directly and indirectly influence the change levers of policies, programs, practices, and the child welfare workforce. Our demonstration work can lead directly to effective policies, programs, and practice and has an indirect

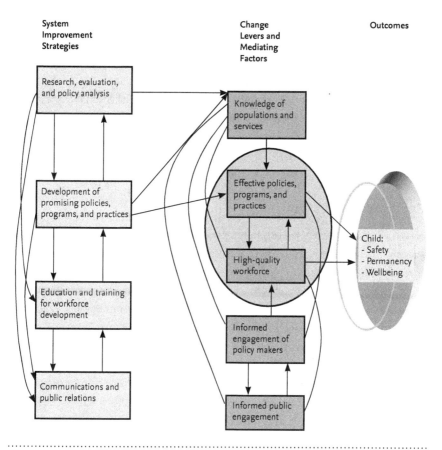

System Improvement Strategies   Change Levers and Mediating Factors   Outcomes

Figure 14.1

influence through its contribution to knowledge about child welfare populations and services. Likewise, our efforts to support workforce excellence can contribute directly to improvement in the effectiveness of that workforce. Some of POC's efforts only affect the change levers indirectly through their influence on mediating factors: for example, research and evaluation only influences the change levers through the ways in which it informs our other strategies and its effect on our knowledge of child welfare populations and services. Similarly, our communications work, while influencing our other strategies, can also have an impact on the change levers through its ability to inform and engage child welfare stakeholders (e.g., policy-makers and the public).

KEY CHILD WELFARE COMMUNITY STAKEHOLDERS

POC engages in its work a wide range of stakeholders in the child welfare system. However, since POC expects to mobilize change primarily through its impact on policy, program, practice, and the child welfare workforce, it considers its key stake-holders (i.e., those through which it expects to have its greatest impact) to be pol-icy-makers, program administrators, and child welfare practitioners. Stakeholders include: the Department of Social & Health Services (Secretary, Assistant Secretary, Regional Directors, Front-Line Workers), allied programs within DSHS (e.g., wel-fare-to-work programs, food assistance, heath and mental health services), the legislature, the Governor's office, legal systems, the service provider community, tribal governments, children's advocates, family advocates, organized labour, foster parents, birth parents, children in care, the media, and the public.

Early Activities (2007)

As with any initiative of this kind, not everyone at every level in the public agency supported the partnership. There are many reasons, some perfectly valid, to be suspicious of collaborative partnerships. Child welfare agencies frequently oper-ate in an environment of public blame where they are held responsible for actions both outside their control and beyond the scope of their public duty. Thus, it is easy to understand a desire within the agency for less openness. Likewise, private child welfare services providers and advocates were skeptical that the partner-ship promised by POC would actually develop; Washington state had seen many new organizations and initiatives directed toward child welfare reform come and go, sometimes with little lasting impact. However, shortly after the found-ing agreement was signed and the executive director hired, a public and widely reported launch event was organized. The launch event was a very early public statement by the DSHS Secretary that a strong and visible leader was investing in the research partnership and established an expectation for all staff from the public agency to collaborate with POC.

After the public launch, the first task was to establish a joint research agenda with the public child welfare agency that reflected the priorities of the Children's Administration. The range of the priorities chosen included both the interests of and the pressures on the public agency. This shared research agenda is an attempt to develop a model that includes the priorities of agency staff and sets the ground-work for collaborative interpretation and dissemination. It signals to the practice community that this is not purely an academic exercise, but an honest attempt to understand and to respond to agency concerns and ultimately to build a rel-evant knowledge base. It also means that drawing practice implications from the research will be more likely, as the issues are important to the people who provide the services and they have a shared understanding of what findings may mean in their specific context. The initial shared agenda included the following priorities, all of which have generated research and development projects with our partners:

- Recruitment and retention of both foster parents and kinship care providers
- Family reunification
- Placement stability
- Birth parent engagement
- Family assessment

Another early accomplishment was a signed data sharing agreement between POC and DSHS. The data-sharing agreement gives POC access to all administrative records on the families served by DSHS for the purposes of conducting a shared research and evaluation agenda. It describes the process for generating the shared agenda, and provides for agency review of POC dissemination products (i.e., papers, presentations, and press releases). In Washington this broke new ground and required establishing a level of trust and shared understanding regarding the dissemination and use of agency data.

Project Case Study: Family Reunification

Although it is not always appropriate or feasible, safe reunification of children in out-of-home care with their families is one of the primary goals of child welfare services. While it has long been the case that about three-fifths of children entering out-of-home care in the US will return home, there remains great between- and within-state variability in the timing of family reunification variability that begs explanation. Who should be reunified, and when, are two of the most perplexing questions facing child welfare practitioners and courts. POC developed a project to work with the Children's Administration to better understand how reunification decisions are made in Washington, to learn from efforts outside of Washington to understand family reunification, and to identify promising practices directed at improving family reunification practice and related court processes.

Figure 14.2 illustrates the process POC used to develop this project with its partners, a process that informs all of our work to date. We started broadly with the priority area we established with our public agency partner to increase the rate at which children returned home to their families (i.e., improving permanency) while maintaining or reducing the likelihood that they would be returned to care (i.e., improving safety). We engaged a wide range of stakeholders in the reunification process to identify challenges to improve reunification outcomes and opportunities for positive change in the institutions involved. We formed an advisory committee made up of professionals involved in some part of the reunification process, including public child welfare agency staff; private service providers; child and family advocates, including an advocacy organization representing parents who had been reunified with their children after their placement

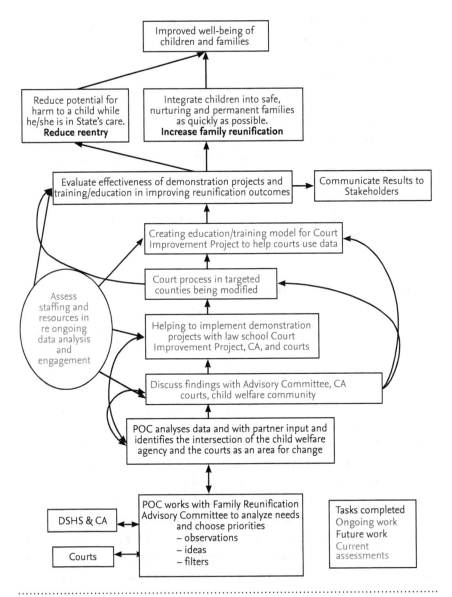

Figure 14.2

in foster care; a juvenile court judge; a state's attorney; an attorney responsible for representing parents; and public agency staff with expertise in mental health services, substance abuse treatment, and services to tribal communities. The advisory committee identified a wide range of potential opportunities to improve family reunification outcomes, but there was little evidence to support any given opportunity over another. Beginning with the hypotheses generated by the advisory committee, over the course of two years a small team of researchers, data experts, and practitioners used administrative data to analyze the reunification process in Washington and engaged the field in interpreting what the data meant in the context of Washington's child welfare and legal systems.

Our early analyses of administrative data on children's paths toward reunification identified significant between-region and between-county[1] variation in the rate at which children were returned home from care, variation that could not be readily explained by differences in the characteristics of the populations served. Digging deeper into the data with agency and court staff at the regional and county level, including sharing and discussing our findings in a wide variety of public and private settings, we identified interactions between the juvenile courts and child welfare agencies as central to much of the inter-jurisdictional variation we observed in outcomes. These engagements with the practice community led POC to involvement in developing and providing technical assistance to demonstration projects intended to streamline and improve court processes and in developing training materials for the juvenile court improvement project operated by the University of Washington School of Law. As these projects evolve we intend to evaluate their impact in order to assess whether they are improving outcomes for children and families.

EARLY LESSONS AND A FEW CHALLENGES FACED BY THE PARTNERSHIP

We have laid out the ideas behind the founding of the centre and the early goals for the organization. POC is still very young and remains a work in progress. In the spirit of reflective practice, we want to lay out some of the lessons learned along the way that might provide guidance to others interested in developing similar public-private partnerships.

Adapting to an Ever-Changing Context

The context in which the organization was founded has changed, as would be expected. Since the launch in 2007, Washington has suffered the consequences of the economic downturn. The budgets of DSHS and the university have been severely cut, leading, among other things, to the discontinuation of direct funding of POC with state funds, though POC has continued to benefit from the state's ability to pass through federal funds for evaluation and program development. Senior leadership at DSHS, the Children's Administration, and POC has changed as people move on to other opportunities, and these changes in leadership have resulted in changes in the organization's priorities. While working to establish the partnership, the Children's Administration has implemented a new practice model and switched to a new data system, all in a time of increasingly scarce resources. These factors underscore the need for POC to maintain a long-term focus in order to reach its goals. Both the promise and the challenge for POC is to create a long-term approach to system innovation and the organizational capacity to sustain that approach. The organization must be nimble enough to seize the opportunities that arise, while building knowledge over the long term in key areas and continuing to strengthen the relationships between the partners.

Need for New Strategies to Disseminate Research and Engage the Practice Community and Broader Audiences

We recognize that data analysis and research alone are weak change agents. We continue to follow the lead established by other organizations (e.g., Research in Practice in the UK) to support the field to use evidence in policy and practice. Increasingly, a key part of our work relates to both dissemination of research and translation into messages for the practice community. We are still learning the most effective ways of going about this and have experimented with a wide range of strategies, from printed and online issue briefs to webinars. Our experience so far is that engaging the practice community at every level is necessary for success and this in turn provides rich ground for new conversations, offering an opportunity for practitioners, researchers, policy-makers, and the public to refine their understanding of the challenges of this work and the limitations of our knowledge base. This exchange of understandings offers the research community an opportunity to be part of an ongoing dialogue that can enrich and inform their own inquiry.

Building Trust and Building Partnerships

Developing and maintaining the trust of public agency partners is a work in progress. Rosenfeld and Chaskin (2008) suggest these partnerships require new roles:

> Rather than providing information and stepping back to become bystanders in the policy and implementation process, they [researchers] instead [must] remain involved as "learning companions" to those involved in policy and practice. This is not always a comfortable position, and it requires the ability to balance among the implications and limitations of evidence, the interests of various actors, and the possibilities for action, while retaining integrity and independence. (p. 161)

While POC has developed a good working relationship with the Children's Administration senior management, the lasting legacy of decentralization within

Washington's state-administered system means that much action happens at the regional or office level. POC needs to be seen as a partner to *all levels* of the public child welfare bureaucracy and beyond. POC's work on family reunification is an example of the kind of project that leads naturally to local engagement, and we will need to continue to develop these kinds of opportunities. Just as this new way of working together requires a set of new attitudes and behaviours of researchers, policy-makers, and practitioners must also change. They need to engage in dialogue around research and evaluation findings and practice, allowing new information to challenge assumptions. Our experience of going into the field to share the findings from the reunification project provided a demonstration of the practice community's strong appetite for this type of engagement.

Balancing Short-Term Expectations and Longer-Term Results

One of the most important lessons has been the difficulty of managing the high expectations of the wide variety of stakeholders that POC could make a meaningful difference in the immediate future. While these high expectations no doubt contributed to POC's ability to engage key system stakeholders, it is also true that the child welfare system is very complex and is subject to a great deal of bureaucratic inertia. Significant reform requires changes to happen at the policy level, but also "on the ground" in interactions between social workers, court personnel, birth families, foster children, foster families, and service providers. Key public agency partners were close enough to the challenges at hand to generally maintain a patient commitment to our work together, but the pace of change in large public systems can seem maddening to those who normally operate outside that process, including legislators, policy advocates, and private sector partners used to the pace of change in the corporate world. Thus, balancing short-term expectations with long-term results will be an ongoing challenge for POC.

Ensuring All Voices Are Heard

Washington state has a rich array of local and specialized services, many meeting critical needs for children and families. The organizations providing these services have perspectives and experiences that are important to understand in both the development and interpretation of research, as well as practice and policy issues at the statewide level. However, the complex and sometimes fragmented nature of the child welfare services provider and child advocacy communities in Washington has made it challenging for POC to know who should be involved in any given project to objectively represent the interests of children and families. In addition, Washington does not have a strong child welfare services provider association.

Moreover, advocates sometimes find themselves needing to balance the promotion of their agency's business interests with advocating on behalf of children and families. As it moves ahead, POC needs to be more active in engaging a diverse group of child welfare services and policy players in its work. Increasingly, we must identify and shape strategies to engage a broader range of stakeholders than just public and private child welfare services providers, including the broad legal community dealing with the court dependency process, professionals who assist vulnerable families with housing and economic services, and, perhaps most importantly, the recipients of child welfare services themselves.

Distinct Organizational Cultures Create Challenges

The distinct cultures of POC's partners both enrich the partnership and pose their own challenges for organizational leadership. One unique strength of the partnership is a change-from-within strategy, which assumes and ultimately relies heavily on the development of mutual trust between key stakeholders and requires that all the partners learn to better understand the others' cultures and what they bring to the collaboration. These distinct cultures create tensions that have to be managed in the course of day-to-day work.

University administrators want their faculty to be distinguished independent scholars and expect a university-based research and development centre to provide opportunities for faculty to develop and maintain their scholarship, yet faculty members sometimes have research agendas that are at best peripheral to the pressing concerns of policy-makers, program managers, and social service practitioners. Our hope is to avoid this situation by engaging our partners in discussion about our work agenda and priorities from the earliest stages and by allowing our partners to help us shape the research questions. Another frequently heard criticism is that faculty members are not always sensitive to the implications of public disclosure of research findings for agency managers, program staff, and populations served. POC avoids this by systematically and deliberately sharing findings with partners and seeking help to interpret findings as the work is completed. In this way, practice partners have time and support to generate practice and policy responses and communications strategies as necessary. It is imperative that POC actively involve university faculty in its work in order to maintain the scholarly integrity of the work and institutional support for POC within the university.

Equally, public agency directors can be very committed to generating knowledge about the needs of the populations served by their agencies and the effectiveness of the services they provide, but may be less enthusiastic about the work when it is time to release research findings that may call into question the priorities of current political leadership. For their part, private sector leaders may not be sympathetic as to why public bureaucracies operate the way they do and can come to believe that inducing bureaucracies to change through policy advocacy is the most expedient path. While such advocacy is certainly useful, active engagement in generating outside pressure on its public agency partners may risk undermining the relationships that allow an organization like POC unparalleled access to agency data, agency personnel, and client populations.

These competing cultures represent real challenges for the kind of public-private partnership that POC seeks to create with implications for everything from the selection of strategies for the work we do, for example, balancing an agenda that includes research and advocacy, all the way to how we define success. Grappling with these challenges is key to producing new understandings and about the nature of change and some opportunities for innovative thinking.

Resource Issues

In the current economic climate, many organizations are facing harsh funding realities. The core private funding for the work at POC is a luxury and a privilege that few organizations have. Our private funding has leveraged other financial support from the university and government, has enabled us to build an internal organizational structure around the needs of the work itself, and has provided us with time to develop a new culture of collaboration with key partners, allowing us to ask hard questions about issues that are of great importance to improving child welfare services for families and children. Sadly, these activities are rarely funded either through local or national governments or private philanthropic grant-making. However, private funding also brings with it challenges for the kind of public-private partnership represented by POC, given the understandable desire of all three parties (i.e., the university, the state, and private funders) to maximize the value they derive from the partnership. University and public social service agency administrators are increasingly expected to demonstrate that they can enlist financial support from private partners, especially in the current economic climate when there is very little public funding available for demonstration projects or testing new ideas. Engaging private sector funders in these partnerships requires ongoing dialogue to ensure that everyone is clear about the quid pro quos associated with taking on public partners and thus avoid unrealistic expectations related to a funder's understandable desire to maximize the influence that their support can have on the behaviour of public institutions. A private gift that is seen as a significant sum by university administrators and philanthropists accustomed to sitting on the boards of not-for-profit human services agencies can seem less important to administrators running public institutions that spend hundreds of millions of dollars per year in public funds on services for children and families. The challenges for POC are to continue to leverage its core private funding, to manage the sometimes competing expectations of its partners, and to diversify its funding sources to avoid overdependence on any one source while maximizing the impact of its resources.

Measuring Success

Measuring success in this type of effort is notoriously difficult, but the early promise of POC was recognized by the American Public Human Services Association, which presented POC with its 2008 Academic Excellence Award. Ultimately, the real measure of POC's value in fostering and supporting a child welfare learning community is whether POC's work leads to improvement in the lives of foster children and their families. POC must show the relationship between the work that it does, the outcomes measured at the service provider or system level (changes in practice, program, and/or policy), and outcomes for children, and time will tell whether the early promise of this partnership inures to the benefit of children and families. This will require no small measure of perseverance in the face of challenges, resolve to maintain the spirit of the partnership, and willingness to adapt to new opportunities.

ENDNOTES

1. DSHS organizes its service delivery across six administrative regions, but there are 33 separate juvenile courts in Washington, most of which handle one county but a few of which handle multiple sparsely-populated counties.

REFERENCES

Rosenfeld, J.M., & Chaskin, R.J. (2008). Charting a course for fuller engagement: Toward a framework for action. In R.J. Chaskin & J.M. Rosenfeld (Eds.), Research for action: Cross-national perspectives on connecting knowledge, policy, and practice for children (pp. 158–169). New York: Oxford University Press.

CHAPTER 15

IMPLEMENTING EVIDENCE-BASED PROGRAMS IN CHILD WELFARE AND OTHER HUMAN SERVICES

DEAN L. FIXSEN, Karen A. Blase, Michelle A. Duda,National Implementation Research Network

JACQUIE BROWN, Kinark Child and Family Services

ABSTRACT

If the benefits of evidence-based programs are to be realized in child welfare, attention must be paid to implementation science and practice. It is only when innovations are implemented in child welfare practice settings that children, families, and society can benefit. Implementation science points to the importance of implementation stages (exploration, installation, initial implementation, and full implementation) and implementation drivers (staff competency development, organization supports, and leadership). The rationales for implementation stages and drivers are summarized and some examples from experience are provided to illustrate key points.

INTRODUCTION

Children and families cannot benefit from interventions they do not receive. For children and families to benefit from evidence-based programs and other innovations in child welfare and human services, leaders, managers, and practitioners need to pay close attention to implementation. Implementation is the art and science of incorporating interventions into typical human service settings to benefit children, families, and communities. The term "intervention" is used to include programs and practices that have a strong research base (e.g., "evidence-based programs") as well as other programs and practices that have potential benefit to children, families, communities, or provider organizations (e.g., data-based decision support systems, new human resources recruitment and hiring methods). In recent years, two comprehensive reviews of the diffusion and dissemination literature and of the implementation evaluation literature have been completed. A synthesis of those literatures resulted in new ways to view the methods needed to make better use of science in typical human service settings. In this chapter we will summarize the syntheses of the literature and highlight the findings from an ongoing review of effective implementation practices (Blase & Fixsen, 2003; Blase, Fixsen, Naoom, & Wallace, 2005; Fixsen et al., 2005; Greenhalgh et al., 2004). Implementation knowledge can be used to guide child welfare planning and preparations for the full and effective uses of evidence-based programs in practice to benefit children, families, and communities (Wilson, 2005).

Letting It Happen, Helping It Happen, Making It Happen

Greenhalgh et al. (2004) reviewed the diffusion and dissemination literature in human services and arrived at a classification system. In their view, theory and practice can be divided into three broad categories: letting it happen, helping it happen, and making it happen. For many years, science to service has been seen as a passive process that involves "knowledge diffusion" and "dissemination of information" that somehow makes its way into the hands of enlightened champions, leaders, and practitioners who then put these interventions into practice (Rogers, 1995; Simpson, 2002). In this approach, researchers do their part by publishing their findings; it is then up to practitioners to read the literature and make use of the interventions in their work with consumers. This passive process is well accepted and serves as the foundation for most federal and provincial policies related to making use of evidenced-based programs and other human service interventions. For example, federal technical assistance (TA) grants fund information gathering, publications and meetings to share information, and training sessions to provide more detailed information in a lecture-discussion format. Federal TA efforts feed this information to provincial TA representatives, who pass the information on to provider groups and other potential users (e.g., the Canadian Child Welfare Research Portal[1]). Using this process, millions of dollars are spent each year on the diffusion and dissemination of information in child welfare, education, health, mental health, and other human service domains. This by far is the most common mechanism for providing "professional development" or "continuing education" for administrators and staff.

Over the past four decades, others have taken a more active and effective approach to moving science to service (e.g., Blase, Fixsen, & Phillips, 1984; Chamberlain, 2003; Fairweather, Sanders, & Tornatzky, 1974; Havelock & Havelock, 1973; Schoenwald, Brown, & Henggeler, 2000; Slavin & Madden, 1999; Wolf et al.,

1995). These groups and others "make it happen" by using thoughtful methods that include attention to the stages of implementation and drivers of implementation. The remaining sections of this chapter will review the stages and drivers.

STAGES OF IMPLEMENTATION

Implementation does not happen all at once. It is a process that takes two to four years to complete in any provider organization. It is a recursive process with steps that are focused on achieving benefits for children, families, provider organizations, human service systems, and communities. It appears there are four functional stages of implementation: exploration, installation, initial implementation, and full implementation. While the stages are described in a linear fashion, the stages are not linear as each impacts the other in complex ways. For example, an organization may cycle from exploration to initial implementation and back to exploration as philosophical or values issues are encountered. Or, an organization may move from full implementation to initial implementation in the midst of unusually high levels of staff turnover. Once full implementation has been sustained for several years, implementation of interventions becomes standard practice and fades from memory until a new intervention is introduced and the process begins again.

Exploration Stage

The passive processes of diffusion and information dissemination are important parts of the exploration stage. Information sharing in various formats is important to increasing awareness of interventions and beginning to consider making changes in current services. Prochaska and DiClemente (1982) describe this process as moving from pre-contemplation to contemplation, preparation, and action. In human services, information is most often shared in publications and conferences. Rogers (1995) noted that the diffusion literature takes us up to the point of deciding to adopt an intervention and says nothing about what to do next to implement that intervention with good outcomes. Rogers observed that fewer than 30 of the more than 1,000 articles he reviewed pertained to what happened after an "adoption decision" was made (i.e., implementation). Twenty years later, Greenhalgh et al. (2004) stated that "the most serious gap" in the diffusion, dissemination, and implementation literature they reviewed pertained to the processes by which implementation occurred in health service delivery organizations. Thus, diffusion and dissemination play an important role in starting the implementation process but should not be confused with implementation itself.

Sustainable and effective implementation efforts are firmly rooted in the activities that occur during the exploration stage (Panzano & Roth, 2006). Given that, it is important to allow sufficient time dedicated to exploration stage activities and attempt to gain consensus from key stakeholders on the following questions: What problems exist? What interventions exist that might help solve that problem? Which interventions best align with the culture and values of the organization? How are these interventions viewed by consumers and the community? How will implementation expertise be accessed? What changes will have to be made in the provider organization to make full and effective use of the intervention? What changes will have to be made in related partners and bureaucracies to make full and effective use of the intervention? What are the costs and sources of funds to pay for implementation supports and intervention start up? What data systems need to be in place to detect intended changes in consumer outcomes and organizational and bureaucratic supports?

The process of collecting and analyzing all of this information is a critical part of the exploration stage. Early in this stage, a team needs to be formed (e.g., Barratt, 2003). The team members need to be tied closely to the power structure, freed of their other responsibilities, and allowed to spend the time and resources needed to collect and consider the information necessary to decide on the problem to be solved, the intervention that might help to solve that problem, and the plans to implement the intervention with performance and benefits to consumers (e.g., Barratt, 2003; Kaiser, Hogan, & Craig, 2008; Rhim, Kowal, Hassel, & Hassel, 2007). In some cases, an intervention such as an evidence-based program has an established "implementation team" (Rapp et al., 2008) that has been formed for the sole purpose of helping provider organizations, human service systems, and communities consider the implications of implementing the intervention (e.g., Chamberlain, 2003, describes the implementation team formed to help communities implement Multidimensional Treatment Foster Care). Implementation teams that have the benefit of experienced purveyors will find their jobs much easier to perform. The exploration process, if involving members of the organization, also has the potential to provide the opportunity to start the "buy-in" process within an organization that will develop a foundation that has greater capacity to support the organizational changes required for implementation.

The exploration stage "ends" (as noted earlier, implementation is not linear so stages are never "over") when the decision is made to implement a particular intervention. The time required to carry out exploration tasks seems to vary widely from a few months to several years. However, 6 to 15 months seems to be a fairly common time frame (often shorter with the help of an experienced implementation team that knows what to look for and can facilitate the decision-making process). One organization (Kinark Child and Family Services) embarking upon the identification of interventions for all their services experienced a range between 3 and 18 months from creating the team charged with the exploration process and taking the decision on which intervention to use.

Installation Stage

The installation stage is the period of time between deciding to implement an intervention until the intervention is used for the first time with the first child and family. This is a planning process that is frequently omitted when an organization moves to implementing new interventions. It takes time and resources to start up any intervention, and the lack of planning for these costs has doomed many attempted implementations in human services. Planning for and accomplishing the many tasks in preparation for service delivery is the work to be done during the installation stage. Hiring new staff (e.g., job descriptions, salary scales, special recruiting and interviewing), re-deploying existing staff, arranging office space, purchasing communications equipment (e.g., cell phones, laptop computers), creating new referral mechanisms, securing new funding sources, arranging initial training for staff, preparing for responsible supervision and coaching, and so on during the installation stage can determine the difference between successful implementation or failed implementation. Resources to accomplish the installation tasks are needed before the first consumer is seen and before any revenues are realized, but these resources are a very sound investment. Experienced implementation teams can help provider organizations anticipate and consider the installation tasks during exploration and make sure that adequate resources are brought to bear during the installation stage.

The installation stage "ends" when the intervention is used with the first consumers. The time required for installation varies widely depending upon the nature of the intervention and the quality of implementation supports, but two to six months is typically sufficient time for installation for many attempted implementations.

Initial Implementation Stage

This is where the "rubber meets the road." Initial implementation is the time when practitioners, supervisors, managers, system partners, and others are learning how to do/relate to a new way of doing things (i.e., the intervention). It is called the "initial" implementation stage because practitioners, provider organization managers, and system bureaucrats and policy-makers are not going to be very good in their new roles at the beginning of the implementation process. Learning any new set of skills does not go smoothly in the beginning. It takes experience to gain competence and confidence when learning to play a musical instrument, play a sport, work in a new way with a distressed child and family, provide skill-based coaching, or revamp the methods used by the human resources department. Successful implementation relies on people learning new skills and approaches individually, then learning how to use those new skills and approaches together in an integrated and aligned manner.

Currently, most attempts to implement interventions fail during the initial implementation stage because the intervention is poorly understood, the support processes required are not adequately developed, and implementation expertise in the form of established implementation teams is absent. For those efforts that survive this stage, the initial implementation stage may require one to two years.

Full Implementation Stage

Full implementation of an intervention is reached when at least 50 percent of the currently employed practitioners simultaneously meet the performance criteria for both implementation fidelity and intervention fidelity. This definition may sound like it is easy to meet but in our estimation it is not. Staff turnover occurs at the practitioner level. Each practitioner who leaves must have his or her replacement selected, trained, and coached and have his or her performance assessed one or more times in order to meet performance standards for an intervention. This sequence of activities takes time. In addition, there is no assurance that having met the performance criteria once predicts meeting the criteria the next time in an ongoing process of quality assurance. Staff turnover occurs at the interviewer, trainer, and coach levels. Learning to be a competent interviewer, trainer, or coach takes time so the practitioners who receive services from inexperienced trainers and coaches may not reach performance criteria readily. Turnover occurs at the management and administration levels. Practitioners, interviewers, trainers, coaches, and performance assessors may not receive the support they need from inexperienced managers and directors, and these inadequacies also impact the practitioner's ability to meet performance criteria. Mid-level bureaucrats and policy-makers turn over or move on, resulting in varying levels of support for provider organizations that are working hard to fully implement an intervention. This, too, can be reflected in fluctuations in practitioner performance as referrals, documentation requirements, funding issues, and other circumstances change.

Persistent and full implementation of an intervention leads to sustainability. Creating understanding and building a constituency to support an intervention begins in the exploration stage, and the depth and breadth of support is expanded at every opportunity in every ensuing stage (Khatri & Frieden, 2002). Gaining access to external expertise to assure a quick and successful start and making use of that external expertise to build local capacity impacts sustainability over the long term. Working to develop and maintain quality assurance systems that include practical measures of outcomes impacts sustainability (Fixsen et al., 2010). The conditions under which human services are provided are in a constant state of change. Sustainability depends upon staying tuned into the changes, anticipating the next set of changes, and continually maintaining high performance services in the midst of a sea of change. Creating and maintaining "buy-in" continues until "an innovation" becomes "standard practice" that is done as a matter of course.

Currently, based on the literature and our collective experience, most attempts to implement interventions never reach full implementation. For those that do, the process from the exploration stage to the point of first achieving full implementation may take from two to four years to complete.

IMPLEMENTATION DRIVERS

The stages of implementation are not just about the passage of time and sequencing of events. They represent the implementation activities occurring during each stage that significantly impact the uses of evidence-based programs and other innovations. Based on the commonalities among successfully implemented programs, implementation drivers have been identified (Fixsen et al., 2005). The sources of the implementation drivers are discussed and identified during the exploration stage, resourced during the installation stage, and used to accomplish the goals of the initial implementation and full implementation stages. Implementation drivers are often not part of the conversation about "using evidence-based programs." However, the evidence is becoming clearer; implementation drivers are important to the successful uses of evidence-based programs and other innovations in human services.

The goal of implementation is to have practitioners (e.g., foster parents, caseworkers, therapists, teachers, physicians) use interventions effectively. To accomplish this, high-performance practitioner behaviour is created and supported by use of the implementation drivers. The implementation drivers, identified by our research team, are staff selection, pre-service and in-service training, ongoing coaching and consultation, staff evaluation, decision-support data systems, facilitative administrative support, and systems interventions. These interactive processes are integrated to maximize their influence on staff behaviour and the organizational culture. Once the implementation drivers are well established in a provider organization, they also compensate for one another in that a weakness in one component can be overcome by strengths in other components. These drivers provide a framework that can be used to guide and govern the installation process. At Kinark Child and

Family Services, each installation team developed an initial implementation plan that considered and spoke to all the implementation drivers and the interdependence of them. This ensured that all organizational processes were reviewed and the required changes identified and planned to support implementation.

Staff Selection

Recruitment, interview methods, and selection criteria are part of staff selection. The focus of this driver is to identify who is qualified to carry out the evidence-based practice or program and what the methods are for recruiting and selecting practitioners with those characteristics. Some programs have specific requirements for practitioner qualifications (e.g., Chamberlain, 2003; Phillips et al., 2001; Schoenwald et al., 2000) and methods for assessing competencies (e.g., Blase et al., 1984; Reiter-Lavery, 2004). However, beyond academic qualifications or experience factors, certain practitioner characteristics are difficult to teach in training sessions so they must be part of the selection criteria (e.g., knowledge of the field, basic professional skills, common sense, sense of social justice, ethics, willingness to learn, willingness to intervene, good judgment, empathy). The move toward evidence-based practices and programs in human services has prompted concerns about advanced education, the availability of a suitable workforce, and sources of funding for highly skilled practitioners (O'Connell, Morris, & Hoge, 2004).

Pre-service and In-service Training

Interventions such as evidence-based practices and programs represent new ways of providing treatment and support. Practitioners (and others) at an implementation site need to learn when, where, how, and with whom to use new approaches and new skills. Practitioners should also have some understanding of the theoretical underpinnings for the identified evidence-based program or practice so that they can make informed practice decisions that still fit within the scope of this new way of work. Even though they are ineffective implementation strategies when used alone (e.g., Azocar, Cuffel, Goldman, & McCarter, 2003; Schectman, Schroth, Verme, & Voss, 2003), pre-service and in-service training are efficient ways to provide knowledge of background information, theory, philosophy, and values; introduce the components and rationales of key practices; and provide opportunities to practice new skills and receive feedback in a safe training environment.

Coaching

Most skills needed by successful practitioners can be introduced in training but really are learned on the job with the help of a coach. A coach provides "craft" information along with advice, encouragement, and opportunities to practice and use skills specific to the intervention (e.g., engagement, treatment planning, clinical judgment). Implementation of human service interventions requires behaviour change at the practitioner, supervisory, and administrative support levels. Training and coaching are the principal ways in which behaviour change is brought about for carefully selected staff in the beginning stages of implementation and throughout the life of evidence-based practices and programs. It is important that an organization and the supervisors in the organization understand the difference between supervision and coaching. One of the critical changes at Kinark Child and Family Services was changing the support and supervision process to enable ongoing expert coaching and peer coaching for each evidence-based practice implemented.

Staff Performance Assessment

Staff evaluation is designed to assess the use and outcomes of the skills that are reflected in the selection criteria, taught in training, and reinforced and expanded in coaching processes. Assessments of practitioner performance and measures of performance also provide feedback useful to interviewers, trainers, coaches, managers, and purveyors regarding the progress of implementation efforts and the usefulness of selection, training, and coaching. For example, at Kinark the implementation of new interventions was the catalyst for the development and implementation of a new and standardized process of clinical supervision throughout the organization. This then led to the development of a new supervisory structure that affected every level of the agency.

Decision-Support Data Systems

Other measures (e.g., quality improvement information, organizational performance measures, consumer outcomes, social validity) assess key aspects of the overall performance of the organization and provide data to support decision making to assure continuing implementation of the core intervention components over time. For many service-providing organizations, this may introduce the need for new systems with which the organization has little experience and drawing on the assistance and experience of an implementation team may be of great value.

Facilitative Administration

Facilitative administrators provide leadership and make use of a range of data inputs to inform decision making, support the overall processes, and keep staff organized and focused on the desired intervention outcomes. In facilitative administrative organizations, policies, procedures, structures, culture, and climate are given careful attention to assure alignment of these aspects of an organization with the needs of practitioners. Practitioners' interactions with consumers are the keys to any successful intervention. It is up to administrators and others to make sure the practitioners have the skills and supports they need to perform at a high level of effectiveness with every consumer.

Systems Intervention

Finally, systems interventions are strategies to work with external systems to ensure the availability of the financial, organizational, and human resources required to support the work of the practitioners. Again, alignment of these external systems to specifically support the work of practitioners is an important aspect of systems intervention (see Mihalic & Irwin, 2003, for examples of the interaction of administrative and external system variables with successful implementation and benefits to consumers).

INTEGRATED AND COMPENSATORY NATURE OF DRIVERS

The importance of integrated implementation drivers was illustrated by a meta-analysis of research on training and coaching carried out by Joyce and Showers (2002). They summarized several years of systematic research on training teachers in the public schools. They found that training that consisted of theory and discussion coupled with demonstration, practice, and feedback resulted in only 5 percent of the teachers using the new skills in the classroom. These findings are similar to those of Rogers, Wellens, and Conner (2002) who reviewed the business literature and estimated that only 10 percent of what is taught in training is actually transferred to the job. In the Joyce and Showers (2002) analysis, when on-the-job coaching was added to training, large gains were seen in knowledge and teachers' ability to demonstrate the skills and, most importantly, about 95 percent of the teachers used the new skills in the classroom with students. Joyce & Showers (2002) also note that training and coaching only can be done with the full support and participation of school administrators (facilitative administration) and works best with teachers who are willing and able to be fully involved (selection factors). Despite what the research tells us, most funding for professional development is for "training" alone.

The integrated and compensatory nature of the implementation drivers represents a challenge for implementation and sustainability. Organizations are dynamic, so there is ebb and flow to the relative contribution of each component to the overall outcomes. The feedback loops are critical to keeping the evidence-based program "on track" in the midst of a sea of change. If the feedback and feed-forward loops (staff performance evaluations and decision-support data systems) indicate needed changes, then the integrated system needs to be adjusted to improve effectiveness or efficiency (see Bernfeld, 2001, for a more complete description of these interactive variables). That is, any changes in process or content in any one of the implementation drivers requires adjustments in other implementation drivers as well.

The compensatory nature of the implementation drivers helps to ensure that there are multiple systems, procedures, and opportunities to support high-performance implementation. For example, in an implementation infrastructure that has minimal training opportunities for practitioners, intensive coaching with frequent feedback loops may compensate for the lack of training. Or, careful selection and very well designed staff performance evaluations may compensate for less training and coaching. The integrated implementation drivers also compensate for the fact that practitioners acquire skills and abilities in different ways over time. For example, one practitioner may significantly benefit from sound skill-based training and require less frequent coaching while another practitioner may leave the pre-service training a little overwhelmed and require significant on-the-job coaching. Though time limited, the integrated and compensatory nature of the implementation drivers provides a robust and flexible approach to ensuring effective implementation of an intervention.

Conclusions

The descriptions of the implementation stages and drivers provide a template for analyzing and attending to implementation. Implementation takes careful attention, time, and occurs in stages. Recognizing the recursive nature of stages helps implementation teams recognize what is needed to assure successful implementation. Exploration requires more attention to gathering/providing information and establishing buy-in. Initial implementation requires more work on rapidly developing leadership and staff competence and confidence while changing organizational structures. This is a critical stage that helps with the removal of barriers, and facilitates the uses of a new intervention in a provider organization. Trying to do initial implementation work in an organization that is still in the exploration stage is a waste of time and resources.

As the review of the literature and the review of current implementation best practices have shown, there is nothing really new about the implementation stages or any one of the implementation drivers. What is new is the realization that the stages and drivers are highly integrated parts of a whole new thing that is identifiably "implementation." What is new is finding that closing the science-to-service gap requires attention to both the evidence-based intervention practices and to evidence-based implementation practices. To more rapidly advance the field of child welfare, three seminal issues must be resolved:

1. Reliable and practical measures of the implementation stages and implementation components are needed to provide useful feedback for implementation teams, common outcomes for researchers to assess, and serve as practical sign posts for policy-makers and funders.
2. Training academies need to modify their curricula to systematically, effectively, and efficiently educate a whole generation of implementation team members. These members must have the requisite knowledge and skills to do implementation work competently.
3. Policy-makers and politicians need to be engaged in a deliberate and determined effort to defragment human service systems and fully align funding, licensing, accreditation, monitoring, and bureaucratic functions with the needs of effective practitioners working in the context of facilitative provider organizations. Current state/provincial and federal systems are "legacy systems" more attuned to the past than to the future.

The practice and science of implementation have improved to the point where more is known, and we now have the ability to provide evidence-informed services to consumers. However, to bridge the gap between research and practice in child welfare and to allow for the benefits of these practices to be sustained over time, we need to be as empirically sound in choosing our implementation strategies as we are in choosing effective interventions. Where do we start? We start with the end in mind.

Authors' Note

Preparation of this chapter was supported, in part, by funds from the Centers for Disease Control and Prevention (9211973-2513-2005) and the U.S. Department of Education Office of Special Education Programs (H326K070002). The views expressed are those of the authors and should not be attributed to either funding source. We would like to thank our National Implementation Research Network colleagues who provide continual inspiration and delight: Allison Metz, Sandra Naoom, and Melissa Van Dyke.

Endnote

1. Canadian Child Welfare Research Portal: www.cecw-cepb.ca.

References

Azocar, F., Cuffel, B., Goldman, W., & McCarter, L. (2003). The impact of evidence-based guideline dissemination for the assessment and treatment of major depression in a managed behavioural health care organisation. *Journal of Behavioural Health Services and Research, 30,* 109–118.

Barratt, M. (2003). Organisational support for evidence-based practice within child and family social work: A collaborative study. *Child & Family Social Work, 8,* 143–150.

Bernfeld, G.A. (2001). The struggle for treatment integrity in a "dis-integrated" service delivery system. In G.A. Bernfeld, D.P. Farrington, & A.W. Leschied (Eds.), *Offender rehabilitation in practice: Implementing and evaluating effective programs* (pp. 167–188). London: Wiley.

Blase, K.A., & Fixsen, D.L. (2003). *Evidence-based programs and cultural competence.* Tampa, FL: National Implementation Research Network, Louis de la Parte Florida Mental Health Institute, University of South Florida.

Blase, K.A., Fixsen, D.L., & Phillips, E.L. (1984). Residential treatment for troubled children: Developing service delivery systems. In S.C. Paine, G.T. Bellamy, & B. Wilcox (Eds.), *Human services that work: From intervention to standard practice* (pp. 149–165). Baltimore, MD: Paul H. Brookes Publishing.

Blase, K.A., Fixsen, D.L., Naoom, S.F., & Wallace, F. (2005). *Operationalizing implementation: Strategies and methods.* Tampa, FL: University of South Florida, Louis de la Parte Florida Mental Health Institute, University of South Florida.

Chamberlain, P. (2003). The Oregon Multidimensional Treatment Foster Care Model: Features, outcomes, and progress in dissemination. *Cognitive and Behavioural Practice, 10,* 303–312.

Fairweather, G.W., Sanders, D.H., & Tornatzky, L.G. (1974). *Creating change in mental health organizations.* New York: Pergamon.

Fixsen, D.L., Blase, K.A., Duda, M.A., Naoom, S.F., & Van Dyke, M. (2010). Sustainability of evidence-based programs in education. *Journal of Evidence-Based Practices for Schools, 11,* 30–46.

Fixsen, D.L., Naoom, S.F., Blase, K.A., Friedman, R.M., & Wallace, F. (2005). *Implementation Research: A synthesis of the literature* (FMHI Publication #231). Tampa, FL: University of South Florida, Louis de la Parte Florida Mental Health Institute, The National Implementation Research Network. Retrieved [AQ: Date?] from nirn.fmhi.usf.edu/resources/publications/Monograph/index.cfm

Greenhalgh, T., Robert, G., MacFarlane, F., Bate, P., & Kyriakidou, O. (2004). Diffusion of interventions in service organisations: Systematic review and recommendations. *The Milbank Quarterly, 82,* 581–629.

Havelock, R.G., & Havelock, M.C. (1973). *Training for change agents.* Ann Arbor, MI: University of Michigan Institute for Social Research.

Joyce, B., & Showers, B. (2002). *Student achievement through staff development* (3rd ed.). Alexandria, VA: Association for Supervision and Curriculum Development.

Kaiser, R.B., Hogan, R., & Craig, S.B. (2008). Leadership and the fate of organisations. *American Psychologist, 63,* 96–110.

Khatri, G.R., & Frieden, T.R. (2002). Rapid DOTS expansion in India. *Bulletin of the World Health Organisation, 80,* 457–463.

Mihalic, S.F., & Irwin, K. (2003). Blueprints for violence prevention: From research to real world settings: Factors influencing the successful replication of model programs. *Youth Violence and Juvenile Justice, 1,* 307–329.

O'Connell, M.J., Morris, J.A., & Hoge, M.A. (2004). Intervention in behavioural health workforce education. *Administration and Policy in Mental Health, 32,* 131–165.

Panzano, P.C., & Roth, D. (2006). The decision to adopt evidence-based and other innovative mental health practices: Risky business? *Psychiatric Services, 57,* 1153–1161.

Phillips, S.D., Burns, B.J., & Edgar, E.R. (2001). Moving assertive community treatment into standard practice. *Psychiatric Services, 52,* 771–779.

Prochaska, J.O., & DiClemente, C.C. (1982). Transtheoretical therapy: Toward a more integrative model of change. *Psychotherapy: Theory, Research and Practice, 19,* 276–287.

Rapp, C.A. Etzel-Wise, D., Marty, D., Coffman, M., Carlson, L., Asher, D., et al. (2008). Evidence-based practice implementation strategies: Results of a qualitative study. *Community Mental Health Journal, 44,* 213–224.

Reiter-Lavery, L. (2004). *Finding great MST therapists: New and improved hiring guidelines.* Paper presented at the Third International MST Conference, MST Services, Charleston, SC.

Rhim, L.M., Kowal, J.M., Hassel, B.C., & Hassel, E.A. (2007). *School turnarounds: A review of the cross-sector evidence on dramatic organizational improvement.* Lincoln, IL: Public Impact, Academic Development Institute.

Rogers, E.M. (1995). *Diffusion of interventions* (4th ed.). New York: The Free Press.

Rogers, R.W., Wellens, R.S., & Conner, J.R. (2002). *White paper: The power of realization.* Retrieved October 10, 2007, from www.ddiworld.com/pdf/ddi_realization_whitepaper.pdf

Schectman, J.M., Schroth, W.S., Verme, D., & Voss, J.D. (2003). Randomized controlled trial of education and feedback for implementation of guidelines for acute low back pain. *Journal of General Internal Medicine, 18,* 773–780.

Schoenwald, S.K., Brown, T.L., & Henggeler, S.W. (2000). Inside multisystemic therapy: Therapist, supervisory, and program practices. *Journal of Emotional and Behavioural Disorders, 8,* 113–127.

Simpson, D.D. (2002). A conceptual framework for transferring research to practice. *Journal of Substance Abuse Treatment, 22,* 171–182.

Slavin, R.E., & Madden, N.A. (1999). *Disseminating success for all: Lessons for policy and practice* (No. 30). Baltimore, MD: Center for Research on the Education of Students Placed at Risk (CRESPAR)-—Johns Hopkins University.

Wilson, C. (2005). *Guide for child welfare administrators on evidence based practice.* Washington, DC: National Association of Public Child Welfare Administrators, an affiliate of the American Public Human Services Association.

Wolf, M.M., Kirigin, K.A., Fixsen, D.L., Blase, K.A., & Braukmann, C.J. (1995). The teaching-family model: A case study in data-based program development and refinement (and dragon wrestling). *Journal of Organisational Behaviour Management, 15,* 11–68.

CHAPTER 16

INTEGRATIVE THEMES, LESSONS LEARNED, AND FUTURE CHALLENGES

KATHARINE DILL and WES SHERA

INTRODUCTION

This volume provides a comparison of policies and practices focused on the implementation of evidence-informed practice (EIP) in the provision of care for children and youth in eight countries: Australia, Canada, England, Finland, Ireland, Scotland, Sweden, and the United States. When considering the utility of international comparisons, Baistow (2000) maintains that these comparisons are very useful in enabling us to:

- gain an understanding of another country's system;
- "de-construct" our own system;
- use the feedback from others as an alternative yardstick of the worth of our policies, practices, and ideas;
- make us more reflexive and able to identify the assumptions underlying our policies and practices.

We contend that the concept of evidence-informed practice can act as a catalyst for much-needed change in the focus and performance of child and youth care systems in all countries. These changes also have profound implications for both the providers of care and the children and families who are the beneficiaries of such services.

Each of the chapters in this volume provides an example of how the concept of knowledge utilization in human services, particularly as it relates to our work with vulnerable children and families, is operationalized in a program or service within their respective country. We began the journey by encouraging our colleagues to write their chapters, as their contribution for attending the international conference, using the multi-dimensional evidence-based framework employed by Petr (2009). As discussed earlier, this conceptual framework embraces not only the traditional evidence-based academic research and litera-ture but also promotes the inclusion of practitioner wisdom and client voice. Authors were urged to move beyond the more traditional way of approaching evidence-informed practice, which can at times be overly focused on rigorous quantitative approaches, and consider a more holistic perspective. While many of the authors did speak to this more holistic framework, their contributions typi-cally followed the definitional grounding that had been articulated in the devel-opment of the initiatives that they describe in each of the chapters. In addition to this core conceptual issue, a number of themes related to the implementation of evidence-informed practice emerged from the chapters that demonstrated an array of ideas and alternative perspectives related to evidence-informed practice. The remainder of this chapter provides a distillation of these major themes.

ORGANIZATIONAL LEARNING AND THE LEARNING ORGANIZATION

Alexanderson and her colleagues examine the critical importance of a learning culture for creating a linkage to evidence-based/informed practice. The authors explore the theoretical underpinnings of the organizational excellence model (Alexanderson et al., 2009) and examine how this model has merit for embed-ding evidence-informed practice within organizations. This model is strongly linked to the social work profession, which promotes empowerment and creating change from within. They strongly support the need for using an empowerment approach (Hardina, Middleton, Montana, & Simpson, 2007) in implementing evidence-informed practice and underscore the importance of leveraging the organizational context to affirm the importance of evidence-informed practice. This is seen as particularly important in the context of a challenging organiza-tional culture. Julian and Proykov from RiPfA explore the notion of the learning organization, with a particular emphasis on tacit knowledge and illustrate how structured storytelling and communities of practice can be used to cope with information overload and rapid organizational change.

RiP (Research in Practice) is a world leader in promoting the use of evidence-informed practice within the context of busy social service organizations. Authors Bowyer and Moore provide a framework for creating organizational learning and change through various mechanisms, one of which includes the use of case study workshops. This type of learning process promotes peer-to-peer learning based on different research implementation scenarios. Peers wrestle with these scenarios and bring the ideas forward within the context of their own organiza-tional culture. Dill and Shera also explore the landscape of organizational change that includes the peaks and valleys of implementing a substantive new way of thinking and practicing and the challenges of layering this initiative alongside the busy work of child welfare practice. Fixsen and his colleagues also highlight the importance of paying attention to fidelity in the implementation of evidence-informed practices and identify coaching as a pivotal activity in ensuring robust implementation. Austin and Claassen (2008) argue that the central components of organizational culture that promote evidence-based practice (EBP) are leadership, the involvement of stakeholders at all levels, the nurturing of cohesive teams, organizational resources, and the readiness to become a learning organization.

POLICY AND SOCIO-POLITICAL CONTEXT

This edited book, by its very nature, explores the policy and socio-political context of implementing evidence-informed practice within the international landscape. Indeed, the evidence from many of these authors is that the government and policy-makers are the key drivers that promote an attitude of acceptance and belief in the use of EIP. Sweden's government has promoted the use of evidence-based practice in children's services since 2000, and did so by promoting systematic reviews. Swedes speak to a national appetite for outcomes and producing results; hence the movement toward EBP. The Georgetown chapter, by Goldman and her colleagues, concludes with real-world examples for promoting an outcomes-driven system that applies EIP within the context of a national and statewide infrastructure. Dean Fixsen and his colleagues from the National Implementation Network also speak to the systemic level of implementation of policy-based evidence-informed programs and argue that implementation science and an understanding of the four major stages of implementation (exploration, installation, initial implementation, and full implementation) are critical to success. This framework of stages and the identification of drivers at each level can be adapted to the implementation of evidence-informed practice in most human service systems.

Canavan and colleagues explore the socio-political context of Ireland's children's services. The authors conclude that it is essential to employ an evidence-informed practice orientation as the strategic framework for addressing practice and policy issues in Ireland. Humphreys and colleagues from Australia make the point, however, that research can sometimes create policy and political change and sometimes it cannot. The authors' case studies provide a lens for understanding when research can influence change as an alternative to government policy-makers creating change from the top down. The chapter by Courtney and Keating from Partners for Our Children (POC), in Seattle, Washington, focuses on the creation of an organization (POC) that promotes the linkage between policy and child welfare practice. Courtney and Keating explore the complexities of creating an organization that tries to bridge the two distinct worlds of policy and practice. Dill and Shera argue that we need to take a more multi-level evidence-informed approach that would include evidence-informed policy-making and evidence-informed management. They also note that there are other critical factors in decision making such as politics, resources, labour relations, and community pressure that may impede leaders from making evidence-informed decisions.

Use of Technology

Ever since the 2008 conference held at Dartington, it has become clear that many of our international colleagues have begun to pioneer the use of a range of technologies as mechanisms for promoting the use of evidence within the context of their organization and the services they provide. Watson, O'Neil, and Petch from IRISS in Scotland use Web 2.0, which promotes an interactive set of tools for practitioners to engage with online materials. Bowyer and Moore from RiP explore the use of online forums for promoting dialogue and exchange of ideas between practitioners at the various member organizations. Dill and Shera expand our understanding of how to engage practitioners on a province-wide basis through the use of online webinars. These authors identify several challenges and successes in engaging practitioners in the use of this rapidly spreading technology. Barwick and her colleagues in the Child and Youth Mental Health Information Network are experimenting with a range of technologies including: using a wiki to support clinician practice change; developing virtual communities of practice (VCoPS), a school-based mental health learning e-forum; a mental health information resource for teachers known as Bottom-Line Actionable Messages (BLAMs); You Magazine, a web-based interactive health and mental health literacy program for youth, parents, and teachers; and other resource websites. They highlight the importance of assessing the learning preferences of the knowledge recipients to tailor social networking strategies more effectively. A major challenge for those involved in the dissemination of evidence-informed practice knowledge is to keep abreast of how the continually emerging new technologies can be used effectively to support their work.

Human/Organizational Factors in Implementation

While technology has been a very useful tool in the transfer of evidence to practice, it is often the important organizational processes of supervision, coaching, teamwork, and peer discussion that are the critical factors in utilizing evidence in everyday practice. It is also important to note that we can gain helpful insights from areas other than child welfare and children's mental health. In the field of adult mental health, an investigation of the implementation of supported employment and integrated dual diagnosis treatment in Kansas found that the following were critical to the successful implementation of EBPs: instituting expectations; upper level championing of EBP; making supportive structural and policy changes; creating intra-agency synergy (through leadership teams, work teams, and supervision); systematic use of information to monitor and evaluate fidelity and outcomes of interventions; and the provision of training and consultation (Rapp et al., 2008). This combined approach includes increasing the capacity of individual practitioners and making modifications in organizational processes and procedures to integrate evidence-informed practice into the daily operation of agencies (Austin & Claassen, 2008).

Watson, O'Neil, and Petch from IRISS in Scotland highlight the development of *Confidence through Evidence*, "a tool kit that promotes: acquiring, interpreting and implementing evidence in order to improve practice and service outcomes." This tool kit is an excellent on-the-ground example of how to implement the concept of evidence-informed practice within the context of human service organizations. Practice and Research Together (PART) has recently developed a guidebook for supervision, which assists supervisors to integrate evidence-informed practice into their supervisory activities.

Fixsen and his colleagues note that the most effective pedagogical process for ensuring uptake of evidence in day-to-day practice is coaching. Kinark Child and Family Services changed their support and supervision process to enable ongoing expert coaching and peer coaching to accelerate the implementation of evidence-based practice.

Law and McDermid (2008) argue that practitioners that are competent in EBP have skills for appraising and applying evidence; have extensive knowledge of available evidence; consistently use evidence in their practice; and have positive attitudes toward an evidence-based approach. Aarons (2004) developed the Evidence-Based Practice Attitude Scale (EBPAS) and concludes that attitudes toward adoption of EBP can be reliably measured and vary in relation to individual differences and service context. More recent research by Nelson and Steele (2007) found that practitioner training, the perceived openness of the clinical setting toward EBPs, and the practitioner's attitudes toward treatment research were significant predictors of self-reported EBP use. Other conditions that have been found critical to developing practitioner competence are personal and organizational readiness, personal and organizational expectations, defined timelines, and the availability of support (Law & McDermid, 2008). Horwitz, Chamberlain, Landsverk, and Mullican (2010), with reference to the field of child welfare, identify the continued inability we experience in attempting to implement evidence-based practice in routine service settings. They also contend that in comparison to the fields of health and mental health, child welfare systems have only recently had access to evidence-based practice information, and are only beginning to understand and become comfortable with the EBP implementation process.

Paradigmatic Approaches to EIP—Multi-dimensional EIP

A number of the chapters in this volume describe the history of the evidence-based practice movement in their respective countries. These approaches range from an emphasis on the use of evidence from randomized controlled trials to the inclusion of client voices in the decision-making process. This continuum of approaches includes both a wide variety of methodological tools but also has various degrees of inclusiveness vis-à-vis stakeholders involved in the process (managers, researchers, practitioners, clients). While many of the authors did try to be more inclusive with their reflections, most were embedded in the approach that had been used at the outset of their respective initiatives. In many cases this approach was strongly influenced by policy-makers, and those providing the resources for their programs. Shlonsky and Ballon nicely identify the recent influence of systematic reviews and capture some of the nuances of contextualizing evidence.

The emergence of the multi-dimensional model of EIP is an important development and not only places value on research, practitioner, and consumer evidence but provides criteria for the evaluation of the evidence emerging from each of these perspectives (Petr, 2009). As one example of this approach, Hognobba and her colleagues showcase a model called The Voice of the Child Development Program, which explores the utilization of children's voices in the integration of research into practice. Humphreys and her colleagues explore the theoretical framework of the knowledge diamond that includes the integration of research evidence, consumer, practitioner wisdom, and policy perspectives. Mildon and her colleagues from Australia provide very useful examples of participatory knowledge translation and exchange strategies to enhance evidence-informed practice in child and family services.

Interdisciplinary and Intersectoral Dimensions of Evidence-Informed Services

The notion of interdisciplinary (Abramson & Bronstein, 2006) and intersectoral linkages have become a foundational theme throughout many of the chapters. The deployment of interdisciplinary capacity building typically comes in the form of linking research academics with practitioners. Our Irish colleagues, Canavan et al., describe how they forged an alliance between academics and policy-makers to promote a genesis of ideas for their chapter. The authors wrote a literature review that addresses the intersectoral challenges of working between these two different systems of practice. This type of collaborative work is showcased in the Praxis project, a Finnish model that creates linkages between academics, government policy-makers, and practitioners. Bowyer and Moore from RiP discuss the development and work of the Local Authorities Research Consortium (LARC). This program engages practitioners in large-scale research studies. Other examples of this type of activity, discussed in chapters by Fixsen and Barwick and their colleagues, include the National Implementation Research Network and the Child and Youth Mental Health Information Network. PART, in Ontario, has participated in discussions regarding priority areas for the development of a research agenda in child welfare, and has consulted with and used academics in its webinar series. In terms of intersectoral initiatives, Canavan and his colleagues from Ireland examine the interface between Child Protection and Welfare and the Child and Adolescent Mental Health sector and help us to understand how evidence-informed perspective can shed light on critical intersectoral issues.

TOP-DOWN VERSUS BOTTOM-UP APPROACH

Watson, O'Neil, and Petch outline a key example of a top-down approach to moving evidence-informed practice forward. The Scottish government commissioned a report entitled *Changing Lives: Report of the 21st Century Social Work Review* in 2006, which strongly encouraged the use of evidence-informed practice. This is a good example of a top-down approach where politicians and policy-makers mandate the use of evidence to develop programs and influence practice. Other chapters support a "bottom- up" approach (Australia, Ireland, and the UK) and claim that practitioners and clients need to be co-collaborators in both the creation and application of new knowledge for practice. Austin and Claassen (2008) argue that combination approaches can be effective in helping organizations to develop a culture of evidence-informed practice. Humphreys and colleagues make the important point that, not only does change take time, but that timing is also very critical. The authors use case study analysis to demonstrate how sometimes research studies "hit the mark" because the evidence comes at the right time within the context of the practice and policy milieus.

The PART chapter explores the changes that have occurred in the area of evidence-informed practice in Ontario with child welfare practitioners and caution that lasting and substantive changes take time and patience—an element that is sometimes in short supply in the rapidly changing context of human service programs.

PARTICIPATORY MODELS OF IMPLEMENTATION

Bowyer and Moore explore the participatory action approach to integrating EIP within systems and organizational contexts through the implementation of change projects, or as they are referred to in the PART model, guide books. This participatory model explores the engagement of practitioners in the development of publications that promote organizational and systemic change. This participatory model, first pioneered by our UK partners, RiP and RiPfA, has been replicated by the PART program and demonstrates how practitioners can become engaged in the deployment of tools and resources that are developed by and for practitioners. Mildon and her Australian colleagues explore how higher levels of utilization can be achieved with different knowledge transfer and exchange strategies and varied levels of participation by practitioners in child and family services. These approaches are generally more congruent with Petr's (2009) model of multi-dimensional evidence-based practice.

Cunningham and Duffee (2009) argue that there are at least three major styles of evidence-informed practice in child welfare: adoption, developmental, and compliance. These approaches vary primarily in terms of their assumptions, how evidence is obtained and used, and who sets the agenda regarding the utilization of this evidence. Participatory approaches are most congruent with a developmental style of evidence-informed practice.

LESSONS LEARNED

The chapters in this book provide testimony to the fact that the process of implementing evidence-informed practice is not easy and often encounters various barriers to its success. In reflecting on some of the lessons learned from these chapters, the following major themes emerge:

- Building an organization's capacity to significantly implement evidence-informed practice takes time; you have to be in it for the long haul.
- While leadership can change, it is important to maintain continuity in the level of commitment by senior leaders to the promotion and implementation of evidence-informed practice.
- Change of this significance cannot be isolated to one sector of the organization. It must be comprehensive and multi-level and be embedded in organizational culture.
- When and where possible use external forces to create a sense of urgency and increase motivation to change.

- When undertaking systemic or organizational initiatives it is important to do a scan of the policy environment.
- It is critical to hire practitioners and supervisors who are trained in evidence-informed practice and to assist those who are not to develop the requisite competencies.
- Understand that organizational members need support and incentives to move in the desired direction of change.
- While the importance of evidence-informed practice needs to be upheld by the organizational leadership, it is only through the participation of those involved (in delivering or receiving services) that these changes can be achieved.
- Redesign organizational processes such as supervision, teamwork, and client/community partnerships to align them with the evidence-informed practice agenda.
- Implement a systematic approach to tracking implementation and hold managers and supervisors accountable for meeting agreed-upon objectives.
- Establish an evidence-informed hub (office, committee, and website) that provides practitioner support and acts as a catalyst for evidence-informed practice and creates partnerships with academics and other sectors of the practice community.
- When creating research partnerships with community agencies and academic institutions custom tailor the agreement and focus on the unique strengths and areas for development that are required using a wide range of context-appropriate strategies.
- Participate in national and international networks to keep abreast of new developments in the art and science of implementing evidence-informed practice.

Future Research and International Collaboration

This edited book provides an excellent framework for understanding some of the important research issues that have emerged from our in-depth analysis of this substantive topic. All of the contributing chapters have helped us to recognize that there is a very significant need for future research on the implementation of evidence-informed practice both at the individual and organizational level.

At the 2010 conference, a unique initiative entitled "Special Projects" (SP) was developed. The goal of the SP was to provide participants with the opportunity to collaborate and work together on international projects in areas of interest to them and of importance to the knowledge base of evidence-informed practice.

The SP will culminate in presentations at the next biennial event scheduled to be held in the spring of 2012 in Ireland. In planning for this upcoming conference in Ireland, we are expanding our involvement to include other countries with more diverse perspectives. The current group of international participants is limited to North American and European countries. A more global perspective on evidence-informed practice is required.

There are a total of six special international research projects, which include the following:

1. **Support to the Global Implementation Initiative** is being sponsored by the National Research Implementation Network, a conference that is scheduled for the fall 2011. The group has created an international consortium of members who will move ideas forward at this upcoming event and provide the genesis for more specialized practice groups at the conference that will address the issue of implementation at a systemic and organizational level.

2. **Engagement with Children, Youth and Families** promotes the consumer dialogue in the context of evidence-informed research studies. The work of the group includes conducting a literature review that explores the ambiguous concept of engagement and related terms from various disciplines, and identifies effective strategies for engaging consumers in applied social research. The group also plans to explore and document real-world mechanisms for engaging consumers in evidence-informed initiatives.

3. **Evidence-Informed Decision Making** seeks to embed the use of research in key child welfare–related decision-making processes. Decision making in mandated child protection processes in many countries occurs at similar points (e.g., at intake, assessment, investigation, child removal, and placement). This project aims to identify and map the evidence that can be used to inform decision making at each of these points.

4. **Framework for Critical Decision-Making to Achieve an Outcome-Driven System** is an extension of models presented by Goldman and her colleagues. The workgroup's goal is to develop a critical decision-making framework to guide the development of an outcome-oriented system that will enable agencies to document the outcomes of their services for youth and families.

5. **Frameworks and Tools for Measuring Knowledge Uptake and Impact** is aimed at increasing the global understanding and measurement of impact of knowledge utilization activities and their ultimate outcomes for children and families across both Child Welfare and Children's Mental Health settings.

6. Engaging Front-Line Workers in Evidence-Informed Practice intends to complete a literature review on what we currently know about factors that promote the engagement of front-line workers in evidence-informed practice. Out of this review will come an agenda for future research by various stakeholders participating in the groups.

A project manager has been hired, and this person coordinates monthly conference calls to ensure that the work of the special projects is moving forward. These projects are an excellent example of international collaboration. The research and development that is emerging from these groups is gaining momentum and should result in significant new findings and new collaborative research initiatives that are sustained and driven by experts in the field of evidence-informed practice. These continuing international linkages are invaluable in further developing our expertise in this important area.

References

Aarons, G.A. (2004). Mental health provider attitudes toward adoption of evidence-based practice: The evidence-based practice attitude scale (EBPAS). *Mental Health Services Research, 6*(2), 61–74.

Abramson, J., & Bronstein, L. (2006). Group processes and skills in interdisciplinary teamwork. In C.D. Garvin, L.M. Gutierrez, & M.J. Galinsky (Eds.), *Handbook of social work: Social Work with groups.* New York: Guilford Press.

Alexandrson, K., Beijer, E., Bengtsson, S., Hyvonen, U., Karlsson, P.–A., & Nyman, M. (2009). Producing and consuming knowledge in social work practice: Research and development activities in a Swedish context. *Evidence & Policy: A Journal of Research, Debate and Practice, 5*(2), 127–139.

Austin, M.J., & Claassen, J. (2008). Implementing evidence based practices in human services organizations: Preliminary lessons from the front-lines. *Journal of Evidence Based Social Work, 5*, 271–293.

Baistow, K. (2000) Cross national research: What can we learn from inter-country comparisons. *Social Work in Europe, 7*(3), 8–13.

Cunningham, W.S., & Duffee, D.E. (2009). Styles of evidence-based practice in the child welfare system. *Journal of Evidence-Based Social Work, 6*, 176–197.

Hardina, D., Middleton, J., Montana, S., & Simpson, R.A. (2007). *An empowering approach to managing social service organizations.* New York: Springer Publishing Company.

Horwitz, S.M., Chamberlain, P., Landsverk, J., & Mullican, C. (2010). Improving the mental health of children in child welfare through the implementation of evidence-based parenting interventions. *Administration & Policy in Mental Health, 37*, 27–39.

Law, M., & McDermid, J. (2008). *Evidence-based rehabilitation: A guide to practice* (2nd ed.). Thorofare, NJ: Slack Incorporated.

Nelson, T.D., & Steele, R.G. (2007). Predictors of practitioner self-reported use of evidence-based practices: Practitioner training, clinical setting, and attitudes toward research. *Administration & Policy in Mental Health & Mental Health Services Research, 34*, 319≠330.

Petr, C.G. (2009). *Multidimensional evidence based practice: Synthesizing knowledge, research, and values.* New York: Routledge.

Rapp, C.A., Etzel-Wisel, D., Marty, D., Coffman, M., Carlson, L., Asher, D., et al. (2008). Evidence-based practice implementation strategies: Results of a qualitative study. *Community Mental Health Journal, 44*, 213–224.